FAMILY,
DRAMA,
AND
AMERICAN
DREAMS

FAMILY, DRAMA, AND AMERICAN DREAMS

TOM SCANLAN

CONTRIBUTIONS IN AMERICAN STUDIES, NUMBER 35

GREENWOOD PRESS

WESTPORT, CONNECTICUT • LONDON, ENGLAND

Library of Congress Cataloging in Publication Data

Scanlan, Tom, 1937-
   Family, drama, and American dreams.

   (Contributions in American studies ; no. 35 ISSN 0084-9227)
   Bibliography: p.
   1. American drama—20th century—History and criticism. 2. Family
in literature. I. Title.
PS338.F35S3   812'.5'09   77-83896
ISBN 0-8371-9827-5

Library of Congress Catalog Card Number: 77-83896
ISBN: 0-8371-9827-5
ISSN: 0084-9227

First published in 1978

Greenwood Press, Inc.
51 Riverside Avenue, Westport, Connecticut 06880

Printed in the United States of America

10   9   8   7   6   5   4   3   2   1

ACKNOWLEDGMENTS

Any intellectual enterprise has debts too myriad for repayment. But some obligations are so great they must be named.

This book owes much to the American Studies Program at the University of Minnesota, where I was fortunate enough to study under a splendid faculty.

More especially, I wish to thank Professor J. C. Levenson, now at the University of Virginia, for his unfailing encouragement, sympathy, and perceptive counsel. He saw this book from its beginnings to its present form. No prospective author has had a better critic or friend.

Susan Mudge typed the manuscript and cared about it.

What I owe to my wife, Mary, cannot be measured.

I acknowledge the Executors of the Eugene O'Neill Estate, Random House, Inc., and Jonathan Cape, Ltd. for permission to quote from *Ah, Wilderness!*, *All God's Chillun Got Wings*, *Mourning Becomes Electra*, *Desire Under the Elms*, and *Welded* in *The Plays of Eugene O'Neill*, 3 vols., copyright 1952 by Eugene O'Neill and renewed 1955 by Carlotta Monterey O'Neill.

Yale University granted permission for the extracts from *Long Day's Journey into Night* by Eugene O'Neill, 1956.

The excerpts from *All My Sons, Death of a Salesman,* and *The Crucible* are from *Arthur Miller's Collected Plays* by Arthur Miller, copyright 1947, © 1957, by Arthur Miller. Reprinted by permission of Viking Press. Other excerpts from Miller's plays are from: *After the Fall,* copyright © 1964 by Arthur Miller. Reprinted by permission of Viking Press. *The Price,* copyright © 1968 by Arthur Miller and Ingeborg M. Miller, Trustee. Reprinted by permission of Viking Press.

Permission to quote from the plays of Tennessee Williams is acknowledged as follows:

From *the Glass Menagerie* by Tennessee Williams. Copyright 1945 by Tennessee Williams and Edwina D. Williams and renewed 1973 by Tennessee Williams. Reprinted by permission of Random House, Inc.

From *A Streetcar Named Desire* by Tennessee Williams. *The Theatre of Tennessee Williams.* Vol. I. Copyright 1947 by Tennessee Williams. Reprinted by permission of New Directions Publishing Corporation.

From *Summer and Smoke* by Tennessee Williams. *The Theatre of Tennessee Williams.* Vol. II. Copyright 1948 by Tennessee Williams. Reprinted by permission of New Directions Publishing Corporation.

From *The Night of the Iguana* by Tennessee Williams. *The Theatre of Tennessee Williams.* Vol. IV. Copyright © 1961 by Tennessee Williams. Reprinted by permission of New Directions Publishing Corporation.

In the British Commonwealth exclusive of Canada:

A Streetcar Named Desire by Tennessee Williams. *Four Plays* by Tennessee Williams. © Copyright 1947 by Tennessee Williams. Published by Secker & Warburg (£3.10). Reprinted by permission of Elaine Greene Ltd., Literary Agency.

Summer and Smoke by Tennessee Williams. *Four Plays* by Tennessee Williams. © Copyright 1951. Published by Secker & Warburg (£3.10). Reprinted by permission of Elaine Greene Ltd., Literary Agency.

The extracts from Thornton Wilder are used by special permission of the publisher and are from *Three Plays by Thornton Wilder:* Excerpts from pp. 10, 47, 78, 81, 99 in "Our Town." Copyright © 1938, 1957 by Thornton Wilder. Excerpts from pp. 143, 200-201,

238, 240, 243-244 in "The Skin of Our Teeth." Copyright © 1942, 1970 by Thornton Wilder. Excerpt from p. xiv, "Preface." Copyright © 1957 by Thornton Wilder. By permission of Harper & Row, Publishers, Inc.

A portion of this book first appeared in slightly altered form as "The Domestication of Rip Van Winkle: Joe Jefferson's Play as Prologue to Modern American Drama." I acknowledge the permission to reprint that article: Copyright, *The Virginia Quarterly Review,* The University of Virginia, Winter 1974.

To Mary
   Because of Whom Our Family Thrives

CONTENTS

FAMILY, DRAMA, AND AMERICAN DREAMS

INTRODUCTION

In the following study I am arguing that the family situation is the crucial subject of American drama. In our plays family life embodies an important dilemma, one which reflects the strains of a changing family structure. By looking at how the family is portrayed in American drama, perhaps we can discover a habit of mind, a pattern of values and ideology, which has larger implications. The image of family life, then, may be a revealing point at which social history and literature intersect.

The history of America coincides with the emergence of the modern family system. This fact is important to the study of American culture. It should not suggest that in America family life is unique; rather, the opposite, that in general terms it is part of western history. The American family experience seems to be a more extreme example, a purer case, so to speak, of the social forces at work in the western world. In America, we can see family response to these forces in a less qualified and less inhibited form.

My argument begins, then, with a discussion of American family patterns as modern in structure and function. William J. Goode has described the emergence of modern family life in the following way:

> Wherever the economic system expands through industrialization, family patterns change. Extended kinship

ties weaken, lineage patterns dissolve, and a trend toward some form of the conjugal system generally begins to appear—that is, the nuclear family becomes a more independent kinship unit. [1]

The independence of the nuclear family system both emphasizes family life and leaves it vulnerable to many sorts of strains. This is especially true in a culture as distrustful of institutions and hierarchies as America has been. The isolation of the nuclear family—and the corresponding intensity of family feeling—has made the family a source of great hope and of great disappointment. The first signs of these family-centered attitudes actually predate industrialism. We began to sound the theme that our fulfillment is dependent on family life in the Puritan era. And often since, we have assumed an attitude toward the family when we have thought about who we are or what we wish to be. From this perspective the highly publicized concern over the American family in recent years is another example of a long preoccupation.

We demand much of the family, making it the focus of our dreams of harmony and the chief obstacle to their realization, the nightmare to be escaped. Our thoughts and dreams are ambiguous, however. Our attitudes toward family life cluster around contending family ideals. We are at war with and dependent on these ideals. We strive for freedom and are appalled by loneliness; we reject family structure and yearn for its security. Our dominant culture presents us with these conflicting images in a variety of forms. Especially in our drama, both serious and sentimental, we reenact our anxieties about family life.

American drama in the twentieth century has been strikingly preoccupied with problems of family life. Its most characteristic moments are realistic scenes of family strife and squabble and bliss wherein conflicting themes of freedom and security recur and are expressed as dilemmas of family relations and personal psychology. It is both the form and the substance of our dramatists' obsession which I link to the general familialism of our culture. In the following chapters I will show that American drama has inherited and transmuted the tangle of assumptions and desires about the family which have characterized American culture.

The degree to which our playwrights have taken up the subject indicates our overwhelming concern for the family. And since American drama reached its maturity half a century ago when Eugene O'Neill first matched serious intent with accomplishment, our playwrights have been zealously devoted to the problems of family life, most often rendered in a realistic style. As a result, whatever other themes and concerns one can identify (and there are many), American drama is also, and in a fundamental way, domestic drama. Note that our best playwrights are best remembered for their family-centered plays: O'Neill, Arthur Miller, and Tennessee Williams head my list; and I have added Thornton Wilder, Clifford Odets, Lillian Hellman, Edward Albee, and Lorraine Hansberry. Any number of interesting if not outstanding writers might also have been included. Sidney Howard, for example, provides a forceful image of "momism" in *The Silver Cord* (1927). For Elmer Rice, family oppression is part of a larger structure which weighs down his little people, as in *The Adding Machine* (1922) and *Street Scene* (1929). And there are others, such as William Inge, whose work is relevant.

However we draw the list, American drama is dominated by plays of family life. In fact, of those usually cited as our important dramatists, only Maxwell Anderson and William Saroyan remain apart from this preoccupation. And neither has been a counterforce of influence. Anderson's career ranged over many types of plays, including a realistic family comedy, *Saturday's Children* (1927), but his most strenuous attempts were in the field of verse tragedy.[2] Saroyan, the problem child of American drama, has remained the special case he wishes to be. In his one undoubted achievement, *The Time of Your Life* (1939), homeless characters dream of home, but the play is actually a celebration of a life of spiritual anarchy and serendipity apart from the family. If Saroyan belongs to a tradition, it is one distinct from American drama. His sweet acceptance of the unrespectable world, which tempts one to talk about his talent rather than his accomplishment, is really in the Whitman vein—as if Walt had written a comedy.

What is remarkable is not only that Americans write domestic drama but that they write little else. In Europe, the realistic family plays of Ibsen, Strindberg, and Chekhov, important as they are, did not exhaust the possibilities of modern drama. European drama

and theater abound in new forms and styles: futurism, theatrical-
ism, poetic drama, symbolist drama, epic theater. We have no
comparable history. We have flirted with expressionism—in order
to intensify the emotions of family life—and, more recently, with
absurdism. We have a busy avant-garde theater. But if accomplishment is a measure, our heart is in the realistic family play. Can
anyone imagine an American Pirandello?

Of all the European moderns, it is Strindberg in his realistic
phase who is closest in spirit to American drama. Plays such as
The Father (1887) and *Dance of Death* (1909) show obsessed,
frenetic, and warring families of a type we now know well. (O'Neill
knew them, too, and said that Strindberg had the greatest influence
on him.) By contrast, the "tasteless parlor" of Ibsen and the country estate of Chekhov each contains a family life less singular, isolated, and egalitarian than does the multiple-exposed house which
makes up the archetypal set of American drama.[3] In American
family plays, connections with an outer society are tenuous, often
merely a matter of surface verisimilitude, and the impulse is toward
the private life of the family even in our supposedly social playwrights.

A simple but crucial difference with Ibsen and Chekhov is
the social density of the family plays. The relatives, friends, and
neighbors are there not merely to set the scene in the opening moments but are part of the most intimate struggles and scenes as well.
They are not brought on stage occasionally for the sake of realism
but are the result of a vision of the family as part of a larger social
fabric. The society in which the family exists may be a trap or a
constraint but it is not simply more families or a generalized condition of life as it tends to be in an American play. Similarly, Ibsen's
ironic sense of human fate and Chekhov's perspective on life as
suffering comedy are always larger than the family emotions being
dramatized. These playwrights of family life have digested the
experience, have made sense out of it for the world of the play.
In contrast, in our best plays family experience tends to be overwhelming. The drama of family life is so crucial that the greatest
act for the playwright is to make peace with it rather than to understand it. The family becomes the whole world rather than one
aspect of it.

In subsequent chapters I will show that this world is made up of family struggles and disappointment. The protagonist searches for freedom and longs for security. He may escape from the family, may triumph over its oppression, or may be destroyed by it. If he survives, he recapitulates the struggle in his own marriage or with his own children. Or, as survivor, he is left alone and anguished by the loss of family. In a particular play (or career) the American dramatist typically chooses some portion along this continuum of family life to present on stage as the dramatic action. He may choose a broad or a narrow segment; he may choose different phases in the action. Whatever else his play is about, it is likely to be rooted in these struggles. Experience outside the family is explained away in terms of large abstractions about life and through generalizations which assume a democratic sameness in the rest of the world. Or such experience is ignored. The crucial action is that which goes on within the family.

The world of American family drama shows a concern for family failure and destruction. The power of our plays comes from the intensity of this concern. When we write other sorts of plays, we seem less inspired, less able to fuse form and content. Our comedies of family life, where one might expect to find a benign view of domesticity, underline this fact. Our achievements in family comedy are relatively few and unimpressive. To begin with, there are the sentimental comedies which the popular theater has always provided. In these versions ideas are untested and unexamined in order to soothe us. In general, the images are concerned with the past goodness of family security rather than freedom but the variations are endless. Occasionally, the formula has been just right and the power of the nostalgia is so strong that the play takes on a special life in terms of its very naïveté. *Life with Father* (1939) by Howard Lindsay and Russel Crouse and *I Remember Mama* (1944) by John van Druten evoke such sweet family memories.[4] As I will show, the play version of *Rip Van Winkle* (1865) is the nineteenth-century anticipation of this sort of longing, and O'Neill's *Ah, Wilderness!* (1933) is the modern self-conscious quintessence.

We do have an excellent writer of farces in George S. Kaufman, who is probably our funniest playwright. But farce, as Eric Bentley has noted, is unlike comedy. It embodies "wishes to damage the family, to desecrate the household gods."[5] Comedy, on the other hand, is marked by a spirit of compromise and social healing.

One has only to watch Sheridan Whiteside wreak havoc in the Stanley family in Kaufman's *The Man Who Came to Dinner* (1939) or note his cynical parody of his own happy ending in *Beggar on Horseback* (1925) to catch the spirit of guerrilla warfare being carried on against the adult world of domesticity. In *You Can't Take It with You* (1936) the entire Vanderhof family is engaged in an assault on the established norms, a farceur's dream of the family of freedom.

Two of our best comedy writers are S. N. Behrman and Philip Barry. Their careers show the difficulty not only of writing on manners in a country which professes democratic classlessness but also of affirming American family life without sentimentally avoiding its contradictions. Barry's *Holiday* (1929) is a particularly good example of what happens when high comedy meets the American spirit, in this instance embodied in the character of Johnny Case, orphan and self-made genius of the stock market. Young Case is infatuated with rich and beautiful Julia Seton but discovers that he cannot compromise with the conventional values she and her tycoon father represent: "I suppose the fact is, I love feeling free inside even better than I love you, Julia."[6] Julia's sister, Linda, is a rebel, too, and wants to be done with the sort of life she has been leading. She knows that the Seton family is more than stuffy; for all its riches it represents a life that is emotionally bankrupt. "The touch of the ashman," as she and her few like-minded friends call it, has driven her brother to alcoholism and her acquaintances to suicide.

Barry neatly measures the inner vitality of the characters by their improvised gaiety. He show us how much life they possess beneath the surface of social conventions by testing their ability to trade light-hearted banter. As it turns out, Linda is the fit partner for Johnny's Thoreauvian desires to go on a spiritually serious holiday, and she leaves to follow him at the final curtain. We are sure they will be united, and we are equally sure that the point of the play is that the hero does not accommodate to the family or to the social values it represents. Case is the embodiment of self-reliance, consciously linked to the pioneer spirit. He makes his capable way into the drawing room and quite victoriously finds his way out again. The woman he wins hopes in the end that she can come back and rescue her drunken brother.

A similar motif can be seen in Behrman's *End of Summer* (1935), where the young radical, Will, in love with rich Paula Frothingham, also goes off to prove his self-sufficiency with the young lady in hot pursuit. Here again the ingenue's family is equated with false social values. Will's temptation is not whether to make more money than he needs but whether to take what is there. He decides against it. Behrman sees more value in the old social order than does Barry, and so his rich family has more virtues. Leonie, the mother, has grace, innocence, and a loving heart, which the Setons lack. Yet it is clearly shown that her life and the values it represents are badly flawed, dangerously thoughtless, and must be discarded by the young lovers. Behrman is wistful. He would like some social healing and a place for Leonie, but the young lovers achieve their personal salvation by breaking with the family system.

In these plays, Barry and Behrman seem uncomfortable with images of family reconciliation. Their example provides us with a clue. It may be that comedy involves attitudes which are inimical to our deepest feelings about family life. There is an implied renewal in the wedding scene that typically ends a comedy, a renewal of the social order through marriage. The blocking elements, those few characters who disrupt the action, are subdued or cast out. Marriages may be awkward and families troublesome, but accommodation, not destruction, is the solution of comedy. American playwrights shy away from such inclusiveness. Even our comedy writers prefer individual gestures of freedom.

Yet it is not simply freedom, either, but a matter of what resources are available to the characters in American plays. Freedom is not necessarily at war with accommodation, as the English comedies of George Bernard Shaw demonstrate. His attitudes toward the family highlight our own, for Shaw has plenty of iconoclasm:

> All that one can say is, roughly, that the homelier the home, and the more familiar the family, the worse for everybody concerned. The family ideal is a humbug and a nuisance: one might as reasonably talk of the barracks ideal, or the forecastle ideal, or any other substitution

of the machinery of social organization for the end of it, which must always be the fullest and most capable life. [7]

If we look carefully at such attacks, however, we see that they are aimed at the cant and sentimentality of public "official" views of family life, not really at the family itself. In this sense, Shaw, the great debunker and champion of progressive and liberated ideas, is very much an institutionalist. No American playwright would use a term such as "social machinery" about the family except to say that if it is social, it is corrupt; and if it is machinery, it is unnatural. To Shaw the family is neither natural nor unnatural. Shaw's assumption is that social machinery is necessary, even useful, although an old-fashioned machine creates aggravating friction and needs a good-natured kick now and then to make it work. In Shaw's plays outdated ideas and useless conventions of love, marriage, and family life are shown up for what they are and ridiculed. But social conventions per se make up the necessary condition of social—which is to say, human—life.

Behind the social conventions is a spirit which Shaw, in *Man and Superman* (1905), calls the "Life Force." The Life Force uses courtship, marriage, and the family to further the evolution of the human species. John Tanner, the hero of *Man and Superman,* loves to denounce the domestic system. For example, one very long speech ends with this flourish:

The law for father and son and mother and daughter is not the law of love: it is the law of revolution, of emancipation, of final supersession of the old and worn-out by the young and capable. I tell you, the first duty of manhood and womanhood is a Declaration of Independence: the man who pleads his father's authority is no man: the woman who pleads her mother's authority is unfit to bear citizens to a free people. [8]

By itself Tanner's speech could be an American manifesto on the family. But all the while he is talking, Ann Whitefield, who wishes to marry him, is calculating to what use she can put his inclination to talk. Her deflation of Tanner at the end of what seems to him a triumphant speech is delicious:

ANN *(Watching him with quiet curiosity):* I suppose
you will go in seriously for politics some day, Jack.[9]

Tanner, who can convict others in the play of foolishness, is himself convicted. Shaw then demonstrates the Life Force operating through Ann, and thus puts the characters in a larger frame of reference, as Ann pursues Tanner in this world and the next, and tricks him into marriage with a conventional Victorian fainting spell at the final curtain. In other words, Shaw, the life force behind the play, uses the conventional theater to *his* own ends.

This approach is the essence of *Misalliance* (1910). Lina Szczepanowska literally crashes into the drawing-room comedy world of the Tarletons when the airplane she is flying in ends up in their greenhouse. This world is taken up with complicated plots of who will marry whom and, consequently, who will be pleased or put out. It is a way of life which Lina, a Polish acrobat who lives by her skill and daring, despises for its conventionality. Here we have a situation common to American drama, the individual defying family institutions. Lina is a woman whose allegiance to freedom makes her more than a match for Johnny Case and Will Dexter combined. Clearly the superior character, Lina soon dazzles all the men in the household, each of whom secretly proposes to her. True to form, she turns them down, rising to witty indignation at the insult of having been asked to marry.

But if Lina is superior and lives at a level above the rest of the characters, they, too, have lives worth living. Lina might reject their conventions, but Shaw does not reject their humanity behind the conventions. None of the men can stand up to the vigorous calisthenics Lina puts them through at the exercise bar. But neither could most of us in the audience. (Linda, in *Holiday,* recalls swinging from her exercise bar to spit at her relatives.) The fun comes, in part, from our sympathy for the men. Indeed, Lina's vigor, physical and spiritual, has its own ridiculous side to balance the satiric picture of the Tarletons carrying on.

In the end the daughter Hypatia still must choose the better match, Percival, over Bentley, and we are meant to be glad when she does. After all, according to Shaw, that is part of the machinery by which life moves us closer to the superior level of Lina. And if Bentley seems potentially left behind by such an evolutionary schema, why, Lina will take him under her wing (as mother Tarleton has done the distraught clerk Gunner, who comes to shoot her husband) and fly him through a storm to put some spirit in him. Thus the ending is both proper (as a social and theatrical convention) and fitting (as a way to go beyond this conventional life). "Well," says Tarleton, who has up to this point had a remark for all occasions, "I suppose—er—I suppose theres [sic] nothing more to be said." "Thank goodness," answers Hypatia, now engaged, who gets the last word on everyone, including Shaw.[10] When all is said—all the talk in the family, in the play, in drawing room comedies, in the life they represent—marriage and family are for Shaw the way things get done. They are the machinery of the theater and of life.

American playwrights are not attracted to such a vision. Their imaginations are stirred by other family possibilities—heroic opposition or tragic oppression or agonized longing—but not by the joyous release of setting things right within the family. There is a touch of the exposé about our family plays. The audience sees what life is "really" like, that is, the family battleground. Reconciliation is not often part of this reality,[11] and few images of family life from our comedies convince us the way our family dramas do. The most powerful impulse in our plays comes out of the dilemma of family escape and loss.

In my argument, the method is twofold: I am looking at plays as an index to society; and, also, I am looking at represented social structure as a key to the plays. Harry Levin has remarked that:

> Literature, instead of reflecting life, refracts it. Our
> task, in any given case, is to determine the angle of

refraction. Since the angle depends on the density of the medium, it is always shifting, and the task is never easy. [12]

Following Levin's suggestion, I have tried to approach the plays under discussion as having density; that is, as vital creations rather than inert artifacts subject only to content analysis. And if their density helps to determine the angle of refraction, so, too, does the cultural context from which they come, especially those values and ideals about family life which have been inherited.

For this reason, in the following chapters I begin with a brief discussion of the sources of our attitudes toward family life and go on to show how the resultant images have been expressed in our popular culture. In the main, however, my evidence is from significant individual plays. Although I am searching for what I have called a habit of mind by which to link drama, intellectual history, and social history, I will try to see literature in Levin's sense, as part of history but expressing it in a special way with its own special rules, translating life through its "formalities and assumptions."

I am hoping to demonstrate a common denominator of modern American drama. To establish such a baseline, and to test out interdisciplinary techniques and interconnections in a manageable way, I concentrate my discussion of American drama on selected plays of Eugene O'Neill, Arthur Miller, and Tennessee Williams. These artists will be examined for their capacity to test existing "formalities and assumptions." The choice is calculated but not, I hope, arbitrary. O'Neill is the chief dramatist of America, and any study which ignored him would be rightly suspect. Miller and Williams represent what seem to me the major artistic and intellectual reactions to O'Neill's achievement. In my final chapter I suggest ways in which other American playwrights are part of this tradition. (Dates which appear in parentheses refer to the first major production of a play.)

I am using the family as a way into the plays, but my critical point of view toward each work will emphasize its dramatic action—that is, the shape of the events represented on stage—rather than a play's language structure. Dramatic character I take to be a function of this action, and language and setting complementary gestures. The totality expresses a dramatic image.

A word about the terms "realism" and "expressionism." Most of the plays I discuss are realistic. I use the term in a broad sense and attempt no strict distinction between it and naturalism (there is very little "pure" naturalism in American drama). The term has no connotations as to the reality of the images presented by a play but refers to a style of literature; in this case, drama. Realism has had a short life thus far in western drama, emerging only recently at the end of the nineteenth century with Ibsen, Strindberg, and Chekhov. In historical terms one can argue a relation between it, the Sophoclean tradition, and the classical unities of time and place. Also, it should be noted that realistic *family* drama has its roots in eighteenth-century England and the domestic drama of Lillo's *The London Merchant* (1731). In addition, the French "well-made play" of the nineteenth century, with its logical plot structure, was an influence on realistic drama, which often adopted its three-act pattern of introduction, complication, and resolution. The pattern is particularly evident in realistic plays of character development where the final revelation of the deepest motives of the protagonist is the truth aimed at. But whatever its antecedents, realism as a critical term refers to a modern style. The general qualities of the realistic drama are: prose speech of an everyday sort; a coherent plot; a specific setting of stable time and place; the passage of time represented as objective; events within the range of experience of the audience; and characters with identifiable motives. The realistic drama invites empathy with its characters. They are to be seen not as higher (tragedy) or lower (comedy) but as on the same level as a middle-class audience. To convince us the play has to stay within a range of emotions, language, and experience which gives it the appearance of verisimilitude. Artistic constriction is balanced by an intensity of identification as we are asked to put ourselves in the place of others.

Expressionism, as I use the term, is less precise than realism. It refers not to a particular movement in German drama of the early twentieth century, but generally to many of the principal anti-realistic devices of modern drama. Such an umbrella term is crude but useful, and I take comfort in the fact that most critics of modern drama use it in a wide sense as I do. Expressionism suggests the subjective, inner, or dream life. Its characteristics are: illogicality; self-conscious symbolism; abstractions made literal and concrete; unstable, shifting, and dissolving personalities, locales, and time frames; characters which may be deliberately two-dimensional; stylized choral effects; action and dialogue of non sequitur; an episodic structure often illustrating theme rather than developing character; and a frank theatricality of a presentational rather than representational sort. Expressionism is an assault on commonsense notions of reality and on the literary conventions of realism. It lends itself to satire. It puts you at a distance emotionally rather than drawing you close. It offers the dramatist the possibility of wild energy rather than intense concentration.

Drama has seldom been used by those who explore literature in relation to intellectual and social history. Sven Armens has written an excellent book on a related subject, the family in classical drama.[13] His approach is an attempt to identify psychological archetypes and so, in method, there is a radical difference between his study and my own, a predisposition toward different questions and answers. The universals Armens demonstrates are recommended as a valuable corrective to the specific, historical patterns I am identifying. Books, articles, and theses abound on the literary treatment of the American woman, the child, the themes of loneliness and of personal freedom, and the nature of modern tragedy. Similarly, the literature on the sociology of modern family life has become massive in recent years, and the social history of family life is a new, growing field. My attempt is to bridge these areas of study. As will be obvious in the notes which follow, my own thinking draws heavily on the insights of drama critics as well as scholars of family life. Raymond Williams, Dennis Welland, John Sirjamaki, Talcott Parsons, and William Goode are but a few on whose work my own depends. This study is not one which offers new scholarship but one which attempts to make something new out of what certain critics and scholars—isolated from each other— have already suggested. If it has any separate merit, it is that of affirming the possibility of intellectual community.

NOTES

1. William J. Goode, *World Revolution and Family Patterns* (New York. 1963), p. 6.

2. It is interesting that *Winterset* (1935), usually regarded as Anderson's most successful verse tragedy, has a domestic theme in its treatment of the legacy of the Sacco-Vanzetti case. T.S. Eliot also attempted to revive verse in the modern theater, and he borrowed elements of the popular domestic comedy of the London stage.

3. For the quoted phrase, derived from Henry James, see Francis Fergusson, *The Idea of a Theater* (Garden City, N.Y., 1949), pp. 170-174. Dennis Welland noted the archetypal American stage set in Welland, *Arthur Miller* (New York, 1961), pp. 63-64.

4. Neither play is original material since both were taken from collections of short stories. The quintessential nostalgia they represent may be related, in part, to the desperate times, just prior to and during World War II.

5. Eric Bentley, *The Life of the Drama* (New York, 1967), p. 226.

6. Philip Barry, *Holiday* in *States of Grace: Eight Plays* (New York, 1975), p. 265.

7. Bernard Shaw, "Preface" to *Misalliance* in *Complete Plays with Prefaces* (New York, 1962) IV, 87.

8. Bernard Shaw, *Man and Superman* in *Complete Plays,* III, 574.

9. Ibid.

10. Shaw, *Misalliance,* p. 204.

11. There is some reconciliation to be seen in our comedy-dramas such as Tennesse Williams's *The Rose Tattoo* (1951). As I will note in Chapter 5, the "picturesqueness" of immigrant family life seems to give Williams a special dispensation from family anguish. A similar point can be made about one of the better domestic comedy-dramas of an earlier era, Sidney Howard's *They Knew What They Wanted* (1924). Howard's usual mode was the drama of family oppression. In this play it is naturalized Tony who, in his Italian accent, teaches Amy that family life has a sustaining power. Joe, the footloose American Wobbly, gratefully leaves his paternal responsibilities in their hands and lights out for the territories. Perhaps William Inge's *Come Back, Little Sheba* (1950) can be said to affirm family life, though in a guarded and heavily qualified way. At least, in it—and in other plays of the 1950s—domesticity is preferable to annihilation by loneliness (or the Cold War).

12. Harry Levin, "Literature as an Institution," in *Criticism: The Foundations of Modern Literary Judgment,* ed. Mark Schorer, Josephine Miles, and Gordon McKenzie (New York, 1958), p. 552.

13. Sven Armens, *Archetypes of the Family in Literature* (Seattle, Wash., 1966).

1

THE AMERICAN FAMILY: SECURITY OR FREEDOM?

> *In proportion as the circle of public society is extended, it may be anticipated that the sphere of private intercourse will be contracted; far from supposing that the members of modern society will ultimately live in common, I am afraid they will end by forming only small coteries.*
>
> Alexis de Tocqueville [1]

> *Many constellations of sentiment are, however, possible within any given structure, and because the crisis of the family today is a crisis of emotion—of attachment and rejection—it is incumbent upon the family historian to trace the tale of sentiments.*
>
> Edward Shorter [2]

Social analysts from Karl Marx to Karl Polanyi have noted the fundamental shift in social relations which has occurred under the modern economy of the western world, a shift from status relations to market relations, from feudal ties to the "cash nexus." [3] This change in social relations has had profound effects on the family institution. First, the family had been jarred loose from long-standing social patterns in which it appeared to be the indispensable center of life. [4] This change in the family's place in society has meant that in one sense the family's importance has diminished. As Talcott Parsons has said, "it is not [as it once was] a major direct agency of integration of the larger society."[5] For example, the family today no longer performs a producing economic function. Where the household was once the center of an entire family's work, it is now a place the wage-earner leaves each day. Also, in an atomistic, homogeneous, "leveled" society, the family has lost its extended kinship relation and shrunk in on itself. Where the household depended on (and may have contained) several generations and an assortment of relatives, it now comprises two generations and these for but part of their lives.[6]

The second principal effect of the changing social fabric has been on the internal functions of the family and is a corollary to the first. If the family is in one sense less important, it is in another more crucial. The very process of contraction has also produced a concentration which intensifies those important social and psychological relations which still occur in the family. As a result of the reduction of its traditional survival functions, notes John Sirjamaki, "the importance of the family as a primary social group and of its child-bearing, child-rearing, and personality functions have come to the fore."[7]

The modern family pattern, then, begins to take shape.[8] It stresses, as Goode puts it, "the relative exclusion of a wide range of affinal and blood relatives from its everyday affairs."[9] This has meant fewer controls over the family by the kin network, a "freeing" of the nuclear unit to seek its own fortune. In addition, when fortunes are bad it has meant less support from others. Fortunes, moreover, are emotional as well as financial. The uncertain young parents are freed from the help and support of a wide range of experienced relatives just as they are freed from a prescribed—usually subordinate—relation to them.

With this independence from others has come mobility in residence and a courtship system based more on mutual attraction and less on family necessity.[10] Such egalitarianism is also extended to the status of women and to their work roles, though of all changes in the family pattern surely this has been the slowest. Finally, a high divorce rate, a lower birth rate, and a smaller family size have come to characterize the modern family.

Exactly how and why these changes first came about is not certain. Theories of natural evolution, which writers once held—such as an orderly historical progression from indiscriminate mating through polygamy to Victorian monogamy—are no longer credible. [11] Furthermore, the history of the family in America has been only lightly touched by the professional scholar [12] and what has been written is often as caught up in the mystique of the family as the very phenomena it describes. It is clear that the changing family is, in part, a response to the new technology. The factory system and capitalism destroyed the land-value culture, which gave stability and an aura of permanence to family life. Industrialism accelerated the pace and extent of these changes. The new order required "both geographic and social mobility," [13] and the family responded to these demands, becoming smaller and more individualistic as it moved into urban centers to work. [14]

But not all changes in the family were the later results of industrialism and urbanization. Some changes preceded the factory system and may be thought of as preparing the way for it. [15] Philippe Ariès has written that the concept of the modern family is a notion which emerged in the seventeenth century when the family began to be noticed and to inspire art. "This powerful concept was formed around the conjugal family, that of the parents and children." [16] The prototype of the modern family began to emerge at this time. Ariès has located it in what he calls the "big houses" of leading middle-class citizens. [17] Here a new grouping of domestic life came into being, one which was made up of the nuclear family and servants.

At first, life in the big house was a combination of the public, communal aspects of medieval social intercourse with a new movement toward withdrawal and privacy. [18] Public business, for example, was still conducted in the home. But increasingly in the eighteenth century, the nuclear family came to represent a rejection of sociability and a "new desire to keep the world at bay." [19] The scramble for separation began to affect domestic life in many respects, from the specialization of rooms to new books on family, rather than public, etiquette. The major characteristic of the modern family was, however, its single-minded devotion "to serving the interests of a deliberately restricted posterity":

> The modern family ... cuts itself off from the world and
> opposes to society the isolated group of parents and
> children. All the energy of the group is expended on
> helping the children to rise in the world, individually
> and without any collective ambition: the children rather
> than the family. [20]

Thus Ariès sees the social and intellectual history of the last three
hundred years in terms of the triumph of the self-regarding family.
This history has shown, he says, a basic incompatibility between
"sociability and the concept of the family." [21]

When one looks at American history with Ariès's argument
in mind, the fact of crucial importance is that America was colo-
nized precisely at the time when these changes in the European
family were taking place. And America was founded by English
families who represented the radical forefront of many of these
changes. Consequently, America had from the outset a family
system that was less impeded by traditional structures than its
European counterparts. In this way the history of the family parallels that of the economic system. At a time when western capitalism
had its radical thrust in the American economy, western family
relations had their radical expression in American family patterns.

The Puritans who settled New England are prime representa-
tives of the emerging nuclear family pattern. Their background was
rooted in a dissenting religion which associated English communal
life with the decadence of the Catholic Church and offered as the
bulwark against such corruption, the family and home. [22] They
wished to sever the family from its traditional Christian basis,
rejecting the notion that marriage was a sacrament. To this end
English Puritans attempted in the Matrimonial Act of 1653 to
make both marriage and divorce contractual (and so a matter of
state control). [23] While the law was repealed in England with the
Restoration, it survived in America and prospered with the Revolution. [24]

When Puritans emigrated to America to escape the antichrist
and to make money, they came as families, and through families
they hoped to establish the kingdom of heaven on earth. Indeed,

the family was the very basis of Puritan social theory and practice, as Edmund S. Morgan has shown.[25]

Puritanism had a strong strain of individualism as one of its significant characteristics. There is no doubt that the individual covenant of grace provided a main source of tension and energy in Puritan thought and life. One's salvation and one's responsibility for it were terrifyingly personal matters. Yet Puritans also held to the need for social covenants. Within these, men were obliged to accept places in an institutionalized social hierarchy.[26] For the seventeenth-century Puritan, the primary and primordial social institution was the family.[27] Both Church and State grew out of the family and took their structure from the family. People joined the church on behalf of their households and salvation was a family matter.[28] The law, too, dealt with heads of families. Both Church and State interfered with the family through admonition and laws, but this was a direct measure of its crucial importance to Puritan society. So highly thought of was family life that its alternatives were forcibly discouraged through taxation or banishment. In some ways, such as marriage and divorce, the family was above even the church—until late in the seventeenth century ministers were forbidden to marry couples.

The Puritan family was in large part "a property institution" for a rising middle class.[29] Puritans emphasized strict discipline, sobriety, industry, and self-denial in family life, virtues in keeping with a class in need of capital and with an environment where survival was a desperate struggle. The domestic household was made up of servants, bound children, natural children, and parents.[30] The father was its head, spiritually, morally, and legally; the Puritan family drew upon the Mosaic law for its justification. The wife was subservient to the husband, the children and servants to the wife.

Internal family relations were not, of course, so neatly arranged in practice. For example, one writer has pointed out the paradox in the status of children.[31] The child was an individual with his own soul and destiny, but the father was patriarch. Full of sin, the child needed to be brought to grace. Wretched as he was, he had the great potential of being saved. New England colonial law was thus strongly in support of parental authority to the point of one colony's providing the death penalty for a disobedient child. But it also abolished feudal inheritance practices which reinforced such authority, and this in a culture which associated property with grace. Children, then, were seen both as important and subordinate.

A contradictory situation existed for Puritan wives as well. They, too, were to be strictly obedient to their husbands. Education beyond domestic skills was not given to most women; and once married, they found their sphere limited to the home. Further, the English common law which America adopted during the colonial period reduced a woman who married to the state of having few legal rights, beyond being protected from abuse. [32] Yet, in other ways, wives did have a new status. [33] For one thing they were considered equal with their husbands before the rest of the household. More importantly, marriage was a contract, and breaking its provisions—such as committing adultery—was not the mild prerogative of the male. Any offender was equally guilty and punishable. Any injured party was entitled to divorce, which was a legislative matter.

These incongruities in Puritan family life are often explained as the effect of individualism hard at work on the oppressive, anti-democratic aspects of an earlier society. [34] Such a one-eyed view distorts our perspective, for it implies that the changing family is only an effect rather than a cause as well. What seem to be paradoxical qualities are less so if the Puritan family is seen to be in the process of separating itself from society. Morgan has traced such a process in the family life of the Saints, showing it to be a rejection of the larger New England society. [35] And other writers have noted that even in the early years of dedicated colonization, common work offended feelings of family separateness. [36] With a weakening of communal ties came an emphasis on internal ones, and this two-way movement of family relations explains the changing status of family members. Women gained esteem for their household management even while they had no legal selves. Children gained importance for their spiritual potential, even while responsibility for their upbringing fell heavily within the family, particularly on the father.

Seventeenth-century Puritans retained one medieval practice

which balanced their family exclusiveness. Many parents put their children out into other families at a young age, [37] retaining ties and authority through frequent visits. Just how often this happened is not known. The practice was partly related to economy, but, as Morgan has shown, even well-to-do families sent their children away while taking others in. [38] He suggests that parents were motivated to put children out for fear "of spoiling them by too great affection," and that this had psychological validity in preserving affection while ensuring discipline. [39]

Morgan's explanation makes eminent sense, for with an emphasis on internal ties came an intensification of them. Thus, while Puritan life was severe, it was not drab. In the poetry of Anne Bradstreet there is expressed a rich emotionalism:

> If ever two were one, then surely we.
> If ever man were loved by wife, then thee;
> If ever wife was happy in a man,
> Compare with me ye women if you can.
> I prize thy love more than whole mines of gold,
> Or all the riches that the East doth hold.
> My love is such that rivers cannot quench,
> Nor ought but love from thee give recompense.
> Thy love is such I can no way repay;
> The heavens reward thee manifold, I pray.
> Then while we love, in love let's so persever,
> That when we live no more we may love ever. [40]

Another good example might be the letters of John Winthrop to his wife. In either case, remarkable gentleness and love can be pointed to as counterbalancing the austerity and authoritarianism of Puritan family life. It would be more accurate, however, to see both qualities together, each as part of the other. The exclusive family life of the Puritans nurtured emotional intimacy but demanded authority to preserve its coherence. [41]

In other colonies the family life of the dominant culture reflected many of the same tendencies, though not to the same degree, as the Puritan family. In the middle colonies there was a great variety of types, [42] dominated for a time by the Quakers with their large, but very exclusive, concept of the correspondence between family and meeting. [43] In the southern colonies the patriarchal pattern of the country English manor approached the aristocratic mode, and in this regard was very like the "big houses" that emerged in seventeenth- and eighteenth-century Europe. [44] But two crucial differences existed. One was the slave work force, the other the isolation of farms. [45]

Both factors worked to give an appearance of self-sufficiency to the southern family quite beyond that of the European household. [46] Black slaves meant a work force, from field hands to artisans, much more alien and separate from the managerial family than were European household servants. [47] Also, the fullness of economic activity on these upper middle-class "farms" was paralleled by the necessity for social and church functions to be carried on in the home—activities such as learning to read, to dance, or to play music, and religious events such as baptisms, weddings, and funerals. It was family-centered life in the fullest sense. [48] William Byrd likened himself to a Biblical patriarch, living "in a kind of Independence on everyone but Providence." [49]

The significance of the Puritan family pattern, then, is in those impulses of intensity, withdrawal, and self-sufficiency which characterized it. In this regard the Puritan family was the most extreme example of forces at work in Colonial America as a whole, just as America became the most extreme example of social patterns for the industrialized West. Of course, there was not such actual uniformity among families as my generalizations might imply. Not only during colonial days but particularly after the Revolution immigration brought new family patterns, often tied to a variety of religions and sects, which made for great diversity of family type. In the nineteenth century wave after wave of these families arrived here. Still, for most immigrants such diversity gave way, at least in part, to the effects of "Americanization," that is, traditional ties were weakened and families moved *toward* the nuclear type. [50] And it is just in this process that they were anticipated by the Puritan family.

For example, the conditions of the frontier in the nineteenth century repeated those of the seventeenth and eighteenth centuries and made for a tight familial culture. The economic asset of a large family, along with its isolation and the necessity of welfare and survival functions being carried on in the home, made for a rather discretely functioning unit:[51]

> This constant enclosure by the family inevitably bred into its members a strong family-mindedness and built up their estimation of both family and kindred more strongly than is the case today.[52]

Perhaps more important was the initial support which an accelerating capitalism gave to the family in revolutionary and nineteenth-century America:

> Capitalism strongly supported the stability of the family, first by providing a means to harness family members in common enterprise but yet permit each person to be economically acquisitive as an individual; and second by motivating them to engage in hard, ceaseless work as an end in itself, which was necessary to them in any event if they were to survive and prosper.[53]

In agriculture, the family farm was the means by which land exploitation and food production for Europe were initially carried on.[54] And, as in Europe, artisans produced at home and factories hired families as units.[55]

But such primary support did not last beyond the mid-nineteenth century. The constant movement westward made for an unsettling impermanence as the small land entrepreneur struggled from homestead to homestead.[56] Family farms gave way to large agricultural "factories" as the chief producing units.[57] The increasing differentiation and specialization of technology first separated members of families and, of greater importance, removed job control from the parents, particularly the father.[58]

As industrialization became the dominant mode of production, the economic basis of the family was removed and a process of dispersion and disorganization began: the modern family pattern emerged. Industrialization demanded mobility and independence.[59] The breadwinner left home each day, and the home followed the job, usually into the city. There was no longer an economic advantage to large families and, in fact, the cost of living penalized them. The wage system meant that young men and, to a lesser extent, young women were less under the control of parents, whose authority had already been weakened by the disappearance of primogeniture. The status of children began to rise dramatically as the government took over the functions of education and, later, of protection through child labor laws. The status of women also rose somewhat with the winning of certain property rights and with the political agitation for equality from the mid-nineteenth century on.

The sum of these changes meant that our acquisitive society was not pressuring the family to produce mobile entrepreneurs—self-sufficient, self-reliant, self-interested individuals. Where previously the Puritan family had separated itself from society, now individuals began to separate themselves from the family. The "fit" between the Puritan pattern of family solidarity—with its opposition to society—and the new economic order was no longer a neat one.[60] In the new shape of things such a family was a rather square peg. Its unified structure, once radical, was now often the conservative opposition. "The need for placing individuals in their jobs on the basis of individual merit rather than family position... [means] that the family gives way before industrializing forces."[61]

Of course, the family did not completely give way. Rather, contrary forces of contraction and dispersion were at work on the family, which continued to perform certain basic—and crucially emphasized—functions. The history of these family changes is not one of the progressive triumphs of individualism and democratic liberation. Families were the scenes of assaults within assaults. "Individualism" and "democracy" were profoundly ambiguous forces in their effect on the family.

In sorting out the confusions of family patterns, one comes to the complex of values and ideals which surrounds and infuses family life. For the family is not only the structure and functions by which we describe it. It is also a cultural unit which creates history out of desires and beliefs. Edward Shorter has remarked: "The nuclear family is a state of mind. . . ."[62] And certainly he is correct that formulations of ideology and value have been at work on the family. As these formulations interacted with the changing structure and functions of the family, two ideal models of the family have emerged. These models are, of course, ideological counterparts to the dominant family patterns; but they are not related in a simple way. The mechanism of cultural justification may have called them into being, but once activated they took on lives of their own. The power of the longings these models represent can be felt to the present day, for they link the family to the center of American thought. The study of family life is itself conditioned by deeply felt attitudes.

Each of these two models has been accompanied by what we might call an ethos which animates, justifies, and perpetuates it. One model is that of a stable, ordered family life lost (or being lost) to the past; the other model is of a spontaneous, natural family life to be gained in the future. The first is animated by nostalgia and pessimism; the second by apocalypse and hope. I shall refer to these two models as the family of security and the family of freedom, for they represent, I think, the urge toward the safety of mutuality along with the contrary urge for independence and selfhood.[63] Both involve a strong sense of self-sufficiency along with a rejection of social institutions. In a curious way these two models depend on each other even as they clash and are antagonistic.

If the structure and function of the family pattern of self-containment can be traced to the Puritans in our culture, the ideal of the family of security is not located in their specifically religious family context. True, overtones of pious Christianity often accompany images of the family of security, especially in the nineteenth century, but these are not Puritan, and not even essential. The real roots of this ideal model are in our agrarian, democratic dreams.

We are a middle-class culture with a strong tradition of family values, derived in part from an agrarian ideology with a central ideal of "family-owned, family-sized farms."[64] Many writers have pointed out the importance of farming in American thought, locating the sources of this habit of mind in the eighteenth-century physiocrats and in Jefferson. But the fact that these farms were thought of as *family* units has not been emphasized. Jefferson's ideal America depends on the family as much as it does on the farm. Writing to his daughters, Mary and Martha, he repeatedly expressed the ideal that the family was the one truly meaningful, happy, or important society. [65] Indeed, when he was Vice-President, he longed for his family as a quiet refuge of security in contrast to the wrangling of public life, in a way anticipating a recurring motif of the nineteenth century:

> Environed here in scenes of constant torment, and oblo-
> quy, worn down in a station where no effort to do men
> service can avail anything, I feel not that existence is a
> blessing, but when something calls my mind to my
> family or farm. [66]

That last conjunction is significant, for the two ideas of family and farm are interchangeable to Jefferson. When reading him, you can usually assume "family" whenever you read "farmer" or "farm." The same association showed itself when he was Secretary of State, agriculture calling to mind the home. And when he was abroad, too, he wrote:

> I am savage enough to prefer the woods, the wilds, and
> the independence of Monticello, to all the brilliant
> pleasures of this gay capital [Paris]. [67]

The desire to retreat to Monticello led Jefferson to urge James Madison to follow the example of his other friends and build nearby so that together they could form a "private rational society." [68]

The idea of the cosmopolitan Jefferson thinking of himself as "savage" and going on about the pleasures of the hearth might lead one to suspect that he wanted only to quiet the ladies back home with such sentiments. But his protest was also in keeping with his notion that political freedom depended on independence and self-reliance—owning property and tilling your own soil made you free.

The small family farm was the best means for Americans to attain and preserve such freedom. The land was there to inspire benign instincts; equally important, one lived with others but free from society. In this way an harmonious balance would be struck. Each family, independent on its farm, meant that each citizen, free in his thinking and protected by a document which hedged the government in, would enjoy the good life. The family farm was a refuge for good men, a bridge between the extremes of despotic society, with its hierarchies of wages and manufactures, and anarchic nature, with its distasteful barbarity and unfulfilled potential. It was, as Leo Marx has shown, a political pastoral.[69] Jefferson wanted Americans to move out of society into the halfway world of the pastoral where the best of nature and of civility could be captured and held in balance, to live in static harmony rather than dynamic interchange. He wanted a civilized life (like the good eighteenth-century man he was); he did not want society. The family farm seemed the ideal answer.

Perhaps the fullest literary expression of the Jeffersonian family farm was made not by Jefferson but by one of his contemporaries, J. Hector St. John Crèvecoeur. In his *Letters from an American Farmer,* Crèvecoeur extends Jefferson's notion of America as a special place and a special time. The lesson we learn is that through ownership of the land, hard work, and a free economy, individuals such as Andrew, the Hebridean, and communities such as Nantucket prosper. Crèvecoeur makes it plain in the first two letters that the family situation is central to the good life. The growing family on the farm is seen in splendid simplicity, interfering with and bothered by no one. A farm, a wife, and a family to bind one to the farm—this is the recipe for the good life and the basis for Crèvecoeur's effusion in the famous third letter: "we are the most perfect society now existing in the world."[70]

In the second letter, Crèvecoeur draws a mural of family life which later America was to long for:

I married, and this perfectly reconciled me to my situation [as a farmer]; my wife rendered my house all at once chearful [sic] and pleasing; it no longer appeared gloomy and solitary as before; when I went to work in the fields I worked with more alacrity and sprightliness; I felt that I did not work for myself alone, and this encouraged me much. My wife would often come with her knitting in her hand, and sit under the shady trees, praising the straitness of my furrows, and the docility of my horses....

When I contemplate my wife, by my fireside, while she either spins, knits, darns, or suckles our child, I cannot describe the various emotions of love, of gratitude, of conscious pride which thrill my heart, and often overflow in involuntary tears....

Often when I plough my low ground, I place my little boy on a chair which screws to the beam of the plow—its motion and that of the horses please him, he is perfectly happy and begins to chat. As I lean over the handle, various are the thoughts which croud [sic] into my mind. I am now doing for him, I say, what my father formerly did for me, may God enable him [the son] to live that he may perform the same operations for the same purpose when I am worn out and old! I relieve his mother of some trouble while I have him with me, the odoriferous furrow exhilarates his spirits, and seems to do the child a great deal of good, for he looks more blooming since I have adopted that practice; can more pleasure, more dignity be added to that primary occupation? The father thus plowing with his child, and to feed his family, is inferior only to the emperor of China ploughing as an example to his kingdom. [71]

The lesson is clear. Through domesticity Crèvecoeur corrects his mistaken longing to go out into the world; and thus he learns the meaning of the good life. For Crèvecoeur the family is a molecule of independence, self-sufficiency, and progress, a repository of private property values, a place where one can reject society without foregoing the security and nurture of a social structure which would care for all. Crèvecoeur, the father, stands within the family as he does over the farmyard in another passage, ensuring by his natural authority that a static harmony prevails.[72] This is the family of security made into a model for all America. The Puritan family pattern of self-enclosed withdrawal and economic production becomes in Crèvecoeur a general social ideal, romantic rather than religious, of a domestic utopia.

The emotional force of such a heightened sense of shining moment depends to some extent on the danger of being cut short. Both Crèvecoeur and Jefferson had gloomy thoughts that the whole social achievement might be lost almost before it was won.[73] With respect to the family ideal, they were right. At least later generations felt so. The decline of the family of security became a central article in the family ethos of the nineteenth century.[74] As William Bridges has pointed out, the culture created hundreds of images "of a closely-knit stable, patriarchal, self-sustaining, well-disciplined family group."[75] Increasingly, these expressions were filled with longing and nostalgia for a time when the family—and so America—had somehow been more pure, more right. Early in the century Washington Irving was fond of such scenes:

> To have seen a numerous household assembled around the fire one would have imagined that he was transported back to those happy days of primeval simplicity which float before our imaginations like golden visions. The fireplaces were of truly patriarchal magnitude, where the whole family, old and young, master and servant, black and white, nay, even the very cat and dog, enjoyed a community of privilege, and each had a right to a corner.[76]

This was whimsical history to Irving but still a very good version of an earlier domestic peaceable kingdom that people liked to feel had existed. Lowell, Whittier, and Longfellow drew on just these sentiments of the bygone hearth for their poetry. [77] Other writers elaborated the lesson to be learned from America's family origins. In the introduction to a volume of inspirational writings— probably compiled by a popular verse and hymn writer of the nineteenth century, Fanny J. Crosby—appears Reverend Theodore Cuyler's sober and tendentious history:

> The real seed-corn whence our republic sprang was the Christian households, which stepped forth from the cabin of the 'Mayflower,' or which set up the family altar of the Hollander and the Huguenot on Manhattan Island or in the sunny South. All our best characters, best legislation, best institutions, and best church-life were cradled in those early homes. They were the tap-root of the republic, and of the American churches. [78]

The early American family—its self-contained qualities emphasized—created and nurtured our virtue and piety.

Some writers, such as C. H. "Whirlwind" Fowler, a nationally prominent Methodist bishop, put the historical source of unified American homes more in racial terms:

> It is one peculiarity of the Anglo-Saxon peoples that they abound in homes. The walls about the hearth shut out all the world and shut in a kingdom. This is the fact; keep it clean and free, and religion will thrive and liberty will dwell in the land forever. [79]

For Fowler and his coauthor, the family unit is the original and only true institution, subsuming all other social groups, including the church.

Yet the champions of this sort of home life wrote their inspirational and guidance books, they clearly implied, to keep the home from further decline. They urged a return to earlier family

forms to recapture the happiness of home life. [80] There was, in
their appeals, a curious mixture of the past with the future. A good
example is Bronson Alcott's cousin, William, who wrote numerous
books touching on the family. *The Young Husband,* written in
1838, ran to at least twenty editions by 1855; in it Alcott enthusias-
tically outlines the possibility of a heaven on earth—"if not angels,
at least angelic beings, even in the humble cottages of New England"—which he has seen "in a few instances." [81] The home would
be such a utopia if only the husband would stay in at night:

> Arrived home, he meets again, with joy, his little family
> group, assembled in his earthly paradise. Supper being
> over, the fireside felicities commence.... No matter
> what..., so the father is present—so he presides in giving
> directions and life to the circle, as it is his bounden
> duty, and his highest happiness at home. [82]

The anxious exhortation on the evils of the absent father betrays
an uncertainty about the state of family life despite its glowing
promise.

The longing for the family of security with its stability and
self-containment became complicated as the century progressed.
In the South it is related to the plantation myth. [83] Prior to the
Civil War such family longings were combined with the need to
justify slavery, and Old Testament partriarchal relations were seen
to provide the model for a natural order of society. For George
Fitzhugh, the plantation family unit needed to be defended against
the effects of the wage system and feminism, both northern imports. [84] After the Civil War the plantation became increasingly
imbued with the gauzy romance of a lost Eden of family solidarity
as well as racial harmony.

In the industrializing North the ideal family of security under-
went even more intricate complications. For one thing, as William
Bridges has argued, the family came to be thought of as a refuge
from the strains of the competitive capitalist world. It was a place
for the father to come back to for solace, a place where he could

be refreshed for the next day's grind. The wife, now often alone within the home, was involved in changing values, too. She was charged with the main responsibility of home management, to which was added the role of preserving the moral and cultural values of society.[85] These changes show that the ideal family of security did not answer the new ideological demands being made on the family. Functionally, the thrust of individuals was away from the family. With the husband gone, family self-containment was weakened. Ideologically, the higher values the wife was to instill were defined as those leading to independence and self-sufficiency. The family of security, then, was increasingly a lost (but not abandoned) ideal. A new model was needed to fit the new entreprenurial culture.

This new model, which I have called the family of freedom, received its most complete statement early in the nineteenth century. It came from that most prescient of American observers, Alexis de Tocqueville. Writing of the effects of democracy on family life in America, Tocqueville paints a predominantly cheerful picture of its prospects. As with social relations in general, family relations will be freed from artificiality, arbitrary authority, and "that bitter and angry regret which is apt to survive a bygone power." They will be "more intimate and more affectionate," more characterized by "confidence and tenderness;" unlike the "aristocratic family," that feudal institution where interests agree but hearts are in disharmony, in the "democratic family" there will be a "free sympathy of opinion and of taste." In short, the family will be natural, spontaneous, and humane: "It would seem that the natural bond is drawn closer as the social bond is loosened."[86] Here, Tocqueville is reluctant to speculate on the social disadvantages of this change. Elsewhere, however, he spells out more clearly what the effect of "democracy" on social relations might be:

> Thus not only does democracy make every man forget his ancestors, but it hides his descendents and separates his contemporaries from him; it throws him back for-ever upon himself alone and threatens in the end to

confine him entirely within the solitude of his own heart.[87]

It may be that democracy separates and isolates the members of the family from each other, too. Tocqueville neatly balances his two attitudes in his summarizing statement on the subject:

> Democracy loosens social ties, but tightens natural ones; it brings kindred more closely together, while it throws citizens more apart.[88]

The emotional solidarity of the family of security can be preserved without hierarchy, without structure, in a spontaneous, unforced domesticity.

The term "democracy," as Tocqueville means it, seems to imply the entire individualized, atomistic social world. If so, Tocqueville's critique of the family combines into a revealing polarity those attitudes toward family life I have been discussing. The dominant note is positive and optimistic, only slightly undercut by a more neutral hint of social disorganization. Here, then, is discernible the new possibility for family life in America. Tocqueville prophesies a family of freedom, an escape from artificial feudal relations into a natural harmony of free individuals. Lurking around the edges of this cheerful prediction is a nagging possibility that this change may have other isolating and destructive effects, that the yearned-for qualities of the family of security might, in fact, be in jeopardy. Tocqueville has outlined the new ideal model and has gone one step further to hint at what will be, to later generations, its weakness and painful vulnerability.

Not all nineteenth-century writers revealed the ambiguities of family freedom as fully as Tocqueville did. T. W. Higginson, for example, saw the matter more simply as one of radical melioration. His attitude was summed up in the quotation he chose to head one of his chapters: "The progress of civilization has changed the family from a barony to a republic; but the law has not kept pace with the advance of ideas, manners and customs."[89] This sentence combined his sense of natural social progress up from feudalism with his demands for institutional reform. Writing in 1882, Higginson asserted that the highest form of family life is that which leads to freedom, which is as truly domestic as any family hierarchy of confinement.[90] At about the same time that the inspirational book *Mother, Home, and Heaven* published an engraving which might have been on the pages of Crèvecoeur,[91] Higginson offered a critique of this dream of family security:

> There are many families, innocent though torpid, where the only dream of existence is to have plenty of quiet, plenty of food, plenty of well-fed children.[92]

Free women, educate them, and then the family will be based on equality, like a business partnership, with each member having an area of responsibility. As with some modern marriage counselors, the problems of female equality are solved by Higginson through his claim that household management is a profession as important as any.[93]

According to another writer of the time, Helen Ekin Starrett, the "Ideal Family" is the most important goal in life. It is characterized by love and freedom, where mothers and daughters teach the soft refinements of life to fathers and sons. "Perfect freedom for all members of the family within the limits of home life is one of the essential elements in every ideal family."[94]

By the turn of the century such sentiments qualifying family authority would seem mild to Charlotte Perkins Gilman, whose great-uncle was Henry Ward Beecher, while they would have been outrageous to Lyman Abbott, Beecher's protege. Gilman writes:

> The home in *its essential nature* is pure, good, and in its due development is progressively good; but it must change with society's advance; and the kind of home

that was wholly beneficial in one century may be largely evil in another. [95]

The home has retarded social development by perpetuating primitive industry and outmoded myths, according to Gilman. Now there is the wider duty and home of mankind. Mother love, shelter, privacy of the home, sanctity of the home—all derive from the fact that the family is the oldest of institutions. But by the same token it is the lowest development of social man. Of the sacredness of maternity Gilman asks: "Is it better than Liberty, better than Justice, better than Art, Government, Science, Industry, Relition?" [96]

Lyman Abbott thought he had an answer, and it is interesting to imagine the sparks which would have flown if, considering their connections, he ever challenged Gilman in person. He asserted the importance of the family of security against all claims, social and individual; yet the claims of freedom are evident, too, though conveniently only for the men. Seven years after Gilman's book, his breathless paean to the virtues of the sober, steadfast, and demure woman who creates a loving home appeared:

As she grows into early womanhood she grows into a clearer comprehension of what the home is; a rest and refuge from the strenuous and stormy life outside, and a tonic to virtue and an inspiration to vigor in that life. [97]

Women want to be subjugated, obedient, and anti-feminist, according to Abbott. When they are, they naturally and intuitively create an order of "Love, Service, Sacrifice." They teach daughters obedience and sons a manly independence. [98]

Abbott's conservative family ideal claims the male prerogative in response to the demands entrepreneurial America was making on the family. But he asserts freedom for men only as long as the ladies are at home to give him a sense of security. In other words, though he opposes it, Abbott must reckon with the claim of family freedom Gilman presents. In fact, such claims were, early on, a key element in our thinking about family life. The progressive attitude toward family melioration, the prophecy which Tocqueville had first set out, became an article of faith, troublesome or not, to writers on the family. And not only to casual essayists. Early scholarship on family life—and a good deal of it since[99]—was conditioned by the habits of mind I am discussing. We can see these patterns in the first history of American family life.

Arthur W. Calhoun's three-volume work, *A Social History of the American Family,* appeared during 1917-1919. In it Calhoun recorded so much fascinating and valuable material that he is often cited by writers who otherwise think him out of date. Although valuable as a source of details and information, Calhoun is of even greater interest as an example of the thought of an early, important professional scholar of the family. The jumble of facts which he collected may seem confused and structureless at first. As one reads through the volumes, however, a point of view emerges. Volume 1 —"Colonial Period"—is fairly straightforward as Calhoun's occasional interpretations seem aimed at pointing out the severity and harshness of Puritan New England family life. For example, he contrasts Puritan attitudes toward children with what he feels to be the more reasonable approach of John Adams and the eighteenth century.[100] His attention to legal equality, divorce, and the status of women and children indicate the modern interest in those questions.

It is in volume 2—"From Independence Through the Civil War"—that Calhoun's view first begins to assert itself clearly. This history of the family in America is going to be the story of the progress of emancipation from "medieval" (his choicest epithet) forms. "Rules and authority recede before tenderness and confidence, and spiritual values in kinship are free to assert themselves." "The emancipation [of children] was a forward move toward family reciprocity, democracy, and spontaneous, unforced loyalty."[101] After a rather forbidding list of those factors destroying family spirit,[102] he says that more important are those leading to a new familialism: Americans are preeminently domestic, and homes here are happy and loving. A kind of utopia is in the making:

Morality was high. Though women received what seemed to Europeans great adulation, they were not spoiled. Flirts settled down into staid and efficient domesticity. After marriage, if not before, women became thoughtful, responsible, and painstaking. Domestic order and comfort were marked. Affection, fidelity, and good management on the part of wives conserved the best interest of husband, children, and home. The very reserve and mutual respect that existed tended to obviate collisions and render the American families largely free from that brutality which too often disgraces the lower class of other nations.[103]

Just what are the forces able to bring about the new American family in the face of modern disorganization? Having made his preliminary prediction in the second volume, Calhoun elaborates and expands it in volume 3, "Since the Civil War." The triumph of the family of freedom will come about through industry. Ever the sharp-eyed observer, Calhoun does not slight evidence of the ill effects of industry, and he shows how it has undermined the home.[104] As if to bid a fond farewell to the family of security, Calhoun writes:

The old, interesting rural social life can scarcely be sustained for want of young folks.... Amusements become more sophisticated and less spontaneous: the moving picture house in the nearest town takes the place of the crude jollities that formerly brought the homes of the neighbors together. In general the family becomes less self-dependent.... The farm hand often is not a neighbor's son but an alien or a tramp.[105]

Alas, though never mind. The future is guaranteed. "All in all there is little doubt that American marriage is happier than any other in the world."[106] If industrialism has had its own enslaving effects, what is needed is *more* industrialism. Take the case of the child. Set free from the family unit, he was then left at the mercy of the market. But now American abundance and know-how are causing such neglect to be replaced by "child care on a social and scientific basis."[107] Although Calhoun is momentarily uneasy about the results of rising childhood status—such twinges are regular in this third volume and relate, I think, to his attraction to the cohesiveness of the family of security—he finally finds it a good thing:

> The American child certainly does develop an independence well adapted to the fierce struggle of individualism—an alertness and resourcefulness that makes the children of other nations seem dull.[108]

Such children keep adults youthful, making them good companions. Thus close family ties are actually promoted by youthful independence. Where mutual confidence is fostered, the father can become the boy's comrade and friend, and the mother, likewise, the daugher's; a strong attachment develops also between mother and sons, father and daughters.

But enthusiasm for one's family is not enough, as Calhoun recognizes. What is needed is the full achievement of the democratic ethos,

> the actual enfranchisement of every member of the family. It is not sufficient that personal freedom be allowed. The work of the household requires to be divided among the members and family projects need to be discussed in open council where even the smallest child may have voice and influence. The young may thus serve an apprenticeship to the coming social democracy.[109]

This turning of the "domestic monarchy" into "spontaneous

democracy" will mean the greater moral purity of the home, but more important it will lead to the socialization of the family. [110] The family of freedom will not withdraw from society but merge with it—hence Tocqueville's dilemma is solved. Calhoun works hard to convince the reader that the casual, cool, incohesive nature of family life as he describes it is the harbinger of a new day. The signs of disorganization, the excesses of individualism and selfishness, the haphazard and impromptu social arrangements—"all these phenomena are preliminary to a recentering of society; they are the clearing of the ground for a broader socialization." [111] A new order of democratic socialism will revolutionize America, and the family's functions will be absorbed by a national "social parenthood." Monogamy will be a matter of individual preference, sex roles in the home and family will be eliminated. Freedom of choice, social and sexual equality, and scientific betterment will be the order of the day.

Yet even at the end of the third volume, where Calhoun is being his most prophetic, he is significantly reluctant to give up the family altogether. Despite statements which imply—logically extended—the diminution and even disappearance of the family in the new order, he finds a triumphant place for the family of freedom as re-emerging in a still newer, more spiritual form. [112] Not only will socialism emphasize home ownership [113] (traditionally a hallmark of the family of security), but

> a new family is inevitable, a family based on a social democracy devoid of artificial stratification based on economic exploitation. Such is the promise of American life, of world life. [114]

Like Tocqueville's, Calhoun's happy prediction for the democratic family rejects old structures and organizations in favor of a more genuine and loving cohesiveness which will come from freeing family members to act out of their natural impulses. Tocqueville's qualifying anxieties about such freedom persist in Calhoun's earnest desire to see the family survive and prosper. Indeed, I would not be distorting Calhoun's argument greatly if I said that, finally, the new industrial socialism is at the service of the family of freedom as much as family change is necessary to bring the larger social order into being.

Throughout the nineteenth century, and since, the two models of the family—security and freedom—vie with each other for a claim on the American imagination. In one, the family is a self-contained unit of relatedness and comfort; in the other, this close-knit quality becomes oppressive and limiting. Yet both models were intimately associated with radical democratic notions of freedom. Both held that self-reliance and self-sufficiency were natural to the family and that democracy could best be realized through the creation of and acceptance of the proper family pattern. When the virtue the family unit possessed for Crèvecoeur became located in the separate members of the family, a new assertion of the democracy of family life took place. Earlier, the family of security was seen as a natural liberating force in contrast to the institutional claims of society, the source of freedom and harmony. Next, the family of security began to seem the conservative, traditional family form, for it had claims to make on its members. A community of privilege was rather fixed and so, in turn, the family of security was arbitrary and unnatural, a feudal anachronism to some, while others decried its passing.

A more spontaneous, freer, and less arbitrary family life seemed to be the true, democratic way to establish harmony in America. But, as Tocqueville had hinted early on, there were shadows in this bright picture. A way had to be found to preserve the warmth, security, and nurture so attractive in the model of the family of security while emphasizing the qualities of independence and self-sufficiency. Such are the ambiguities of the newer American family ethos. The atomism of democratic society, with its tendency to reject institutions, left one exposed to life without support. Yet investing oneself in the primary institution of protection, the family, meant commitment to a social structure, which was what one had fled from initially.[115] A radical, anti-institutional ideology could not easily make peace with the one institution it recognized. But the dream was that harmony would prevail.

NOTES

1. Alexis de Tocqueville, *Democracy in America,* ed. Phillips Bradley (New York, 1945), II, 227.

2. Edward Shorter, *The Making of the Modern Family* (New York, 1975), p. 9.

3. The best succinct statement of Marx's view is this famous one from the Communist Manifesto:

> The bourgeoisie, wherever it has got the upper hand, has put an end to all feudal, patriarchal idyllic relations. It has pitilessly torn asunder the motley feudal ties that bound man to his 'natural superiors,' and has left remaining no other nexus between man and man than naked self-interest, than callous 'cash payment.'

Quotation from *Essential Works of Marxism,* ed. Arthur P. Mendel (New York, 1961), p. 15. Karl Polanyi, *The Great Transformation* (Boston, 1957)—see especially pp. 163-177.

4. Though they may agree on little else, the chief writers on family life are in accord on this point. See, e.g., Philippe Ariès, *Centuries of Childhood: A Social History of Family Life,* trans. Robert Baldick (New York, 1962); Ernest W. Burgess, Harvey J. Locke, and Mary Margaret Thomas, *The Family: From Institution to Companionship,* 3rd ed. (New York, 1963); William J. Goode, *World Revolution and Family Patterns* (New York, 1963); Talcott Parsons, Robert F. Bales, et al., *Family, Socialization and Interaction Process* (Glencoe, Ill., 1955); John Sirjamaki, *The American Family in the Twentieth Century* (Cambridge, Mass., 1963); Pitrim A. Sorokin, *The Crisis of Our Age* (New York, 1941); Carl C. Zimmerman, *Family and Civilization* (New York, 1947).

5. Talcott Parsons, "The American Family: Its Relations to Personality and to the Social Structure," in Parsons and Bales, *Family,* p. 16.

6. Goode warns against excessive emphasis here, asserting that medieval families were more nuclear than historians have assumed, especially in the lower classes, and that today the kin network still obtains in many minor respects—*World Revolution,* pp. 22-28, 31-33, 70-76.

7. Sirjamaki, *American Family,* p. 50.

8. The following discussion of general characteristics draws heavily on Goode, *World Revolution,* and is substantially agreed upon by most scholars, such as those cited in note 4. It is the interpretation of these characteristics and their significance which is disputed.

9. Goode, *World Revolution,* p. 8.

10. Even today, however, parents exercise some control in terms of who is part of the social circle. Ibid., p. 9.

11. Ibid., p. 11.

12. Bernard Bailyn, *Education in the Forming of American Society* (Chapel Hill, N.C., 1960), pp. 75-78. The situation has begun to change in recent years.

13. Goode, *World Revolution,* p. 11.

14. An excellent study of the impact on industrialism on the English family is by Neil J. Smelser, *Social Change in the Industrial Revolution* (Chicago, 1959).

15. Goode, *World Revolution,* pp. 22-28.

16. Ariès, *Centuries of Childhood,* p. 364.

17. Ibid., pp. 391-393.

18. Ibid., pp. 375, 395, 398.

19. Ibid., p. 398.

20. Ibid., pp. 406, 403-404.

21. Ibid., p. 401.

22. Arthur W. Calhoun, *A Social History of the American Family,* I (Cleveland, Ohio, 1917), 37-40.

23. Sirjamaki, *American Family,* pp. 11-18.

24. Ibid., p. 51.

25. Edmund S. Morgan, *The Puritan Family* (New York, 1966). See also Calhoun, *Social History,* I, chapter 3.

26. Perry Miller has argued this paradox to be one of the continuing legacies of Puritan thought: "From Edwards to Emerson," in *Errand into the Wilderness* (New York, 1964), pp. 184-203.

27. Morgan, *Puritan Family,* chapter 6. The remainder of this paragraph is a summary of Morgan's chapter.

28. Ibid., pp. 10-11, is also relevant.

29. Arthur W. Calhoun, "The Early American Family," *Annals of the American Academy,* 160 (March 1932), 7-12.

30. Compare Calhoun, *Social History,* I, chapter 4, with Morgan, *Puritan Family.*

31. Manford Hinshaw Kuhn, "American Families Today: Development and Differentiation of Types," in *Family, Marriage and Parenthood,* ed. Howard Becker and Reuben Hill (Boston, 1963), pp. 136-137.

32. Sirjamaki, *American Family,* pp. 22-24, 32-35.

33. Morgan, *Puritan Family,* chapter 2.

34. E.g., Andrew G. Truxal and Francis E. Merrill, *Marriage and the Family in American Culture* (Englewood Cliffs, N.J., 1953), chapter 2. Other writers such as Willystyne Goodsell, *A History of Marriage and the Family* (New York, 1934) and Calhoun choose the eighteenth century and democracy as the explanation. In either case the logic is the same.

35. Morgan, *Puritan Family,* chapter 7.

36. Calhoun, *Social History,* I, 77-78.

37. Ibid., pp. 123-126. For the medieval custom, see Ariès, *Centuries of Childhood,* pp. 365-367.

38. Morgan, *Puritan Family,* pp. 75-78.

39. Ibid., pp. 77, 78.

40. Anne Bradstreet, "To My Dear and Loving Husband," in *The American Tradition in Literature,* ed. Sculley Bradley et al., 2nd ed. (New York, 1962), I, 38-39.

41. Such a process of self-enclosing had disastrous results for the Puritans. The

family of a saint was in a special position in that its members were already halfway saved. It was a holy unit with a covenant of its own, a relationship made especially crucial by the intimacy I have noted. An inbred quality developed, a "tribalism" which was ultimately self-destructive. The church, built upon these special families, increasingly talked not to others but to itself and so crumbled. Morgan, *Puritan Family,* chapter 7.

42. Calhoun, *Social History,* I, chapters 8-11; Kuhn, "American Families Today," pp. 138-142.

43. Kuhn, "American Families Today," pp. 138-141.

44. Cf. Ariès, *Centuries of Childhood,* pp. 391-393, with Kuhn, "American Families Today," pp. 142-147; Calhoun, *Social History,* I, chapters 12-19; and Edmund S. Morgan, *Virginians at Home* (Williamsburg, Va., 1952).

45. Kuhn, "American Families Today," pp. 145-147; Morgan, *Virginians,* p. 54; Calhoun, *Social History,* I, 241-242.

46. Economically, the upper middle-class southern family was not independent for it was tied closely to the market economy of Europe.

47. An interesting point is the status of such white "servants" as the tutor. The caste system from black field hands to white owner placed the tutor almost equal to the planter and clearly separate from labor (even if the tutor was indentured), and, of course, separate from the slaves. For example, the tutor had the job of discipline, allowing parents to be more indulgent, much in the way of colonial parents, North and South, who sent their children out. Morgan, *Virginians,* pp. 20-25, 51-72.

48. Calhoun, *Social History,* I, 241-242.

49. Quoted in Morgan, *Virginians,* p. 52.

50. Nathan Miller, "The European Heritage of the American Family," *Annals of the American Academy,* 160 (March 1932), 4-6. Also, Sirjamaki, *American Family,* pp. 38-41. For a somewhat different argument see Kuhn, "American Families Today," pp. 152-164, where the emphasis is on the remaining type differences. Kuhn does agree that the differentiation of family types is lessening due to geographic mobility and to mass transit, communications, and education.

51. Kuhn, "American Families Today," p. 147.

52. Sirjamaki, *American Family,* p. 30.

53. Ibid., p. 32.

54. Ibid., p. 31.

55. Arthur W. Calhoun, *A Social History of the American Family,* III (Cleveland, Ohio, 1919), 67.

56. Richard Hofstader, *The Age of Reform* (New York, 1955), pp. 46-59.

57. Sirjamaki, *American Family,* p. 43.

58. The process in the English woolen industries is spelled out in Smelser, *Social Change,* chapter 9, where he demonstrates the importance of job control.

59. The following traits—but again not their significance—are generally agreed on by such diverse writers as Goode, Sirjamaki, Kuhn, Goodsell, and Calhoun.

60. The concept of a "fit" is from Goode, *World Revolution,* pp. 10 ff.; he refers to the "harmony," empirical or theoretical, between industrialization and the family system.

61. Ibid., p. 11.

62. Shorter, *Modern Family,* p. 205.

63. William E. Bridges has made a parallel argument about nineteenth-century attitudes toward family. He contrasts the Adamic symbol with the American mother, establishing a dichotomy of values much like mine, which were arrived at independently. He does not, however, associate Adamic freedom with an ideal *family* of the future. William E. Bridges, "Warm Hearth, Cold World: Social Perspectives on the Household Poets," *American Quarterly,* 21 (Winter 1969), 778-779.

64. Sirjamaki, *American Family,* pp. 31, 32.

65. Sarah W. Randolph, *The Domestic Life of Thomas Jefferson* (New York, 1871), pp. 248, 255, 263, 281.

66. Ibid., p. 256. See also p. 243.

67. See Thomas Jefferson, *The Writings of ...,* ed. Paul Leicester Ford, V (New York, 1895), 417, 442. The quotation is from Thomas Jefferson, *The Writings of ...,* ed. H. A. Washington, I (Washington, D.C., 1853), 427.

68. Jefferson, *Writings,* ed. Ford, III (1894), 406; and IV (1894), 17.

69. Leo Marx, *The Machine in the Garden* (New York, 1964). See also A. Whitney Griswold, *Farming and Democracy* (New Haven, Conn., 1952).

70. J. Hector St. John Crèvecoeur, *Letters from an American Farmer* (Garden City, N.Y., 1961), p. 47.

71. Ibid., pp. 28-31.

72. The very best critique of Crèvecoeur's idealistic picture, particularly of the family, is by D. H. Lawrence; he pricks the bubble with brutal efficiency: *Studies in Classic American Literature* (Garden City, N.Y., 1953), chapter 3.

73. Crèvecoeur's Letters IX, X, and XII are filled with foreboding and gloomy images. Jefferson felt that revolutionary America was at its most lucid and concordant moment for establishing political rights and social order. "From the conclusion of this war we shall be going down hill." Thomas Jefferson, *Notes on the State of Virginia* (New York, 1964), p. 154.

74. Calhoun, *Social History,* II, 66-69; III, 144-156; and William E. Bridges, "Family Patterns and Social Values in America, 1825-1875," *American Quarterly,* 17 (Spring 1965), 4-6.

75. Bridges, "Family Patterns," p. 5.

76. Washington Irving, *Knickerbocker's History of New York* in *Selected Writings of ...,* (New York, 1945), pp. 464-465.

77. Bridges, "Household Poets," 764-779.

78. Reverend Theodore L. Cuyler, "Introduction," *Mother, Home, and Heaven* (New York, 1878), p. 7.

79. C. H. Fowler and W. H. DePuy, *Home and Health and Home Economics* (New York, 1880), p. 63.

80. E.g., William Hague, *Home Life* (Philadelphia, 1855), chapter 1, where both motives seem to apply.

81. William A. Alcott, *The Young Husband* (New York, 1855), p. 153.

82. Ibid., pp. 155-156.

83. E.g., William R. Taylor, *Cavalier and Yankee* (New York, 1961), pp. 145-176.

84. Paul Connor, "Patriarchy: Old World and New," *American Quarterly,* 17 (Spring 1965), 48-62. Connor argues that the attitudes of Fitzhugh are medieval and feudal. I follow Ariès in saying that with regard to the family they are bourgeois and modern.

85. Bridges, "Family Patterns," pp. 9-11.

86. Tocqueville, *Democracy,* II, 202-208.

87. Ibid., p. 106.

88. Ibid., p. 208.

89. Quoted in T. W. Higginson, *Common Sense About Women* (Boston, 1882), p. 87.

90. Ibid., pp. 109-111.

91. The wife sits outside with her work and child, the husband is just in from the fields, which are in sight. Only the minor figure of the hired hand is new, but—*mutatis mutandis*—not irrelevant to Crèvecoeur a hundred years earlier. *Mother, Home, and Heaven,* p. 101.

92. Higginson, *Common Sense,* p. 110.

93. Ibid., pp. 123-130. Cf. Christine Beasley, *Democracy in the Home* (New York, 1954), pp. 111-122.

94. Helen Ekin Starrett, *Letters to Elder Daughters* (Chicago, 1888), pp. 5-13; quotation appears on p. 10.

95. Charlotte Perkins Gilman, *The Home: Its Work and Influence* (New York, 1903), p. 8.

96. Ibid., pp. 10-50; quotation appears on p. 48.

97. Lyman Abbot, *The Home Builder* (Boston, 1910), pp. 13-14.

98. Ibid., pp. 3-8, 21-27, 45-58, 76.

99. The patterns of nostalgia and prophecy can be seen in modern sociologists, psychologists, and family counselors. See Thomas Michael Scanlan, "The American Family and Family Dilemmas in American Drama," Diss. U. of Minnesota 1970, pp. 53-64.

100. Calhoun, *Social History,* I, 119-123.

101. Ibid., II, 54, 71.

102. Ibid., pp. 132-140. He mentions economic opportunity, political democracy, loss of economic functions, competitive stress of the economy, legal changes of obligation and inheritance, loss of educational function, and religious fragmentation.

103. Ibid., pp. 140-141.

104. See e.g., ibid., III, chapter 4, as well as note 102 above.

105. Ibid., pp. 82-83.

106. Ibid., p. 129.

107. Ibid., p. 140; see also p. 131.

108. Ibid., p. 154.

109. Ibid., p. 156.

110. Ibid., pp. 157-162.

111. Ibid., pp. 162-172; the quotation appears on p. 172.

112. See, e.g., ibid., pp. 171, 175.

113. Ibid., pp. 326-327.

114. Ibid., p. 332.

115. Cf. Kuhn, "American Families Today," p. 139. "Each [the family and the individual] was a reaction—and in the same direction—from the class-categorized social, political, and economic structure of feudalism. Perhaps another way to put it would be to say that this society tended to break into family molecules in those respects in which it was not expedient to go all the way to complete individualism." I think expedience is a bit off the point. The tension between the two "natural" family images is a continuing and a deep one, involving attraction and repulsion on both sides.

2

THE CODIFICATION
OF THE
FAMILY DREAM

*If we think of companionship as the
nourishing bread and butter of marriage,
then love is the jam on the bread.*

Ruth Shonle Cavan [1]

Take your finger out of my jam.

Fats Waller [2]

In the American imagination the dream of domestic harmony is fundamental to our self-definition. Images of this dream appear over and over. They pervade our dramatic literature, high and low. Our drama is singularly about family life, and through attention to family images we can better understand it and ourselves. As I will point out in later chapters, the failure of the domestic dream preoccupies our serious dramatists. From O'Neill on, our playwrights have been obsessed with the failure of family harmony and with family disintegration. Similarly, our popular drama is of a family life strained by the conflicting tensions of security and freedom, mutuality and selfhood. Apparently, our drama and our sub-drama have drawn on the same cultural sources. But the popular drama blithely reconciles contradictions, asserting that the dream will prevail or that it is the only dream worth having.

Henry Nash Smith argues that the literature of mass dreams provides us with important insights into our culture:

The individual writer abandons his own personality and identifies himself with the reveries of his readers. It is the presumably close fidelity of the Beadle stories to the dream life of a vast inarticulate public that renders them valuable to the social historian and the historian of ideas. [3]

As with pulp fiction, our popular drama is a literature of mass dreams. It embodies our yearnings and fears for family life. The conception of human nature and life presented is consonant with fundamental, conflicting attitudes we hold toward social institutions. The "ethics" of this consumer entertainment and the ethos of family life are similar. Two different examples of popular drama demonstrate as much. The first is one of the most beloved plays of the nineteenth-century popular stage, Joe Jefferson's *Rip Van Winkle*. Jefferson's play is interesting in that it anticipates the problems of form as well as of content which our serious drama will explore in the twentieth century. The second, the "soap opera," is, in a sense, a reduction of the family conventions of *Rip Van Winkle* into the routinely conventional. This ultimate mechanization of our concern with domestic troubles first appeared in the 1930s.

Joseph Jefferson III (in fact, he seldom went by his formal name) was one of the leading comic actors of his day, and his most famous role as Rip was written largely by himself. The play has a secure place in American theatrical history if not in our dramatic literature since, in an era characterized by productions of spectacular longevity, it was more than merely popular. Plays such as *East Lynne* (1862), *The Two Orphans* (1874) and *Hazel Kirke* (1880) (to name just a few) were repeated in repertory for ten, twenty, and thirty years at a time. The initially modest *Uncle Tom's Cabin* began in 1852, and an endless stream of extravaganza productions continued well into the twentieth century. Often the success of a nineteenth-century "hit" was due to a particular actor, as in the case of James O'Neill—Eugene's father—who performed year in and year out in *The Count of Monte Cristo* (American version—1848; O'Neill began in it in 1883). It made him rich, though he felt it ruined his talent.

But Jefferson's forty years as Rip—from the 1865 opening in London—were different. It was not only a very long run but a very special one. By Jefferson's own account in his autobiography the repetition was no trap for him.[4] By all accounts his performance was rare magic.[5] "So simple, so true, so beautiful, so moral!" enthused a minister in 1868,[6] and a review of other commentary on Jefferson's performance shows a remarkable uniformity of agreement. William Winter, Brander Matthews, Montrose Moses, and Henry James were as captivated. These big fry ranked Jefferson with the best actors of Europe, including the great Italian tragedian, Tommaso Salvini.[7] The small-town audience, which saw Rip on one of Jefferson's annual tours, paid an equal compliment by closing school when he came to town. To see Rip was felt to be an education in itself.[8] The long tenure of the play, its yearly return on the theatrical circuit, only confirmed the timeless mythic quality of the theatrical event. Art and life came together. Ageless Jefferson was Rip, and seeing him became a special ritual.[9]

There is no doubt that Jefferson's play touched a chord in the America of its time. The reason, I think, was that it embodied conflicting ideals of family life and unconsciously expressed certain fears, hopes, and dilemmas concerning this central cultural dream. It set in juxtaposition the individual and the family, two of our most sacred and worrisome ideals. The dream was that the two are naturally harmonious, that family security and individual freedom are compatible. And the dream was not limited to the nineteenth century. As I have suggested, Jefferson's play anticipates twentieth-century drama. By the nature of its contradictions and by its naive style, *Rip Van Winkle* prefigures our later dramatic tradition, crudely embodying what will subsequently be our major conventions of family subject matter and of style.

I have referred to the stage version of *Rip Van Winkle* as Jefferson's play, yet Jefferson himself was anxious to acknowledge other authors before him. "Its flow was gradual," as he put it.[10] The play stretches back through a variety of actors and writers to Irving's story, which in turn can be traced to German folklore. After Irving's *Rip* appeared in *The Sketch Book* in 1819, the addition and subtraction of characters, the changes in plot and action, and the shifts in tone are many and their history is obscure and tangled. [11] At least three major stage versions—one by Jefferson's half-brother, the actor Charles Burke—and as many minor ones, not to mention an opera, are known to have existed before Jefferson's first attempt in 1859.

He was lying in a hayloft one rainy afternoon in rural Pennsylvania, dreaming over a book of Irving's which contained a complimentary reference to his acting, when, he recounts in his autobiography, it struck him to try his own hand at such "American" material. [12] Jefferson's account is a lovely story, a myth about a search for a myth, but it is inaccurate as history. He was much more involved with earlier dramatizations of the tale than his hayloft inspiration suggests. He had, for instance, already acted in Burke's version, and several other members of his family had appeared in earlier versions. [13] At any rate, it is clear that Jefferson combined several extant versions, added his own third-act meeting between Rip and the silent ghostly crew of Hendrick Hudson, and tried it out that fall, only to fail. Six years later in London he turned his version over to the melodramatist Dion Boucicault, who rewrote it—he, too, apparently with previous dramas in front of him. This was the version that Jefferson "interpreted and enlarged upon," as he put it, shaping it to suit himself over the next thirty years until its publication under his name in 1893. [14] While it is not, then, entirely Jefferson's play, it is certainly no one else's. It is, in fact, a good case of the dramatic literature of mass dreams, all the more valuable as a cultural repository in its hazy and uncertain origin than if it were written solely by one man. We call it Jefferson's play for convenience.

What the special dream elements are in this piece of sub-literature can best be seen, perhaps, by contrasting the play with Irving's tale. Rip's character in the play maintains the raffish, humorous spirit of freedom from responsibility. He is kind, generous, thoughtless, and lovable. Moreover, he has an essential, if evasive, innocence. A good instance occurs at the end of Act One, when Rip is dancing with a pretty girl. Gretchen, his wife, enters. *"As the curtain descends, Rip is seen pointing at the girl as if seeking, like a modern Adam, to put the blame on her."* [15] In general,

Jefferson has softened and sentimentalized the tougher comic spirit of Irving's tale. Also, he sets the character of Rip and the story of his twenty years' sleep in a framework of melodramatic actions. Around Rip there is villainy and pathos, though relative to other versions of the play, such as Burke's, these qualities are subdued. [16]

In the play Gretchen (Irving gave her only the generalized name, Dame Van Winkle) is kept alive rather than being made to suffer apoplexy, and Rip's son is omitted. Also, his daughter, her name changed to Meenie, is in the later part of the play unmarried but in love. The political references are minimized in the play, while a plot by the village entrepreneur Derrick Von Beekman to gain ownership of Rip's land, marry his wife, and give Meenie away in marriage to a scoundrel nephew is added.

These changes help demonstrate the sentimental conventions of family life in the play. Not only does the audience see very early that Gretchen is in love with Rip and loyal to him, but they also see that her shrewishness comes from a desire to reform him, a sure sign of her good heart. She is, then, justified in her complaints if not in her method of reform. Irving tends to excuse Rip's drinking; indeed, in Irving it is only "habits of idleness." But in Jefferson's play the innocent irresponsibility is carried to the point of potential disaster. The cupboard is bare, and Rip squanders money and time.

The play affirms the importance of family structure in a way Irving's tale does not, for Jefferson is reluctant to kill off Dame Van Winkle and he even redeems her at the end. When she realizes how badly she has acted toward Rip, she assumes a final subservience. She puts Rip at the head of the family in the last scene. The image of family structure is reinforced by the successful reunion of Meenie and her true love. The young couple stand beaming in the background while Gretchen is by Rip's side, having learned her place in the family system. Finally, Rip defeats Von Beekman by producing an unsigned deed. In the end, he is the head not only of the family but of the whole village, the chief landowner, the richest man around, a kind of squire or village patriarch. (One might speculate that the defeat of the villain indicates some uneasiness about the threat nineteenth-century capitalism posed to the family, since Von Beekman represents the new prevailing economic order. Such a reading would be in marked contrast to the emphasis on the new political order and on patriotism in earlier versions of the play, references Jefferson deliberately avoided. [17])

Rip's character on stage has been modified and domesticated in a way that conflicts with his spirit of freedom and irresponsibility. He is still a vagabond, full of good intentions that fail. And he still drinks at every turn. The toast "I'll drink your good health, and your families', and may they all live long and prosper" punctuates the action throughout the play and is its final line. Indeed, the toast is an emblem of the ambiguous action of the play as a whole, for while the drinking is a gesture of irresponsibility, the words are an affirmation of family renewal. The actual words of the toast—its family reference—have a benign meaning for family structure, like the obedient wife and engaged daughter. Rip's domestic vice turns out to be a charming peccadillo. (There were temperance advocates who urged Jefferson to change this, a move he stoutly resisted on the grounds that it would violate the integrity of what Rip stood for. "It would take all the poetry and fairytale element completely out of it ...," he remarked in his autobiography. [18])

The family affirmations at the end divert us from but do not alter the contrary dramatic fact that Rip, though now installed as a father figure, in some ways has not changed:

> GRETCHEN: *(Kneeling by the side of Rip.)* O, Rip! I drove you from your home; but do not desert me again. I'll never speak an unkind word to you, and you shall never see a frown on my face. And Rip—
> RIP: Yah.
> GRETCHEN: You may stay out all night, if you like.
> RIP: *(Leaning back in his chair.)* No, thank you. I had enough of that.
> GRETCHEN: And, Rip, you can get tight as often as you please.
> *(Taking bottle, and filling the cup from it.)*
> RIP: No; I don't touch another drop.
> MEENIE: *(Kneeling by the other side of Rip.)* Oh, yes, you will, father. For see, here are all the neighbours come to welcome you home.

(Gretchen offers Rip the cup.)

RIP: *(With all his old kindliness and hospitality.)* Well,
bring in all the children, and the neighbours, and
the dogs, and— *(Seeing the cup which Gretchen is
offering him.)* I swore off, you know. Well, I won't
count this one; for this will go down with a prayer.
I will take my cup and pipe and tell my strange
story to all my friends. Here is my child Meenie,
and my wife Gretchen, and my boy Hendrick. I'll
drink all your good health, and I'll drink your good
health, and your families', and may they all live
long and prosper!

CURTAIN[19]

Rather than face the issues raised by such freedom as Rip represents and the danger to family structure it implies, the play solves
this dilemma by changing Rip's world for him. He—and by extension the audience—can have the family, the patriarchy, and the
raffish innocence all at once.

What we see in the changed story line of Jefferson's *Rip Van
Winkle* is a divided attitude toward family life. On the one hand,
the escape from responsibility, which continues as a motive from
the Irving story, is now the escape from a more fully developed
family responsibility. Such fear of family life—the resistance to it
as suffocating or destructive of independence—is countered by the
assertion of the worth of family structure with its mutuality and the
secure embrace of obedient love which is meant to overcome all
fears. (For nineteenth-century audiences, one of the most moving
moments in the play was when Rip is driven from the warmth of the
family fire into the cold, stormy night.) Gretchen is conquered, and
by that act she triumphs. When she takes her proper place, Rip
finds himself in his. Yet the play gives the illusion that conflicting
ideals are reconciled and that the freedom force Rip represents has
not yet been subdued. The play both affirms family structure and
freedom from that structure.

If the changed action from Irving's story to Jefferson's play
reveals contradictory ideals, the play's odd mix of styles is also
significant. In this regard, Jefferson's own acting style can be seen

at work shaping the play. Arthur E. Waterman has suggested that Jefferson's place in the development of a more natural comic acting style is roughly parallel to that of Booth in tragedy.[20] Both Jefferson and Booth sought to move away from the exaggerations of the older (sometimes identified as English, sometimes French) style. Jefferson gave up the forced mugging, subdued the display of comic specialties known as "points," and attempted a quiet style that mingled smiles and tears. L. Clarke Davis's comment is typical of the admiration felt for Jefferson's naturalism at the time:

> From the rising of the curtain on the first scene, until its fall on the last, nothing is forced, sensational, or unseemly. The remarkable beauty of the performance arises from nothing so much as its entire repose and equality.[21]

The substantial humanity of Rip was foremost in Jefferson's mind. Whereas Irving does not describe Rip physically in his tale, Jefferson began "writing" the play by setting off for Philadelphia, where he spent a day at a theatrical wardrobe, putting together the entire costume to his satisfaction. Then he returned home and put pen to paper.[22] As he said later, "the action [of Irving's story] had neither the body nor the strength to carry the hero; the spiritual quality was there but the human interest was missing."[23]

What resulted was, for the first two acts, one of those early, crude attempts at what we now call realism in the drama: the dialect speech of Rip; the long sections of quiet byplay preparing for scenes of high pathos; and the simple attempts to motivate character at a level with which the audience could identify. Thus Gretchen's divided attitude toward Rip keeps her from caricature. Also, the fact that Rip is not quite a helpless coward in the face of his wife's attacks makes him more complex and lifelike. He can sometimes cope with her and joke her out of her moods. Moreover, in the scene where she tells him to leave (not in Irving or in the earlier versions), he does so in a gesture that asserts some dignity. The low-keyed realistic style went hand in hand in Jefferson's mind with the emphasis on familiar family life. He says in his autobiography: "As the earlier scenes were of a natural and domestic character, I had only to draw upon my experience of their effect, or employ such conventional methods as myself and others had used before in a character of that sort."[24] Irving's story was domesticated in more than action.

The early realism of Act One and Act Two would hardly be worth more than a footnote in the history of American drama, however, if it were not for what followed. Jefferson himself was fully aware of the radical shift in styles:

> But from the moment Rip meets the spirits of Hendrick Hudson and his crew I felt that all colloquial dialogue and commonplace pantomime should cease. It is at this point in the story that the supernatural element begins, and henceforth the character must be raised from the domestic plane and lifted into the realms of the ideal.[25]

The diction here might sound a bit like shopworn romanticism, and surely there is a good deal of sentimental romantic melodrama in the play. Scenes of self-sacrifice, pathos, fainting, close calls, and plotting villains are there. But it seems to me something very different—and more interesting—is happening as well. Jefferson was no conscious literary theorist but an intelligent and instinctive performer. If he used the terms "supernatural" and "ideal" (he was also very fond of "poetical") in opposition to "commonplace" and "domestic," he did so to express the distinctive quality he had created in the last half of the play.

This quality begins in Act Three with the silence of the ghostly crew set in sharp contrast to Rip's long monologue. Other versions had turned the scene into a rather spectacular song and dance. Jefferson followed Irving's hint of the crew's eerie silence—it is not complete silence in Irving—but added Rip's long speeches. On stage the alternation between the single voice and absolute quiet punctuated with a few gestures is isolating and cumulative. The tension builds as we wait for a human response to human sound.

Realism gives way and a theatrical symbolism takes over in which the creatures seem external representations of the phantoms within Rip's mind. Walter Prichard Eaton noted this effect as well when he said that the scene was "technically" similar to O'Neill's experimental *The Emperor Jones* (1920).[26] Jefferson has created, in a crude preliminary way, the expressionism of a dream play.

A similar effect is produced by Rip's unreality as a character when he again encounters the "real" world of his village. He is bewildered, of course, and the children fear him. After an initial curiosity on the part of the townspeople, he is shunned and nearly driven off. Then he begins an extended symbolic search for his own identity. In Irving this is a crisis hinted at but quickly solved. The play dramatizes Rip's isolation and alienation from his community and from himself. His personality and even his sanity begin to disintegrate. He learns of his own "death," becomes increasingly childish as people fail to recognize him, and refers to himself in the third person, as if he were someone else. His alienation is intensified as his search comes closer and closer to the heart of his family. Hendrick (Meenie's lover) does not recognize him. Nor does Gretchen. Finally, he reaches Meenie and makes his pathetic last plea:

> RIP: Yes, but hear me, my dear, and then you will know. *(Trying to be logical and calm, but labouring under great excitement.)* This village here is the village of Falling Waters. Well, that was my home. I had here in this place my wife Gretchen, and my child Meenie—little Meenie—*(A long pause, during which he strives to re-assemble his ideas and memories more accurately.)* And my dog Schneider. That's all the family I've got. Try and remember me, dear, won't you? *(Pleadingly.)* I don't know when it was—This night there was a storm; and my wife drove me from my house; and I went away— I don't remember any more till I come back here now. And see, I get back now, and my wife is gone, and my home is gone. My home is gone, and my child—my child looks me in my face, and don't know who I am!

MEENIE: *(Rushing into his arms.)* I do! Father!
RIP: *(Sobbing.)* Ah, my child! Somebody knows me
    now! Somebody knows me now!
MEENIE: But can it be possible?
RIP: Oh, yah; it is so Meenie! *(With a pathetic return of
    his old uncertainty.)* Don't say it is not, or you will
    kill me if you do. [27]

With the danger past but not forgotten, Rip begins a return to the
normal world of the play. He becomes increasingly active and
revitalized as he defeats Derrick, wins back his wife, his land, and
his child's destiny. By the end he has recovered enough to take
another cup. Through family he comes to sanity and reality.

    Yet the return from stylization to realism is never complete.
Jefferson is careful to remind us that throughout the last act Rip
never returns to his old laughter even when he makes jokes. Nor
does he eat. [28] And in a tantalizing remark Jefferson explains the
unreality of Rip's other small actions by saying:

> I went to a Chinese theatre once, and after the Chinese
> lady got through her song, they brought her a glass of
> gin; she turned her back to the audience, and drank it,
> as much as to say, 'That's not in the play.' We are
> dealing with the impossible all the time on the stage;
> and we have got to make it appear possible. Drama-
> tically, things may often be right, when, realistically,
> they are wrong. [29]

In other words, Jefferson justifies some of his effects by pointing
to the stylization of the Chinese theater. It reminds one that years
later Thornton Wilder's own experiments in freeing the theater
from realism drew on Oriental drama as well (in his case it was
Japanese theater). Jefferson's instincts as an actor carry him far
at such moments. What he called his "idealism" suggests the effects that later go under the general term "expressionism." As with
our later playwrights, Jefferson is committed to realistic conven-

tions and yet compelled to intensify them with the devices of a modified expressionism. Realism as a style implies a sensible real world, but it seems that our experience of family life is not adequately rendered by such rationality.

After the realism of Act One and Act Two, and the anti-realism in Act Three, Jefferson gradually but never completely returns to realism in Act Four. Popular elements such as melodramatic pathos and plot contrivance do not obscure this main shift of stylistic qualities. Jefferson comfortably worked with the rigid mechanical conventions of the popular stage even as he moved against them in *Rip Van Winkle.* That he was no conscious artist and did not grasp and follow up the implications of what he was doing is certain. But he had a fascinating artistic instinct. He anticipated not only the thematic problems but the stylistic solutions of modern American drama. Jefferson touched on the conflicting claims of freedom and security in family life; he rendered these longings in a style that reached toward a heightened symbolic realism. His naive expressionism was not influential—expressionism came into American drama later via the German playwrights and Strindberg—and there is little indication that he was familiar with or cared about the theatrical avant-garde. But he did instinctively grasp the materials out of which our later family drama was fashioned.

Rip Van Winkle is an instance in which the popular culture anticipates, rather than imitates, the subject matter, the attitudes, and the tensions which concern serious artists. Not that such attitudes disappear from consumer entertainment when taken up subsequently by our best playwrights. Far from it. They persist; and in at least one rather dreary and predictable form, they continue to be immensely popular, for the materials of *Rip,* without the stylistic originality, have become those of the soap opera. Our family dreams and nightmares have been codified, our family anxieties established as formula by the mass media. Perhaps this is one measure of their importance to us.

In 1931 Frank and Anne Hummert, who ran an advertising agency in Chicago, were looking for a new way to promote their clients' household products. With the help of a young writer,

Robert Hardy Andrews, they developed a serialized radio drama called "The Stolen Husband." It seemed such a good format that the following year they put together another. Called "Just Plain Bill," the show remained on the air for twenty years and helped launch that phenomenon of American culture, the soap opera.[30]

Even as advertisers, the Hummerts could hardly have imagined what energies they were tapping with their low-budget competition to the high-powered Hollywood and New York radio talent. Neither, I am sure, did other early writers for radio who had similar instincts in 1932. In that year, Irna Phillips, also from Chicago, created a show called "Painted Dreams," later named "Today's Children"; Elaine Carrington sold "Red Adams," which evolved through four titles into "Pepper Young's Family"; Carleton E. Morse started his weekly effort to save the American family through "One Man's Family"; and Paul Rhymer's comic "Vic and Sade" began. Exactly what title marks the beginnings of soap opera is problematical.[31] What cannot be disputed, however, is the immediate success of such shows in the early 1930s, and the quick emergence of the daytime serial of domestic drama as a successful form of radio entertainment.

The popularity of the daytime serial soared. By 1946 *Fortune* magazine estimated that 20 million women per day listened to them.[32] This figure represented half the women in America who had radios and were at home. There were forty serials on the air at that time (each show lasted fifteen minutes), down from a high of sixty in 1939. The popular shows, such as "Young Widder Brown," pulled 5 million listeners each day. Another favorite, "Pepper Young's Family," was heard on two networks at three different times each day.[33]

The serials made up half of the total daylight programming time of CBS and NBC, the radio networks carrying them, and were arranged in blocks of listening time. NBC had as many as twelve shows and CBS eleven in a row. The economics are equally impressive. In 1946 the shows represented $30 million in time charges, which was two-thirds of the network's daytime revenue.

The soap opera was not only popular and profitable, but it had longevity as well. By 1946 there were fifteen serials that had been on the air ten years or more. "When a Girl Marries" lasted eighteen years in all; and when in 1960 CBS shut down its last six shows,[34] "Ma Perkins" ended, said the announcer, "after more than seven thousand broadcasts and twenty-seven years."[35] In themselves these are remarkable statistics for an ephemeral medium, but the phenomenon was far from dead. Similar programs, usually in an expanded format, were already firmly entrenched on daytime television. The networks had been trying since 1946 to make the soap opera work in this new industry. Lengthening the show to a thirty-minute daily schedule seemed to help, at least economically,[36] and half a dozen radio soap operas came over to television in the early 1950s.

"The Guiding Light," which began as a radio show in 1939, moved to television in 1952 and is still one of the more popular serials. In 1951 two titles original to television—"Love of Life" and "Search for Tomorrow"—were established and are now the longest running television soaps. (CBS seems to be the soap opera network of champions. These three shows, along with "As the World Turns," which is often the highest Neilsen-rated soap, are all on CBS.) In 1964 soap opera invaded evening television and held its own for five years. "Peyton Place," a half-hour serial, was shown twice weekly at prime time.

Soap operas are big business on daytime television. There are fourteen such shows on the three networks, and 20 to 30 million people a day watch them. In addition, a single show usually reaches households with 7 to 10 million people each day, and the total revenue produced by television soaps accounts for a major part of the network's profits, perhaps more than half.[37] With such a money-making potential, it is no wonder that the search for successful programs is continual. There have been soap operas with overtones of campus political protest, soap operas with vampires, soap operas with big-name stars, and even soap operas with stories which regularly came to a conclusion. NBC and ABC have tried longer formats as the networks vie with each other for the market.

Our interest in soaps seems to be growing. On the newsstand, at least eight monthly magazines are devoted almost exclusively to them. Meanwhile, weekly serials with family themes appear on evening commercial television, spurred on, no doubt, by the success of British imports such as "The Forsyte Saga" and "Upstairs, Downstairs." And we even had a successful parody: nightly "Mary Hartman, Mary Hartman" teased us for our devotion to the family serial, which is now approaching half a century.

The soap opera is a drama of mass dreams of family life. The "abandon" which Henry Nash Smith found in the writers of pulp fiction is also apparent in the creators of soap operas. It is reported that:

> Elaine Carrington talked for eight hours a day, five and six days a week, writing fifteen or more individual scripts per week. Miss Carrington's method of work was to talk the scripts out into a recording machine. 'I pour myself into it,' she observed. 'I give everything. I change voices. I laugh. I cry.'[38]

Another writer notes that Elaine Carrington claimed an output of 38,000 words a week and Irna Phillips, 60,000.[39] Neither lady rewrote, apparently, and as the years went on Irna Phillips, who moved on to television soaps, hired assistant writers. Carleton E. Morse said that once he knew his characters, "writing their lines becomes automatic. They just naturally fall into the 'right slot.'" Morse, like Phillips, kept only slightly ahead of the plot, though in his case it was to get the reactions of his actors to the events in the script. In effect, he blurred the line between actor and character.[40] In the writing of soap opera, instinct and spontaneity are prized above editorial reflection.

It was the Hummerts, however, who organized all this dreaming into a rationalized production unit, a sort of writing factory. From them came most of the radio soap operas written (as well as juvenile serials such as "Jack Armstrong" and thrillers such as "Mr. Keen, Tracer of Lost Persons").

> By 1938 they were buying one-eighth of all radio time at a cost of $12 million a year, and they were responsible

for 6.5 million yearly words. Their factory was organized as a rigid hierarchy. At the top were the Hummerts themselves. Laboring on the lower rungs were
approximately twenty writers, six script readers or
editors, and some sixty clerical assistants. [41]

The Hummerts had strict control over each phase of a show's
production from idea to plot line to dialogue, yet it was a corporate
product. Here the family attitudes in our culture were dramatized
in mass-produced images, the final profitable reduction of our
anxieties by the very system that agitates them.

The audience of the radio daytime serial was mostly women,
mostly housewives, and the same appears to be true for television. [42]
Just what qualifications this introduces in generalizing from the
daytime serial audience to the whole culture is hard to determine.
It could be argued that the housewife, since her life is most immediately involved with domestic affairs, is the prime repository of
the family ethos. Far from being biased, a sample of these women
may give a more clear-cut indication of basic, primary attitudes.

A few researchers have tried to discover what kind of women
made up the radio audience. It seems that these radio shows drew
equally from all social levels. [43] Furthermore, in one study the crude
indications show little psychological difference between listeners
and non-listeners in regard to such personality traits as anxiety or
general social participation. [44] Such differences as magazine preference (listeners predictably preferred "true story" and home life
magazines) and voting habits (listeners tended to vote less) were
more clear-cut. Also, there was a difference in educational levels
as to the amount of listening; less education meant a greater number of shows. But some interesting twists developed here which
tend to modify any easy generalizations about the unsophisticated
tastes of the lower educational and social classes.

The difference in intellectual range of serial listeners
and non-listeners would lead us to expect the former to
be considerably less interested in these educational

stations [two university stations in Iowa]. In fact, the difference is negligible (31 per cent of serial listeners and 34 per cent of non-listeners tune in these stations). Apparently if it is the radio which presents somewhat alien subject matter, the day-time serial listeners are willing to accept it. [45]

Shades of Marshall McLuhan!

The soap opera audience enters a world of white, middle-class family strife. There appear to have been some changes in this world during the years that soap operas have been around, but the differences between radio shows and present-day television ones are not, for the most part, fundamental. [46] The announcer-narrator is gone along with his rhetorical questions. There is more frankness in matters of sex, more swearing, and less passivity on the part of men. The television shows are (marginally) less exaggerated and more tied to details which enhance the realistic surface of the stories presented. Whether this is the result of a more sophisticated audience or of the demands of a medium which, by its nature, must have an actual rather than imagined setting is hard to say.

Certainly, a good many things have stayed pretty much the same throughout the history of the soap opera. The town in which the serial takes place is usually a fictional one of middle size. There are virtually no working-class characters, though radio's Stella Dallas was genteelly poor and the Woleks on television's "One Life to Live" have a touch of blue-collar background. (Rudolph Arnheim noted that on radio the wealthy and upper-class characters were often "shown paying courtship to the attractiveness or efficiency, or both, of the middle-class people." [47]) Though Our Gal Sunday married into English aristocracy, she had the same troubles at Black Swan Hall as the wife of England's richest and most handsome lord, Lord Henry Brinthrope, as did other heroines in less glamorous surroundings. Similarly, on television's "All My Children" the Martins and the Tylers, though presumably from different social backgrounds, are indistinguishable in their problems.

Soap opera males are of the professional class, usually

doctors and lawyers. Each television soap opera today has at least one doctor as a main character, most have several, and three of the serials are set primarily in hospitals. Medicine is one area of the television soap opera where women regularly pursue careers. (In this regard, television may be less liberated than the radio shows, which could boast several sorts of careers for strong heroines—senator, lawyer, newscaster, dress designer, social worker, and the heads of a variety of small businesses.)

Even when women have careers, however, their work remains in the background. As protagonists they are seen as girl friends, wives, and mothers (and men as boyfriends, husbands, and fathers). For the soap opera is a world closed in not only by the middle class, but by the theme of domestic crisis. As one radio listener put it, the stories are about people "getting into trouble and out again,"[48] revealing the anxiety of the modern nuclear family system, unsupported from without and locked intensely into itself. The problems which constantly threaten to engulf the characters—Rudolph Arnheim found a rough average of one new crisis every four days on the radio[49]—are private ones created by themselves and complicated by catastrophes and illnesses. This tendency has, if anything, been exaggerated by the move from radio to television. With an expanded format, plot lines on television are multiplied and the general anxiety level raised. The catastrophes which impinge on the characters are similar to those of radio soap opera: rare diseases; murder; alcoholism; paralysis; auto accidents; bigamy (innocent and otherwise); suicide; miscarriage; criminal abduction; and—of course—amnesia.

This constant barrage of troubles is made all the more spectacular by contrast with the life soap opera characters long for. Implicitly, these shows assert that domestic relationships are ideally static. Although this ideal is not achieved, its pursuit animates the characters. What they are after is an harmonious relationship created by a fixed system of unendangered love. For example, "When a Girl Marries" was a radio serial about the troubles of a young couple, Harry and Joan Davis. They are driving down the highway:

JOAN: I'm just married to a guy I love . . . a man who

hasn't a grain of sense so far as the laughing of life is concerned. And . . . oh, I guess what I'm trying to say is that because I love you so much, it's easy to love and understand anyone who is the slightest bit like you . . . someone like Steve. To understand why he loves Betty so much . . . Harry, look out for that car!

HARRY: Sorry, darling. But I shouldn't even try to drive when you're sitting that close beside me saying things that make me feel I'm everything in the world to you, that our love explains everything to you . . .

JOAN: Nothing matters really, but that we love each other. Not being separated. Not even death. It's— why, Harry, it's knowing a kind of immortality . . . and don't you dare laugh at me![50]

Such rapturously harmonious moments are the unifying center to be achieved, the potential nexus of life. But usually the crash, symbolic or actual, is not avoided.

Contemporary television dialogue may be more subdued than the rhetoric of Elaine Carrington I have just quoted—she was famous for her flights on the subject of romance—but the concern with love is the same. As a character on "Love of Life" put it recently: "It's your whole future—whether you'll ever be happy with your life." The speaker, a young lady, was talking about love with her girl friend, who was hospitalized with a broken back. Unlike Harry Davis, the girl friend did not manage to avoid the crash, perhaps because, unlike him, she was not in a state of domestic grace (she had driven recklessly in the fog after her mother had interfered in her affair with an ex-mental patient). At any rate, most troubles are measured on a scale of romantic-domestic love.

Shortly after Kathy Phillips on "Search for Tomorrow" has escaped from being murdered for the second time, she tells her estranged husband that they must talk about "the real life-and-death problem," whether they can get back together again. And the hired Syndicate killer, pistol in hand, paused, wanting to talk to Kathy about her attitude toward men before pulling the trigger. For these, and most soap opera characters, harmonious domestic love is the all-important attainment of life; romantic love is crucial in that it aims at such a domestic state. Even Ma Perkins, given to common-sense advice, will worry if this is not the case: "Is my little Fay so old that she must choose her husband just because it's sensible? . . . The question is, ain't it maybe better to begin leastways with the . . . romantic love?"[51]

Dramatic action occurs because this system of love is jarred continually—perhaps by other individuals, as when another woman becomes a rival, or perhaps by the character's own inability to find a proper mate due to temperamental waywardness or intervening catastrophe (deserved or not). In any case, the implicit motive is to attain fixed harmony, romantic and domestic, which is the true natural order. From one perspective we might say that trouble is the norm in the world of the soap opera, but this is not really so. Trouble is continual, but it is not normal, which is why the characters spend the greatest part of their dramatic lives worrying. Anxiety that the domestic world is not as it should be is their dominant emotional state.[52] It is what they are, in essence, always talking about, the state of their being which the soap opera dramatizes.

One pattern of dramatic action on the radio soap opera is to have the weak cause trouble through the temptations of the bad only to be saved by the good, who suffer as a result of helping. The problems do not come from social forces outside the characters or from their attempts to reach some specific goal.[53] No questions of social or historical cause are raised. It is an atomistic world in which problems are personal, existing purely on a one-to-one basis, and villainy becomes its own explanation. "No community is admitted between the bad people and the listener, no understanding of their motives exists or is desired."[54] There are, perhaps, fewer outright villains on television (aside from those who are simply criminals), but the individualism which Arnheim notes is still true.

The family, existing apart from any larger social environment, is virtually the only social institution of the soap opera world. On television this enclosure is emphasized by the predominance of interior and close-up shots which create a visual claustrophobia. There is, for the most part, no community to which the family belongs. Its problems are very private ones and "the interests of the community fade into insignificance."[55] The domestic issues of courtship, marriage, and family difficulty have no implications for the community just as the sources of tension never originate in the community. Aside from the medical profession, work is important only in terms of its effect on domestic life. The board of directors of the vague corporation controlled by the Collinses on "Search for Tomorrow" worries about its president because of his irresponsible love life (i.e., he doesn't get married), not because of his corporate decisions. This worry is so great for the chief stockholder, the president's brother, that his wife feels it is interfering with *their* home life. Doctors and nurses are occasionally seen at work, no doubt because in this role they can approximate nurturing, parental figures. But when political difficulties face the protagonist, it is only because a politician is individually corrupt. In general, when trouble occurs there is seldom an indication that the community suffers also. [56]

The occasional appearance of community interests or community forces is one which is accompanied by hostility and often scandal. The police are an obvious example. Pursuing arson, they may uncover bigamy. The community pries into the private affairs of the family. On "Love of Life," Felicia, who has confessed her frigidity to her new husband, says, "Our secret is seeping out of this household little by little." The family must, in return, present a barrier of respectability to keep the community out. The newspaperman becomes a particular instance of this general threat, trying to uncover secrets which if learned would expose the family and leave it vulnerable to the community. Also, a typical closing scene of a television soap opera—one intended to give it a "strong curtain"—shows an unwanted character entering the background of the set and eavesdropping. Thus, among soap opera characters, one primary mode of encounter is to be defensive, a point which relates to the general conception of human relations as static.

If, as I am arguing, the important value affirmed in a soap opera is a fixed state of romantic-domestic love, then it can be said this ideal excludes, or makes irrelevant, any interest in the larger society or community. Furthermore, the pursuit of this ideal creates a second important mode of encounter. In addition to defensiveness there is a more specifically domestic way in which soap opera characters impinge on one another. In the search for domestic harmony nearly all adult characters are potential lovers when involved with the opposite sex. There is a constant flux of attraction and repulsion, of danger and promise for even the most stable—or least unstable—couples. The air is filled with a sort of dramatic tension peculiar to soap opera since its characters live in a world which family sociologists would describe as "permanent availability." [57] In effect there is a serial polygamy of never-ending marriage, divorce (or death of spouse), and the renewed quest for and with another mate.

The personal relationships which result from such domestic drama are extraordinarily tangled since former spouses, children, in-laws, and lovers continually reappear, which rearranges loyalties and affection. Young children are often step-children and wards, and even become something we might call "step-step children" as a result of the ongoing remarriage process. Further complicating many situations is simple illegitimacy, acknowledged or not, and on several shows the child of one family has been fathered secretly by the head of another family. When soap opera children are grown, a symbolic incest theme emerges in the romances between the young men and their quasi-sisters or in the remarriage of a character to brother-in-law or sister-in-law. It is no wonder that children in a soap opera seldom call their parents by other than given names.

The danger to and dissolution of soap opera families is a reflection of the strains on the nuclear family system and as such it presents us with an image of a laissez-faire marriage market gone mad. But it is important to see that the animating force is the desire for a true love, a better marriage which will lead to a new family, that is, one closer to the domestic ideal. Here is where the promise lies: the characters' agitated domestic lives embody the continual reaffirmation of achieving family harmony, a tenacious longing that it must come true.

It is at this point that the models of the family of freedom and the family of security can be discerned. Elements of both intermingle in the soap opera. The family unit as a whole tends to be withdrawn, as in the family of security. Society at large is rejected in favor of a self-enclosed structure. Yet the characters also tend to be self-contained as in the family of freedom. They struggle toward love as the natural and harmonious state of their lives. But in their spontaneous efforts to achieve genuine domestic love, they collide with one another like random atoms.

If there is no community or only a hostile one; if the conception of social life is individualistic; if relationships are seen ideally to be rigid and fixed—how does the family cope with the problems which beset it with such tedious familiarity? Part of the answer has already been suggested. Most characters do not cope at all, but only react passively. They wait until the problems work themselves out, following predictable and stereotyped patterns of behavior as they do. [58] They are at the mercy of their emotional pursuit of the domestic ideal, and the solutions which occur are accidental and fortuitous, implemented by no one.

But not all soap opera characters have been equally passive. If we look at them in terms of the two family models, one major difference between radio and television characters might be noted. A number of radio shows presented a strong element of the family of security. A leading family figure dominated. The character of a Good Family Leader (usually a Good Woman) acted as a force which aimed at giving structure to the family. This character was striving continually for cohesion and equilibrium among family members, knowing that static harmony was the natural state of affairs. If it could be achieved, the family household would become a home, a place where one has both freedom and security. These two ideals do not conflict in a home because there they are bathed in goodness and love. It was the mission of the Good Family Leader to strive for the home with all the moral powers at his or her command.

The presence of the Good Family Leader brings the benefits of structure and order to a potentially anarchical society. [59] In this world of autonomous, self-sufficient individuals, the Good Family Leader tries to neutralize a chaotic collision of egos. Order constantly breaks down, but through his or her individual efforts it is constantly reestablished. The special feature of this leadership is its innocence. The power which is wielded is not corrupting. It is good power because it comes from a good person. Ma Perkins, who ran a lumberyard, was probably as good a woman as soap operas produced. In the following quotation she is discussing, with her confidante, daughter Fay's choice of a rich (second) husband over a poor one:

> SHUFFLE: Ma, if Fay was making a sacrifice, for the sake of us folks she figures is old and can't take care of ourselves no more, you and me wouldn't let her do it. We'd beat her over the head and lock her in the cellar. But Fay ain't making a sacrifice, she's catching the brass ring . . . she's reaching out her hands and letting the blessings of life fall into em . . .
>
> MA: Shuffle, Shuffle, you're right. Here we sit, and upstairs there's Fay, and the circle comes round again. Losing Paul, but here's baby Paulette. Fay gets married, but we get Carl . . .
>
> SHUFFLE: Be happy, Ma. You and me, we've been on this porch a hundred million times, the lights going off in the houses up and down the street. But what I'm saying—of all the times we've sat here and talked the rest of the town to sleep, maybe tonight is best of all.
>
> MA: Oh, Shuffle. He'll be a wonderful husband for Fay. And I couldn't ask for nothing more than that. [60]

Despite all the troubles, the universe is naturally good, providing accidental poetic justice where the Good Woman Leader does not or cannot. Thus there are two forces acting against difficulties (they often occur in combination), imposing order.

In a world of atomistic individuals, there can be no creative communal power, that is, no institutions and traditions beyond the family which capacitate as well as forbid. But order is necessary and so is maintained by the special power of the leader. The family becomes a defensive unit isolated from the world and held together by the intervention of the Good Leader who is constantly trying to turn it into a home. Because Ma Perkins is good her authority is not arbitrary, and because she has authority there exists some equilibrium in a world of atoms.

Carleton E. More's "One Man's Family" solved the problem of order in the Barbour family in a different way. Morse's program, though it was not a daily one until its final years, may have been the longest running and most popular of the family serials on radio.[61] In it he depicted the rather low-keyed events of an upper-middle-class San Francisco family in a series of episodes subdivided into "books" and "chapters." His initial inspiration was Galsworthy's *The Forsyte Saga*. His motive was consciously didactic:

> To me, home and family stand for the very essence of good living, good character, and good citizenship. So long as family life exists with its love, ideals, and high moral standards and continues as a training ground for young minds, this nation will remain the great country we know and love. But once let the dry-rot of ignorance or indifference or personal selfishness of parents destroy family life, then our whole high moral standard of civilization will disintegrate before our eyes.... People MUST realize the importance of the family. They must know the obligation of man and wife; obligations of parenthood. I have tried to emphasize these factors in "One Man's Family" all these years, because I firmly believe if men and women do not make the home the foundation of today's civilization, tomorrow will find them living in the greatest ruins of hopelessness and despair ever known to mankind.[62]

As Walter Sheppard has shown,[63] the Barbours had, in effect, two heads of family: Father Barbour, conservative spokesman for traditional values, and his eldest son, Paul, a widower of liberal views who gave good advice to his younger brothers and sisters. Father Barbour stood for authority, Paul for individual freedom, a polarity that was repeated somewhat in the other family members with Fanny, the mother, as background mediator. Fanny did not need to figure prominently in the dramatic action since all of Morse's characters were fundamentally loyal to the family. Most often the episodic events revolved around such problems as trying to get Father Barbour to go to the hospital for needed medical attention, with a lot of the dialogue taken up by discussions of marriage and family. The show could be topical as well. Gloomy thoughts of the approach of World War II occasioned the following dialogue:

CLAUDIA: Isn't that getting in over our heads, Paul?

PAUL: Not when you consider that every world problem has its beginning and its solution in the hearts of men . . . not in some vague, complicated system of which the ordinary person has no knowledge . . . What's in your heart and what's in my heart is going to have a lot to do with what happens. . . . Dad . . . what one thing is foremost in your thoughts?

HENRY: Why, Paul, I think 'family.' . . . It's my opinion that the family is the source from whence comes the moral strength of a nation. And disintegration of any nation begins with the disintegration of the family. The family is the smallest unit in society. Millions and millions of these little units make a nation. And the standards of living set up by these family units indicate the high or low standards of a nation. . . . A well-disciplined, morally upright family is bound to turn out good citizens! Good citizens make a good nation.

PAUL: No doubt about that! There's a rising tide of sentiment growing throughout the world, fostered by people who are sick over the way things are going. . . . Perhaps it's the answer we've all been looking for . . . an answer in the hearts of men. [64]

The closeness of these sentiments to Morse's stated credo is clear enough. It only remains to say that Paul's optimism did not sustain

Morse to the end. When the show was finally cancelled in 1959, Morse said that it went off the air because American family life had deteriorated and a close, happy family life was no longer a reality. [65]

There are still good men and women on television soap operas, and even the vague suggestion of family leaders, but they are less powerful, their role is more diminished, and they do not have the same claim on our attention as they once had. Titles have changed to reflect this: "Ma Perkins," "Mary Marlin," "Just Plain Bill," and "The Romance of Helen Trent" have given way to "All My Children," "Days of Our Lives," and "As the World Turns." Perhaps radio figures were more powerful because the programs were done in a more exaggerated style. For example, the following exchange is between Stella Dallas and her daughter, Laurel (who is married to Dick Grosvenor):

LAUREL: Mummy, I can't believe even Mrs. Grosvenor would be mean enough to send you to jail for stealing that Egyptian mummy.

STELLA: Ah, Lolly baby, she'd do it in a minute. You know how she resents you and her son, Dick, bein' close to me.

LAUREL: Yes, I know.

STELLA: Besides, having that Egyptian mummy at her party was an important thing to Mrs. Grosvenor. It was somethin' to impress all her big society friends. She blames me for making her look bad to all those people.

LAUREL: But Mummy, anybody who knows you knows you could never steal an Egyptian mummy. Why, you'd never steal anything!

STELLA: Lolly baby, you're my own daughter. Naturally you wouldn't think I would steal the Egyptian mummy, but I reckon I'm just going to have to prove my innocence to everybody else. [66]

On television a more mundane style is attempted with contemporary stereotypes of psychological characterization modifying the extreme heroines and villains. Sisters Vanessa and Meg are still the light and dark heroines whose stories anchor "Love of Life." Meg connives and remarries (about five times to date) while Vanessa sticks to her husband (as long as he lives) and tries to help others, which gets her into trouble with Meg. But there are too many people to help and she has plenty of troubles of her own. Alcoholics Anonymous and medical experts are as likely to be called upon, and various forms of psychotherapy seem to have the respect the Good Family Leader once had.

The effect of these changes is that television soap operas present an image of family life with even less family structure or authority than did many radio soap operas. Today there are typically three generations of family in an emotional quest for personal happiness based on the achievement of romantic and domestic love. Two or three such families are interrelated and the resultant multiple plot lines in themselves convey a sense of disunity. There is no schema or reason of dramatic structure for the various stories being place side by side. Juxtaposition is for purposes of narrative titillation. Crisis interrupts the daily five scenes which direct our interest among the various plots.

The compromise between anguished freedom and repugnant authority has shifted in emphasis in soap opera. This tendency becomes even clearer when we compare it to Jefferson's *Rip Van Winkle.* In its nineteenth-century popular expression, the family of security was made to accommodate individual freedom. Crèvecoeur's ideal predominated. But in the soap opera, a secure family structure is lost. In its place came the Good Family Leader, who tried to keep some order. Now with this character diminished, we see only glimpses of the ideal family of security in a few background figures of an older generation. In the foreground is the family of freedom, Tocqueville's ideal, not as a represented reality but as an elusive dream of the characters to replace reality.

The American family ethos can be seen to contain significant ambiguities. In a market economy it must make room for familialism; in an anti-institutional culture it must affirm its value as an institution. The strains are obvious when one analyzes such a conventionalized form as the daytime serial. In a setting of atomistic relations there is no conception of communal support to call on.

Power in the name of goodness is one tendency in the dreams of the audience. Lacking this power, characters struggle for family in a world in which the family is constantly threatened. Some prophecy has been unfulfilled in American life, some expectation unrealized. The family of freedom ought to get along very well. Old feudal relations of authority and status have been declared abolished. Free, warm, and spontaneous relations should follow. But what occurs seems fearfully like anarchy. Through the special merits of the Good Family Leader, the extreme of freedom was avoided, but only temporarily.

Not only in content does the soap opera reveal a world charged with contradictions and inadequacies. The action veers compulsively toward non-drama. In its recurring pulsations of crisis there are no solutions, just as there are no active attempts to solve problems (and so connect with some larger reality). One should not dismiss the implications of this for the drama merely because the evidence is from the mass media. It is not because soap opera is popular or poor art that it lacks a dramatic curve. The western is equally conventionalized and stereotyped, yet it has purposeful action, conflict, and resolution, however crude. The soap opera has within it an impulse toward self-destruction as drama, perhaps because endless crises are the inevitable concomitant of a static ideal.

The popular drama is a vital repository of family attitudes. But these formulations are not only (or merely) the property of popular culture and consumer entertainment. Winthrop Tilley has noted similarities between Henry James's *The Spoils of Poynton* and the serial "Young Widder Brown." [67] Both are dominated by the Good Woman and the virtue of gallant suffering; both proceed at a snail's pace and the action consists of "mental-analytical chit-chat"; both show a rejection of the outer world and of sexuality. Ineffectuality is his final judgment on the characters of both worlds. In other words, Tilley uses the soap opera to put James down. If a work of art shares qualities with the soap opera, he assumes, it must be inferior.

I would argue a different point. Literature and sub-literature can and do share the same materials; especially in the drama they draw upon the same dreams of family life. The question is: what does the writer make of such materials? The soap opera is the final formula created from the uncertainties seen in *Rip Van Winkle*. In both, attitudes and value systems concerning the family exist in vague compromises which obscure their conflicting, exclusive, and absolute qualities. These popular forms are in contrast to our serious dramatic literature, which apparently draws on the same attitudes and tests them for their validity, internal consistency, and expressive adequacy. What separates playwrights such as O'Neill, Miller, and Williams from products of our mass dreams of family life such as *Rip Van Winkle* and the soap opera is not the materials dealt with, or even the eloquence of language, so much as the relentless pursuit of the contradictions which the popular culture imagines as compatible and harmonious. The conscious artist is willing, inspired, or perhaps driven, to test these conflicting claims, to push them to their furthest extreme to define their true relation. Popular family drama avoids the implications of its own material. Beginning with O'Neill, our best playwrights bring an intensity and relentlessness to the drama of family tensions.

NOTES

1. Ruth Shonle Cavan, *American Marriage* (New York, 1953), p. 7.

2. Fats Waller, improvised tag line to "Black Raspberry Jam," *Guide to Jazz* (RCA Victor Records, LPM-1393).

3. Henry Nash Smith, *Virgin Land* (New York, 1957), pp. 100-101.

4. Joseph Jefferson, *"Rip Van Winkle:" The Autobiography of Joseph Jefferson* (New York, 1950), p. 347.

5. For a list of references see *Representative Plays by American Dramatists 1865-1911,* ed. Montrose J. Moses, III (New York, 1921), 7-8. In addition see Edward King, "Joseph Jefferson," in *Famous American Actors Today,* ed. Charles E. L. Wingate and F. E. McKay (New York, 1896), pp. 1-17; and Lewis C. Strang, *Famous Actors of the Day* (Boston, 1900), pp. 11-17.

6. Quoted in Montrose J. Moses, *Famous Actor-Families in America* (1906; rpt. New York, 1968), p. 82.

7. James is cited in Bernard Hewitt, *Theatre U.S.A., 1665 to 1957* (New York, 1959), p. 203; Winter and Mathews are cited with Moses's approval in Moses, *Famous Actor-Families,* pp. 81-82. See also the reference to James Huneker in Moses, *Famous Actor-Families,* p. 86.

8. W[alter] P[ritchard] E[aton], "Jefferson, Joseph," *DAB* (1933).

9. For further suggestions on the popularity of Rip see Arthur E. Waterman,

"Joe Jefferson as Rip Van Winkle," *Journal of Popular Culture,* 1 (1968), 371-378. Waterman cites Garff B. Wilson, *A History of American Acting* (Bloomington, Ind., 1966), p. 170, as first proposing that Rip and Jefferson were compounded in the public's mind. Leslie Fiedler dismisses the play for turning Rip's mythical qualities into a stereotype for the ladies: *The Return of the Vanishing American* (New York, 1968), pp. 60-62.

10. Jefferson, *Autobiography,* p. 353.

11. Perhaps the best account is Arthur Hobson Quinn, *A History of the American Drama from the Beginning to the Civil War* (New York, 1923), pp. 324-332. Quinn corrects Moses's version of these changes which appears in *Representative Plays,* ed. Moses, III, 17-26. See also Jefferson, *Autobiography,* pp. 172-177, 353-354; and Dion Boucicault, "Dramatization of Rip Van Winkle," *Critic,* 3 (April 7, 1883), 158-159.

12. Jefferson, *Autobiography,* pp. 172-177.

13. William Winter, *Other Days* (New York, 1908), pp. 76, 90-93.

14. Jefferson, *Autobiography,* p. 353.

15. Joseph Jefferson, *Rip Van Winkle* in *Representative American Plays,* ed. Arthur Hobson Quinn, 7th ed. (New York, 1957), p. 413. All subsequent references to *Rip Van Winkle* will be to Quinn's edition of the play.

16. Burke's version is available, along with a version by the English actor John Kerr, in *Representative Plays,* ed. Moses, III, 27-71.

17. Jefferson, *Autobiography,* p. 350.

18. Ibid., p. 348.

19. Jefferson, *Rip Van Winkle,* p. 431.

20. Waterman, "Jefferson's Rip," pp. 373-374.

21. Quoted in Hewitt, *Theatre U.S.A.,* p. 200.

22. Jefferson, *Autobiography,* p. 173.

23. Ibid., pp. 175-176.

24. Ibid., p. 175. He probably has Charles Burke in mind whose natural style he admired greatly.

25. Ibid., p. 175.

26. Eaton, "Jefferson," *DAB.*

27. Jefferson, *Rip Van Winkle,* pp. 429-430.

28. Quinn, Introduction to ibid., p. 402.

29. Ibid., p. 430, note 1.

30. Madeleine Edmondson and David Rounds, *The Soaps: Daytime Serials of Radio and TV* (New York, 1973), pp. 53-58; Jim Harmon, *The Great Radio Heroes* (New York, 1967), pp. 167-169; Ray Stedman, *The Serials* (Norman, Okla., 1971), pp. 235-236.

I am not arguing that soap operas are exclusively American any more than is the emerging nuclear family pattern. But if changes toward a nuclear family pattern are more highly developed in America than elsewhere, then it is characteristic that a conventionalized form of popular drama, reflecting the attitudes which accompany such change, should originate in America. Soap operas are now popular in other countries as well. For example, it is estimated that "Simplemente Maria," an

Argentinian soap opera *(telenovela),* is seen by 60 million Latin Americans. See Terri Shaw, "The Median Is a Message on Latin American Soaps," *The Washington Post,* Sept. 11, 1975, Sec. B, p. 13.

31. For a discussion of the origins of the soap opera, see Edmondson and Rounds, *Soaps,* pp. 25-41; Stedman, *Serials,* pp. 225-237.

32. Except where otherwise noted, the following figures for radio serials are gleaned from "Soap Opera," *Fortune,* 33 (March 1946), 119-122.

33. Edmondson and Rounds, *Soaps,* p. 51.

34. Ibid., p. 119. The six are: "Rosemary," "Right to Happiness," "Ma Perkins," "Young Dr. Malone," "The Second Mrs. Burton," and "The Romance of Helen Trent." Harmon, *Radio Heroes,* p. 172, says seven shows, but he does not list them. Here, as at a number of points, Edmondson and Rounds appear to be relying on Stedman without specific acknowledgement.

35. Quoted in Harmon, *Radio Heroes,* p. 174.

36. Edmondson and Rounds, *Soaps,* pp. 130-140.

37. Ibid., pp. 186-189, 197-198.

38. Harmon, *Radio Heroes,* p. 178.

39. Edmondson and Rounds, *Soaps,* pp. 51-52, 45.

40. Walter Pierce Sheppard, *"One Man's Family:* A History 1932 to 1959 and a Script Analysis 1932 to 1944," Diss. U. of Wisconsin 1964, pp. 194-200; quotation appears on p. 205. According to Sheppard (p. 200), Morse was told by a psychiatrist that "One Man's Family" may have been Morse's ideal creation to replace personal dissatisfaction with his actual family.

41. Edmondson and Rounds, *Soaps,* p. 56.

42. One television soap with a crime motif, "Edge of Night," claims to draw a sizable male audience. Also, a social worker I know tells of couples who do not wish to have her visits interrupt "our stories." But the statistics suggest that housewives still predominate in the television audience. Edmondson and Rounds, *Soaps,* pp. 184-185.

43. W. Lloyd Warner and William E. Henry, "The Radio Day-Time Serial: A Symbolic Analysis," *Genetic Psychology Monographs,* 37, (1948), 13-14.

44. Herta Herzog, "What Do We Really Know about Day-Time Serial Listeners?," in *Radio Research, 1942-43,* ed. Paul F. Lazarsfield and Frank K. Stanton (New York, 1943), pp. 3-33.

45. Ibid., pp. 22-23. Another study evaluated the psychology of lower-middle class listeners: Warner and Henry, "Day-Time Serial," pp. 3-71. And a third showed that only slight differences existed among serial audiences with regard to primary characteristics (age, education, income, residence): Helen J. Kaufman, "The Appeal of Specific Daytime Serials," in *Radio Research,* pp. 86-107.

In recent years, the popularity of the British shows—"The Forsyte Saga" and "Upstairs, Downstairs"—suggests that when made fashionable, soap operas (or elements of them) intrigue men as well as women, literati as well as plain folk.

46. The following analysis of the content of soap opera draws on plot synopses and dialogue in: Dan Wakefield, *All Her Children* (Garden City, N.Y., 1976); Rudolph Arnheim, "The World of the Daytime Serial," in *Radio Research,* pp.

34-85; Warner and Henry, "Day-Time Serial"; Sheppard, *"One Man's Family"*; Harmon, *Radio Heroes;* Edmondson and Rounds, *Soaps;* and the magazines *Soap Opera Digest, Daylight TV,* and *Daytime TV Super Special.*

Also, I have listened to recorded excerpts of radio shows, a number of which are available commercially, and have viewed the principal television soap operas.

Finally, although it is, in effect, an "inversion of true soap opera" (Edmondson and Rounds, *Soaps,* p. 39) rather than another variation, Paul Rhymer's "Vic and Sade" is available for sampling and is of interest for its special wit as well as for the image of family life presented: *The Small House Halfway Up in the Next Block,* ed. Mary Frances Rhymer (New York, 1972).

47. Arnheim, "World of Daytime Serial," p. 41.

48. Quoted in Herta Herzog, "On Borrowed Experience: An Analysis of Listening to Daytime Sketches," *Studies in Philosophy and Social Science,* 9 (1941), 66.

49. Arnheim, "World of Daytime Serial," p. 44.

50. Quoted in Harmon, *Radio Heroes,* p. 169.

51. "Ma Perkins in the 1940s," on *When Radio was King!* (Memorabilia Records, MLP. 725).

52. Cf. Edmondson and Rounds, *Soaps,* p. 249.

53. Cf. Arnheim, "World of Daytime Serial," pp. 58-61. The exception to the generalization often cited is "Against the Storm" by Sandra Michael in which an attempt to achieve goals was characteristic of the action. Significantly, social and political issues made up much of the content. See Arnheim, "World of Daytime Serial," p. 84; Harmon, *Radio Heroes,* pp. 179-181; Stedman, *Serials,* pp. 332-333. And for a more jaundiced view, Edmondson and Rounds, *Soaps,* pp. 235-238.

54. Arnheim, "World of Daytime Serial," p. 60.

55. Ibid., p. 47.

56. Arnheim, ibid., p. 52, notes only six instances in 166 cases.

57. "In essence, [Bernard] Farber's model assumes the permanent availability of all adults, regardless of marital status, as potential spouses for all other cross-sex adults who are not ruled by the incest taboo. This means, among other things, that even a person already married is a potential spouse. Marriages are not arranged by kinsmen but based on personal choice. Personal welfare is the primary consideration, and as a result marriages take place early, the divorce rate is high, and remarriages are frequent. Having children is an indication, by the parents, that they intend to maintain their marital relationship, but children do not rule out divorce." Summary by Rodman, *Marriage, Family and Society,* ed. Hyman Rodman (New York, 1965), pp. 250-251.

58. And they are expected to do so by the audience. See Warner and Henry, "Day-Time Serial," pp. 20-27, 48-53.

59. Arnheim, "World of Daytime Serial," p. 45, notes in passing that two family types exist in the soap opera, but he is more interested in showing the anarchy of rampant individualism as the central ethic of the daytime serial: "Instead of discussing the question of how a well-built community offers protection to its members, the serials show the individual taking the law into his own hands and

getting away with it.'' Ibid., pp. 81-82. This ignores the whole family context of the soap opera but it is a good deal closer to what happens than is the interpretation of Warner and Henry, who see soap opera values as socially oriented because audience values are reaffirmed. Warner and Henry, ''Day-Time Serial,'' pp. 60, 63-64.

60. Harmon, *Radio Heroes,* p. 178.

61. Sheppard, *''One Man's Family,''* p. 171.

62. Ibid., p. 16.

63. Ibid., pp. 287-349.

64. Quoted in Harmon, *Radio Heroes,* p. 188.

65. Sheppard, *''One Man's Family,''* pp. 55-56.

66. Quoted in Harmon, *Radio Heroes,* p. 165.

67. Winthrop Tilley, ''Fleda Vetch and Ellen Brown, or, Henry James and the Soap Opera,'' *Western Humanities Review,* 10 (1956), 175-180.

3

EUGENE O'NEILL AND THE DRAMA OF FAMILY DILEMMA

> *Like two skilled dancers, the experienced married couple can undertake with the ease and confidence born of long experience the smooth execution of complex movements in which, despite their constantly changing roles, they present an articulated pattern of graceful harmony.*
> David R. Mace [1]

> *[The middle-class male child] is embraced by a psychological Iron Maiden: any lunge forward or backward only impales him more securely on the spikes.*
> Arnold W. Green [2]

Our foremost playwright, Eugene O'Neill, was predominantly a writer of domestic drama. Because his life itself reads like the long, groping, painful script of some raw family tragedy, the psychology of O'Neill—like that of a character in such a play—has been an important basis for understanding his life and work. And an immensely useful one, of that there is no doubt. O'Neill's plays embody much of his personal *angst* in an immediate way, as Arthur and Barbara Gelb and Louis Shaeffer exhaustively demonstrate. [3] O'Neill invites such emphasis not only because of his personal life but because of his own use of Freudian concepts. His achievement is made greater not smaller by our understanding of the intricacies of his feelings for his parents, his brother, his wives, and his own children. But not in a simple way. The more we know, the more we become aware of the power and resonance of his work, of the distance between the "realism" of his art and the psychological reality of his daily world. The temptation, of course, is to concern one's self with the inner agonies of the man as transferred to the stage and embodied in a dramatic image. But I suggest that O'Neill's vision of family life is a symbol not only of personal psychological experience, but of a social history larger than his own.

One could interpret O'Neill's biography in this way. In his parents, Mary Ellen Quinlan and James O'Neill, we have the meeting of two nineteenth-century worlds. "Ella" was the quintessence of the genteel middle class, the provincial bourgeoise with pretensions to the finer things in life. This refined idealism might take the form of artistic ambition to be a pianist or religious ambition to be a nun—no matter. For her, the home was a place of protection and for the nurturing of cultural values. James O'Neill was from the rough and tumble world of the theater, a society on the make in which business values dominated artistic ones. Robust, outgoing, intent on being thought a good fellow, James was engaged in the ruthless struggle to achieve what the Quinlans of America already had. He barnstormed from a rebuilding Chicago to a San Francisco rich on Comstock silver; home was nonexistent for him. At their marriage in a beau monde parish of New York, respectability and status met glamour and energy; it was the gilded age, and certain of its paradoxes became family dilemmas for Eugene O'Neill.

The boarding hotel—that prime symbol of family decay to the nineteenth century[4]—framed O'Neill's life. "Born in a hotel room—and God damn it—died in a hotel room!" was O'Neill's own version of his life story, pronounced on his deathbed.[5] James, always touring (and searching for a hot investment), and Ella, unable to manage a household, sought a compromise in their New London, Connecticut, summer house. "Monte Cristo Cottage," with its alternating periods of family life and family dispersion, continually reenacted an extreme version of modern nuclear family life. Turned inward—especially as the O'Neills came to be snubbed by New London—emotional involvement was intense. Scattered and functionless—with James on the road and the children at boarding school—the family became increasingly estranged, each member absorbed in his own world, whether of drugs and alcohol, or of the theater and literature.

Finally, Eugene O'Neill's own series of marriages and marital difficulties recapitulated the cycle of contraction and dispersion, just as his attitude toward his children showed a more complex version of this pattern of family forces. In such an act as his last will, where he "cut off Shane and Oona, as well as 'their issue now or hereafter born,'"[6] O'Neill, in effect, demanded his independence from what sociologists call the "family of procreation" and its restraints on his artistic and private self. But he also implicitly confirmed the devotion to his "family of orientation," the subject of his plays. One can even say that in this peculiar way his art encompassed both families, for he and his wives referred to his plays as their "children."[7]

The social symbolism of O'Neill's biography extends to his plays. From first plays to last, O'Neill made the domestic situation his primary subject. There are exceptions, of course. Among his better-known works, these would be: the four one-act plays of the sea—*The Long Voyage Home, The Moon of the Caribbees, Bound East for Cardiff,* and *In the Zone*—known collectively as *S.S. Glencairn* (1916-1918; first performed together in 1924); *The Emperor Jones* (1920); *The Hairy Ape* (1922); *Lazarus Laughed* and *Marco Millions* (both 1928); and *The Iceman Cometh* (1946). But even in most of these, family and marriage are noticeable in their absence, missed by the characters. Some, like Yank in *Bound East for Cardiff,* die dreaming of home. Domesticity is a need for O'Neill, the one recurring context in which his people meet and struggle. And since his dramatic world scarcely includes society or community as a larger reality, family and marriage are peculiarly emphasized. They are the only social institutions of force or substance. In the individual's life they are the context of O'Neill's grandiose intention to write about the eternal cosmos and man's condition. They are the structures which exist "between man and God."[8]

O'Neill's attitudes toward domesticity do not change during his career.[9] His work shows a constant return to the same dramatic dilemma even while he refines his imaginative presentation of it.

He is caught between self and otherness, between the family of freedom and the family of security. O'Neill presents us with images of this dichotomy. Both in the obvious "content" of the plays and in the forms their actions create, he depicts families struggling between two possibilities. He elaborates on these from play to play, testing out first one aspect, then another. But the sum of his career shows that he always returns to the deadlocked center.

While it is useful to see, as many critics have, distinct periods in O'Neill's career, the dilemma of family life is the common denominator. In his early plays, O'Neill is mainly concerned with its definition. In his middle period, he begins a search for some larger structure for his plays which would give context to, and so an organizing perspective on, this dilemma. In his late work, he returns with surety and a new richness of feeling to the unadorned family experience. As the following survey will indicate, each period has its masterpiece in which O'Neill struggles to define the implications of his attitudes toward family life. By looking at his family plays, we can see the conflicting claims of the two family models he inherited. In turn, the artistry of his work gives us powerful images which shape our thinking about family life.

In the first phase of his career, O'Neill set out to discover what were the forces at work in family life. The patterns he established recur throughout his career. The prophecy of family harmony had failed. Instead, the family was a battleground, a clash of wills in which the struggle for power over (or escape from) its members involved illusions of peace and harmony. The major ironies of his plays are built on the way self-deception mocks such hopes. *Beyond the Horizon* (1920), O'Neill's first Pulitzer prize winner, attempted to dramatize just such a world.

Two brothers, who love each other without much hatred—a rarity for O'Neill siblings—lead complementary, self-defeating lives. Robert, the poetic dreamer, wants to leave the family farm to find beauty and freedom. Andrew, the staunch man of the soil, want to stay and marry the neighbor girl, Ruth. He cannot plow and read poetry at the same time—Crèvecoeur's yeoman has been split into two dissonant parts. The patriarchal father, a footloose bachelor uncle, and two clinging mothers compound the forces at work on these men, but the catalyst to the action is that Ruth imagines she loves Robert, who then stays to work the farm while Andrew goes off to sea in his place. The result is disastrous. The farm is ruined along with Robert's health. Ruth's love turns to hatred, then indifference, as everyone dreams that Andrew, who has grown rich, will save them. But Andrew is equally unhappy, for his own grasping after material success has proved it an illusion. In the end, Robert dies, "at last—free—free!" And Andrew will take care of Ruth, whom he no longer loves and who is spiritually dead.

It is interesting how close the action of *Beyond the Horizon* comes to implying reassurance: if only each brother had followed his calling, his life would have been prosperous, creative, and sane. The play is then about a pitiable mistake in judgment rather than the bitter irony of life. Perhaps the play's unlooked-for Broadway success came, in part, from just such a viewing. One could participate in fashionable postwar, revolt-from-the-village gloom without giving way to the feeling that things were fundamentally irreparable. It is the sort of appeal that soap operas continually make, and it is theatrically irresistible. But I think O'Neill intended to say something else. He was trying to dramatize the notion that because of our own perversity, and because of the malign nature of life— the two (psychology and fate) are often compounded in his plays— we pursue love and freedom in such ways that each cancels out the other. There is no cure for the world. The family is the quintessential setting for such a struggle between self and mutuality. In effect, everything man is can be seen by what he is in the family.

In the family drama O'Neill occasionally toyed with the possibility of a happy ending, either through sacrifice and submission as a way out of the impasse or, even less often, through a general reconciliation. *Abortion, A Wife for Life,* and *Servitude* (all written during 1913-1914) save the family by the destruction of selfhood. *Anna Christie* (1921) ends with the reconciliation of a prostitute, whose heart is golden, with her lover, and the promise of good days ahead. In the same year *The Straw* more bleakly gives the "hopeless hope" that the hard-won mutual love of two tubercular patients will save one of them. *The First Man* (1922) presents the largest family of any of O'Neill's plays. It shows the acceptance by the father of his infant son, whom he has hated for destroying the freedom of his marriage and separating him from his wife. The theme of submission reappears in the plays of later periods also. In the experimental *Days Without End* (1934) O'Neill split the protagonist between two actors. He combined the domestic dilemma with the struggle between faith and doubt. A happy family, along with religious reconciliation, is the result of submission to a larger reality than the self. And in *A Touch of the Poet* (1957) Nora proudly makes the same choice of submission and loss of self in her love for Con Melody, although it implies no peace or harmony in their marriage.

The plays of reconciliation and hope are so only by comparison with the rest of O'Neill's work. The struggle is modulated by special conditions. In three of the early plays impending or actual death keeps the forces of self and of mutuality from clashing in the family. And in *Anna Christie* O'Neill intended to suggest the temporary quality of the union, even if he didn't succeed. As Barrett Clark says, "What O'Neill may not have seen was that the union of two lovers *is* a happy ending, no matter what is hinted regarding their future." He goes on to quote O'Neill: "'Meaning that I wish it understood as unhappy? Meaning nothing of the kind. Meaning what I have said before, that the play has no ending.... The curtain falls. Behind it their lives go on.'" [10] Again, as in *Beyond the Horizon,* he did not find the precise action to embody his theme, though what he did create was theatrically appealing. In this case O'Neill was looking for a pattern of dramatic action which would structure the play without resolving it. It is a problem that he did not fully solve until near the end of his career.

Not reconciliation but the family destroying the individual is the more usual dramatic subject for O'Neill. *Before Breakfast* (1916), a one-act monologue, established this early in O'Neill's career: a vicious, screeching wife drives her off-stage husband to suicide. The silent, unseen character of the husband rather fully represents the isolation of domestic life which, as I have suggested, runs through all of O'Neill's plays. In *The Rope* (1918), *Gold* (1921), and *All God's Chillun Got Wings* (1924), the destructive forces are allied with greed or race prejudice, but the collision of egos rests on the same longing for mutuality made wholly impossible by the striving to be separate. Final destructions climax similar dilemmas in *The Great God Brown* (1926) and *Dynamo* (1928) as well.

One of these plays, *All God's Chillun Got Wings,* is especially interesting, for in it marriage creates a more than usual isolation. Jim and Ella are cut off from the outer world, their kinship families, and each other because they are a racially mixed couple. The only way they can finally exist together is through a destructive loss of self, a return to the presexual purity of their relationship in which Ella becomes a child and Jim alternates between child and "uncle." Their marriage, in effect, destroys them; and yet O'Neill must mean us to take Jim's submission as a triumphant, if twisted, acceptance:

> Forgive me, God—and make me worthy! Now I see Your Light again! Now I hear Your Voice! ... Forgive me, God, for blaspheming You! Let this fire of burning suffering purify me of selfishness and make me worthy of the child You send me for the woman You take away![11]

What is being celebrated is Jim's recognition of the eternal fixity of their dilemma and his resignation to it. *Welded* (1924) makes a similar thematic point, but in the case of *All God's Chillun Got Wings,* deadlock leads to regression and degeneration. In the conflict between the institutional demand for mutual relation, on the one hand, and individual desire for total freedom, on the other, the self collapses.

Another aspect of O'Neill's attitude toward family life can be seen in his depiction of children. *All God's Chillun Got Wings* is one of the few plays where children have any positive value. Their uncorrupted innocence in the opening scene is the refuge to which Ella must retreat psychologically. Even in *The First Man,* where the entire play depends on the final acceptance of the child, O'Neill lets the protagonist escape to his archeological diggings, leaving the boy (who never appears onstage) to a dotty aunt, who is to keep the boy innocent until he can be taught to be free. In *Welded, All*

God's Chillun Got Wings, and *The First Man,* a childless marriage symbolizes the intensity as well as the isolation of domesticity and family life. If young children do exist they are sickly, die, or leave one lonely, as in *Abortion, The Rope, Beyond the Horizon, The Great God Brown,* and *Strange Interlude* (1928). Children mainly interest O'Neill when they have become full-grown, competing adults. This is true of *Gold* and *Beyond the Horizon,* and of most of his late plays as well.

In addition to self-deception, reconciliation, submission, and destruction, another pattern of conflicting family forces appeared in O'Neill's early work, the possibility that there is nothing but conflict, that deadlock is the result of the clash of mutuality and self. He began to explore this in *Welded.* Here O'Neill shows a playwright and his actress wife striving for what they call their "Grand Ideal" of marriage. In the first act, this is defined for us:

> Not for us the ordinary family rite, you'll remember! We swore to have a true sacrament—or nothing! Our marriage must be a consummation demanding and continuing the best in each of us! Hard, difficult, guarded from the commonplace, kept sacred as the outward form of our inner harmony. [12]

The longing for true peace in marriage is specifically connected with the world of natural cells and the oneness of the deep rhythms of life: "the life of Us—created by us!—beyond us, above us!" [13] This is the ideal, the great urge to belong, to dissolve the self in some greater harmony of nature through marriage.

The remainder of Act One is a shrill attack on that ideal, not as false but as incomplete, for the self cannot abide being swallowed up in the whole—or in the love of another. Eleanor and Michael cannot live with each other without fighting. And in Act Two they learn that they cannot live without one another as each tries with dreary predictability to commit adultery. Act Three brings what for O'Neill is a resolution. Marriage is an inescapable desire for union with a hatred of giving up self. Acceptance is the answer:

And we'll torture and tear, and clutch for each other's souls!—fight—fail and hate again—... but—fail *with* pride—with joy![14]

The Grand Ideal is reaffirmed as the condition of life and as the triumph over that condition, beyond believing or not believing, including love and hate in a violently alternating cycle. Though the emotions are agitated, the action leads to a deadlock. The final crude image spells out this stasis as mutual crucifixion and love:

> *For a moment as their hands touch they form together one cross. Then their arms go about each other and their lips meet.* [15]

Welded is an awkward and clumsy effort, but its theme shows the dead center of the family dilemma as O'Neill represented it. On the one hand, there is the longing for the family of security with its mutuality and protection; on the other, there is the desire for assertion of self which we have seen in the image of the family of freedom. Neither is denied and so both must be subsumed under a generalized, fixed notion of life and human nature.

In his third play of 1924, *Desire Under the Elms,* O'Neill created his most intense expression of the family dilemma to date. The two impulses of self and mutuality become two lines of tragic action within the same play. There is a quality of artistic discovery in *Desire,* as if O'Neill's creative powers took a sudden leap forward. Indeed, it is one of two plays which he said he had dreamed in a night—the other being *Ah, Wilderness!*[16] Not that *Desire* sprang out of O'Neill's head unanticipated. The basic attitudes were not new, as I have been arguing. Moreover, as John Henry Raleigh has pointed out, Ephraim Cabot's character is outlined in several of the early sea plays; and *Beyond the Horizon,* among others, is similarly anti-rural.[17] But O'Neill achieved two interrelated lines of action which embodied his vision more fully than had any of his previous attempts.

Farm life is an endless round of grinding work as O'Neill

portrays it in *Desire,* and the farm family—*pace* Jefferson!—is dehumanized by it. The play, set in 1850, shows that the Cabot family is hardworking and has made a success despite its difficult New England land. But *Desire* is meant to count the cost of this success and to reckon its effect on the family. Two wives have been worked to death, three sons hate their father, and the patriarch of this family, Ephraim Cabot, is so self-reliant as to be cut off from humanity. There is no unity or community of privilege, only greed and autocratic power. The only security is in isolation. The setting is a farmhouse with multiple rooms exposed and full of contrasting action; O'Neill slices into the Cabot household like a surgeon suffering from the same affliction as his patient.

The family farm of the Cabots is confining, limiting, and destructive. The subplot of Simeon and Peter—Ephraim Cabot's sons by his first wife—exists primarily to establish this point. At the play's beginning the sunset reminds Simeon of his lost wife and of "gold in the West," a phrase which echoes throughout the first act. A tension is immediately set up between security and freedom, between lost possibility and the escape from present confining authority.

Abbie, Ephraim's third wife, also struggles for freedom. Left motherless as a child, she was married to a drunkard, saw her baby die, and was widowed:

> an' I was glad sayin' now I'm free for once, on'y I
> disskivered right away all I was free fur was t' wuk agen
> in other folks' hums, doin' other folks' wuk till I'd
> most give up hope o' ever doin' my own wuk in my own
> hum.... [18]

Again freedom and the family are juxtaposed, though here the meaning is somewhat different from the case of Simeon and Peter. Abbie's real freedom—the completion of herself as a person—depends upon making a new family, upon inclusion not exclusion. Her coarse sexuality is the expression of this unfulfilled need.

Ephraim Cabot is the family head—despot would be a better

term, for the Cabots are the most rigidly structured of all of O'Neill's families. Ephraim rules like an Old Testament patriarch with God and property to back him up. Cabot's family is an exaggeration of the authority and structure of the family of security, with personal relations forced and bound to inheritance. It is because of the family's rigidity that Cabot's sons seek to escape. Even the leader of such a family, however, feels the strain of its severity. "Then this spring the call come—the voice o' God cryin' in my wilderness, in my lonesomeness—t' go out an' seek an' find!"[19]

Ephraim responds to the energies of the springtime and journeys west to find a wife. But despite his lonesomeness, family to Ephraim does not mean mutuality and love but the authority of his will. For him it is a means to keep the farm and flout his sons. When he grudgingly agrees with Abbie that the farm is not "mine" but "ours," the compromise clearly settles nothing. Once again the theme of freedom from the family farm is heard like a leitmotif, this time being played off directly against Ephraim's ultimate possessiveness:

> If I could in my dyin' hour, I'd set it [the farm] afire an' watch it burn—this house an' every ear o' corn an' every tree down t' the last blade o' hay! I'd sit an' know it was all a-dying with me an' no one else'd ever own what was mine, what I'd made out o' nothin' with my own sweat 'n' blood! *(A pause—then he adds with a queer affection)* 'Ceptin' the cows. Them I'd turn free.
> ABBIE: *(harshly)* An' me?
> CABOT: *(with a queer smile)* Ye'd be turned free, too.[20]

For Ephraim family is a completion, too, but completion of his absoluteness and power. The family of security is pictured as the rigid product of his arbitrary authority.

Not only is the family of security shown to be oppressively rigid, but it is also a place of selfish greed rather than nurture. O'Neill hints that some moderation of the possessiveness of the Cabot family may exist in his references to Cabot's second wife

(Eben's mother). She represents, apparently, the feminine principle without its possessiveness. She gave kindness and softness to all without its having to be earned. Because of her death, "the atmosphere [of the house] is of a men's camp kitchen rather than that of a home."[21] O'Neill does not develop this suggestion of what a "home" is. It remains only a faint clue.

In *Desire* it is hinted that possessing things and people is connected to nature. Maternity, sexuality, and maturity are all part of a universalized force which gives fundamental rhythms to life (and to the background of the life of the play). The family of security is both the context for these life rhythms and the best example of them. Merging and joining is the rule. Abbie is the most immediate interpreter of these forces, feeding them into the Cabot family, so to speak:

> Nature—makin' thin's grow—into somethin' else—till ye've jined with it—an' it's your'n—but it owns ye, too—an' makes ye grow bigger—like a tree—like them elums—[22]

But this does not lead to family mutuality and relatedness. Man's ego and urge to independence fight against any community of privilege, isolating him and turning the family of security into a battleground. The Cabot family, then, is a private world agitated by the larger pulsing forces of withdrawal and mutuality, isolation and togetherness.

This duality can be seen in Abbie. She has won power over Ephraim and can claim her house with all its belongings; her seduction of Eben begins as part of this general possessiveness. Yet, from the first, Abbie tries to make a place for Eben. She changes from the general possessor to the particular lover, and by the end, in killing her baby, rejects the farm and all else for Eben. She needs him desperately to face her own fate. "I hain't beat—s'long's I got ye!"[23]

This desire to possess is most monolithically developed in Ephraim; nothing intervenes between him and his ego. Ephraim wants to "own" his place in heaven. He does not just own the farm; he has created it, he feels. And Abbie is as much of a thing to be possessed as the farm:

> Sometimes ye air the farm an' sometimes the farm be yew. That's why I clove t' ye in my lonesomeness.... Me an' the farm has got t' beget a son! [24]

So, too, with his family which exists as an extension of his possessive will. His unborn son is the chance to deny his heirs and to transcend his own mortality:

> But har's the p'int. What son o'mine'll keep on here t' the farm—when the Lord does call me?
>
> . . .
>
> A son is me—my blood—mine. Mine ought t' git mine. An' then it's still mine—even though I be six foot under. [25]

Where Abbie feels the creativity and growth of the universe, Ephraim feels its finality at his impending death. "I'm gettin' ripe on the bough," he reiterates. Both respond to cosmic forces of completion but in opposite ways. Ephraim retains strength by giving up nothing. Abbie and Eben learn to give up the ownership of things to find love in each other. It is true that near the end Eben temporarily breaks with Abbie, but not over possession of the farm, which no longer is equivalent to family love for him. "But t'aint the farm so much—not no more—it's yew foolin' me— gittin' me t' love ye—lyin' yew loved me—jest t' get a son t' steal." [26] His final reconciliation with Abbie reestablishes their community of love.

These two modes of action make complex and conflicting claims on us. To begin with, Abbie and Eben are never able to escape the ambiguity of their actions. For all of their growth away from selfish possession and toward the recognition of their need for each other, they remain tainted by their very love. Like the elms which hang over the house, "to protect and at the same time subdue,"[27] their love has a selfish quality. Abbie's sexuality is forever mixed with possessive maternity. At the moment of their final reconciliation, Eben is still—if faintly—"my boy" to her.

Eben completes his growth to manhood in loving Abbie, and his story is very much that of his *rite of passage.* He is released from his mother by Abbie. The act is a passive one on his part, emphasizing the largeness of the forces at work on him. From an old, revengeful role, he comes into a new, accepting one. But at the moment of his seduction by Abbie he still must justify himself in the old terms of his rights. Even though he has learned something of spontaneity from Abbie, he is still tainted by the possessiveness associated with the Cabot family.

Seen in this light the love of Abbie and Eben is not simply an expose of oedipal longings. Psychological myth can just as easily be at the service of social and family myth as the reverse. In the Cabot family possessiveness and destruction accompany liberation and the creation of a new family. The line of dramatic action begins with Eben's initiation into the possessiveness of his family. He buys out his brothers and "takes" Min as the other men of the family before him have done. In loving Abbie, who enters the play already free from family, Eben breaks with his grasping family. But he is functionally part of the family in that he is most in need of committing vengeance on his father and freeing himself from the influence of his mother. With the birth of their son, he and Abbie make up a new family unit in which the child interferes with the mutual absorption which characterizes their love. So this family structure in turn destroys part of itself, only this time for an apparent purpose—to finally reconcile Abbie and Eben as free partners in love on the high plane of tragedy.

The movement toward mutuality on the part of Abbie and Eben is continually subject to the "natural" human dilemma: in searching for some way out of their isolation, they can find no refuge from the corrupting selfishness which goes hand in hand with love. The best they can do is to create their own world of shared guilt and suffering as well as love. Tragic victims of the family of security, they are maneuvered by forces which it embodies and which they attempt to hold at bay by their intense, private consciousness of each other.[28] Yet familialism is a refuge, and belonging a form of withdrawal in the face of this family dilemma. And so they also represent a triumph over the conditions which victimize them.

The story of Abbie and Eben, which seems to repeat a pattern in a never-ending series, is played off against the static heroism of Ephraim. His lonely assertion of self becomes an alternate tragic stance. It is the indomitable will set against the world and attempting to transcend the limits of family through exclusion of everything but self. In Ephraim we are invited to admire the heroic strength and cruelty of his self-centeredness. Ephraim, who calls on the "God of the lonesome," exemplifies the isolation of self with God. To him stones do not mean walls and separation but the domination of his will over the earth. Owning is the right of domination through struggle, and he is proud to be "hard." His sons are "soft"—"them coveting what I'd made for mine." No one else can enter such a system. Hard father and soft sons make up his entire family world.

Almost to the last moment of the play Cabot is a force representing values which nothing can subdue, certainly not Abbie and Eben. They have created their own world, but it is clearly incapable of modifying Cabot's, or what he stands for. Indeed, his strength almost reduces their world of love to his terms, while their love adds poignancy to his loneliness.

When Eben completes the rehabilitation of his character in returning to Abbie and accepting responsibility for his part in the murder, the seal of approval is placed on this act by Ephraim himself:

(He comes forward—stares at EBEN with a trace of grudging admiration) Purty good—fur yew![29]

At this moment the selfish strength of Ephraim comes close to dominating the entire meaning of the play. Eben has triumphed not because he has perceived life differently from his father but because he is so very much like him.

Yet the last image of the play contradicts such a suggestion, and we are finally impressed with the love of Abbie and Eben. The action, a deliberate echo of the play's opening, comes to a close but the only ending is death. Only in the face of destruction is mutuality possible:

> ABBIE: I love ye, Eben.
> EBEN: I love ye, Abbie. *(They kiss. The three men grin and shuffle embarrassedly. EBEN takes ABBIE'S hand. They go out the door in the rear, the men following, and come from the house, walking hand hand to the gate. EBEN stops there and points to the sunrise sky)* Sun's a'rizin'! Purty, hain't it?
> ABBIE: Ay-eh *(They both stand for a moment looking up raptly in attitudes strangely aloof and devout)*.
> SHERIFF: *(looking around at the farm enviously—to his companion)* It's a jim-dandy farm, no denyin'. Wished I owned it!
> CURTAIN[30]

The play offers, then, two lines of tragedy. In neither case is the suffering made acceptable through reference to some larger reality. Ephraim is untamable; this is the essence of his appeal. Abbie and Eben must face punishment, but the law brings no order into the world of the play, only pain. When the Sheriff appears, we see how far removed they are from the law and how different Ephraim's possessiveness is from the mean acquisitiveness that prevails outside the family. In *Desire* the cheerful independence and self-sufficiency of the yeoman family of security is inverted by O'Neill to demonstrate its falsity. The order and power which Ephraim represents is too cruel and hard for humanity. The family of security must give way to the new, freer family. But this is a false hope, for escape from the family structure does not bring renewal but death.

Desire is the capstone of the first phase of O'Neill's career. It fairly bursts with discovery of its own form as if O'Neill quite suddenly found the patterns of action he needed. The play is dense with action, packed with intricate movements and reversals. It is nearly overfull, I think, but perhaps there is an artistic function to this apparent flaw. The resulting sense of compression intensifies the emotional tone of the play, its claustrophobia and repression. There is enough material packed into one play to make up a great number of longer ones as O'Neill was to discover. He has two tragedies, each one of which embodies an extreme of the family dilemma. In this way he has come to a definition of the major elements of the drama of family life. His next move is to extend these elements to give them the largest possible significance.

In his early plays O'Neill treated the family in a realistic manner. He saved his expressionistic experiments for such plays as *The Emperor Jones* and *The Hairy Ape*. But toward the end of this period, he began to use touches of expressionism in his family plays as well. In *All God's Chillun Got Wings* he symbolized the racial forces in the play by two formal lines of hostile people through which Jim and Ella must pass after their wedding. And the suffocation of their lives together is made visual by the actual shrinkage of the room in which they live and by the enlargement of the African mask on the wall. The unrealistic touches are more subtle in *Desire*. Stage directions aside (whatever the style of the play, O'Neill was fond of extreme effects in his descriptions of characters and setting), the symbolism of *Desire* is closely merged with realistic conventions of time, place, speech, and character. People speak of forces at work on them but we don't see such emotions objectified. One major exception, however, occurs just prior to the seduction scene: in the simultaneous actions of Abbie and Eben reaching for one another while in separate rooms, the play conveys in a stylized manner the powerful emotions at work on these two characters. O'Neill wants to evoke to the fullest extent the feelings which will sweep these two lovers into each other's arms despite Eben's struggle to resist.

This raising of the subtext of the play—its implicit structure of feelings and motivations—to the level of literal presentation is one explanation for the drastic experiments of O'Neill's middle period—generally speaking, those plays produced from 1926 to

1934. None is in the mode of the straightforward realism of *Anna Christie* or *Beyond the Horizon*. *The Great God Brown* (1926), the play which came after *Desire*, introduces masks to symbolize the strange, hidden qualities which keep a family from being truly together, suggesting also that they represent cosmic forces. In *Dynamo* (1928) O'Neill combined the older convention of the aside with the modern notion of the subconscious to show the audience what his characters were thinking as they struggled with their family fears, guilts, and possessive loves.

Strange Interlude, which appeared the same year as *Dynamo*, took this experiment to numbing lengths as the interior monologues overwhelm the exterior speeches in an attempt to emphasize the isolation of each character. Along with this sense of isolation O'Neill presents the action as a self-defeating search for the fullness of life. Nina, who has left her parents at the start and is left in turn (after nine acts) by her own son, throughout the play wants to assert the freedom of her personality, but also needs to be totally part of others. O'Neill divides domestic relations from Nina's point of view into multiple characters representing the spectrum of male family roles—provider, companion, lover, and son. He is able to push the action beyond the impasse of Nina's longings by the sheer length of her endurance. At the end of nine acts she comes to a twilight resignation in the hope for death.

In each of these plays literary self-expression replaces an implied enormity of emotion. Self-revelation is no longer struggled for and incomplete. O'Neill's rhetorical clumsiness is not without its own sort of drama in his other plays. The characters mean more than they can say—the effectiveness of realistic dialogue often depends on such a gap—but O'Neill's experiments, in which his characters tell all, leave us feeling that they are reduced by such articulation. These plays are not just the most glaring examples of O'Neill's lack of rhetorical eloquence, then, but show his misuse of the sources of his special dramatic art. It is the struggle of O'Neill's characters to become articulate that is dramatic. Aside from the technical problems of staging these masks and asides, his experiments do not solve dramatic problems but create them. O'Neill is exploring the degree to which he can depart from the realistic style without giving up a sense of realistic character in which motives and feelings, however irrational, can be understood and felt as significant and meaningful. For O'Neill, the world is not absurd. Personality is real and language communicates something worth knowing. These characters are intended to be people like ourselves with whom we can empathize. The experimental theatricality is not meant to put us at a critical distance from the characters—though I think it often does so with fatal results—but to intensify our suffering with them.

Such departures from the realistic style, while staying mainly with the family subject matter, show O'Neill's search for some way to relate the family to larger themes, a structure or a universal principle of life itself. It was both a philosophical and aesthetic question for him. The discovery of such a principle might lead him to a new form within which to cast the family drama, as well as to a new belief about its ultimate significance. The cycles of enclosure and rupture he packed into the action of *Desire* expand as the experiments become more extreme and the plays longer and longer. He develops family life into patterns which are meant to represent the life process itself. Thus, a specific family protagonist not only struggles within the family, but the family itself—even generations of a family—is seen as a continuing, modulating cycle of response to such forces. The family is cosmic history to O'Neill in these middle plays. [31] Achieving this sense of fate is the rationale for their shape.

The most carefully and tightly worked out of these cosmic plays is *Mourning Becomes Electra* (1931). Perhaps it is the most successful because it is the closest to realistic conventions. Masks are reduced to the description of facial qualities in the stage directions. Internal/external monologues disappear entirely. O'Neill was still after the big effect, however, and the structure he adopts derives from a Greek trilogy. But the mythology is less Greek than Freudian, and less either than family paradigm.

Using the *Orestia* of Aeschylus as a springboard, O'Neill produced his own story of a cursed house, which he set in New England in 1865. Ezra Mannon, whose father drove out Ezra's uncle for begetting an illegitimate child, returns from the Civil War to his wife, Christine, and his grown children, Lavinia and Orin. "The Homecoming," the first play, establishes the major patterns of action as well as the values which the Mannon family will embody. Early in the play Christine and Lavinia specifically abandon the parent-child relationship, freeing themselves to compete as equals for the affection of the men in the house. This competition begins with Adam, Christine's lover during Ezra's absence, and continues with Ezra himself upon his return. After Ezra's murder it is extended in "The Hunted," the second play, to Orin. After Christine's death by suicide all these relationships are concentrated and multiplied in the third play, "The Haunted," where Orin and Lavinia represent parent, lover, and sibling to each other. Incest is the dramatic reduction of their withdrawal and self-enclosure. It symbolizes the most heightened (and complex) of intense interconnections. In its denial of family order, it is a grotesque inversion of the family of security. [32]

This inward movement of the family physically and psychologically also means its withdrawal from the outer world. The Mannons always like to hide their feelings, we are told, maintaining their secretiveness as their family pride. And such shrinkage takes the world of the play along with it. The appearance of the townspeople does not open the play outward. As choral characters they give us no view of a larger social reality. Rather we see them as fools, except for the Mannons' servant, who becomes more and more like the family, absorbed as it were by their withdrawal. When the townspeople flee the "haunted" house at the beginning of the third play, we have the inverted comic parallel of Orin's suicide. The nailing shut of the windows at the play's end is the final image of that isolation, the enclosure of those interiors where the vicious and destructive scenes all take place.

All the Mannons wish to escape from that house and the family life within it to a new domesticity which is free and loving. In part, the South Sea Islands represent this longing. Ezra wants to leave the vanities of his life and recapture the love of Christine, which the birth of the children has ruined for him, by taking her away to these islands. Adam feels it is the only place for love and marriage. Lavinia has learned the possibility of pure love and freedom there. All, of course, are mocked by their desire.

It is Hazel and Peter, however, who dramatize the chance for a new family life to the fullest extent. As the fiancés of Orin and Lavinia, they are O'Neill's approximation of a happy world; they typify the virtues of the good and loving family of security while maintaining their independence. They are polar opposites of the Mannons and are the innocents in the play. The Islands allow a freedom that hints at license, but Hazel and Peter are safe within a family structure. They are halfway between repression and expression, inwardness and outwardness, representing the normal sociability of an ideal family home. Lavinia says: "What we need most is to get back to simple normal things and begin a new life. And their friendship and love will help us more than anything to forget."[33]

Before regeneration can be accomplished Orin must free himself from the responsibility of his mother's death. Lavinia urges him to reject his guilt, arguing the moral isolation of Christine's act. "But she chose to kill herself as a punishment for her crimes—of her own free will!"[34] In other words, Lavinia asserts the need for Orin to break away from family to survive. In her own case it will be marriage to Peter which will allow her to live in the isolated happiness she wants, both free and secure:

> We'll be married soon, won't we, and settle out in the country away from folks and their evil talk. We'll make an island for ourselves on land, and we'll have children and love them and teach them to love life so that they can never be possessed by hate and death! *(She gives a start—in a whisper as if to herself)* But I'm forgetting Orin.[35]

In remembering she is bound to Orin, Lavinia realizes she is still enmeshed in the Mannon family. Her own happiness now depends on totally rupturing the family ties, a process that began with her and Orin's joint effort to escape from family. Lavinia turns against Orin. His death is now needed to break the links that bind Lavinia, and his suicide alone will release her. "Oh, won't it be wonderful, Peter—once we're married and have a home with a garden and trees! We'll be so happy!"[36] But her attempt to break this final family relation in the name of future happiness ties her more tightly to the Mannon household.

Early in the cycle Adam had represented the destructive forces within and without the family. He was the threatening lover and the rejected illegitimate Mannon. His destruction implied family destruction as well, a point Orin sensed at the time and tried to explain to Lavinia:

> Do you remember me telling you how the faces of the men I killed [in the Civil War] came back and changed to Father's face and finally became my own? ... He [Adam] looks like me, too! Maybe I've committed suicide!
>
> ...
>
> If I had been he I would have done what he did! I would have loved her as he loved her—and killed Father too—for her sake! [37]

It is, then, no mere dramatic trick of O'Neill's that Orin's incestuous demands on Lavinia become explicit just before his suicide at the cycle's end. If incest is the symbol of the ultimate self-enclosure of family, then its dramatization is not only a prelude to the final self-withdrawal of suicide but also reveals the desperate flight from family for what it is—a flight from the unrestricted clash of free egos. But such a flight is a mockery, for in destroying family Lavinia affirms that she is truly a destructive Mannon. Through denial, she is the essence of what she denies. [38]

Not only has Lavinia fully become a Mannon but her avenue of escape has been cut off. In desiring to create a new family— "I'll be Mrs. Peter Niles"—she is already destroying Peter's happy home life. Hazel tells her:

> He left home and went to a hotel to stay. He said he'd never speak to Mother or me again. He's always been such a wonderful son before—and brother. We three

have been so happy. It's broken Mother's heart. All
she does is sit and cry. [39]

With Peter the cycle would only begin again. There is nothing left
for Lavinia but to rebuff him and to lock herself in the house she
despises. The isolation and death of the Mannons can have no
part of the goodness and love which exists in the family home of
Hazel and Peter. Inward and ever inward is the movement of the
action until the last Mannon, Lavinia, is left with the dead family:

> I'll live alone with the dead, and keep their secrets, and
> let them hound me, until the curse is paid out and the
> last Mannon is let die. *(With a strange smile of gloating
> over the years of self-torture)* I know they will see to it
> I live for a long time! It takes the Mannons to punish
> themselves for being born. [40]

Mourning Becomes Electra presents us with an extended and
heightened example of the dramatic action which typifies O'Neill's
family drama. With careful proportion he works out the lines of
forward movement as murder, incest, and masochism sensationally
embody the family's pain and loneliness. As with *Desire, Mourning
Becomes Electra* is the culmination of the images, attitudes, and
explorations of his preceding work. In a similar manner it points
to his next phase and the direction he will take. The cyclic and
deadlocked action of inwardness, turning escape into destruction,
is a recurring one for O'Neill, especially in his late plays of family
life—those written during 1933-1943 (but, in most cases, not produced until much later). Here, after his one lush evocation of a
loving and redeeming family, its possibility becomes a more hopeless dream than ever. In his last plays the family is even more self-
absorbed, if not so flamboyantly as in *Mourning Becomes Electra*. [41]

After *Mourning,* O'Neill returns to the realistic style and does
not need the help of expressionism to strengthen emotions or to
provide a significance to the family dramas he completed. [42] His

ambitions remained grand, and the long cycles of family agitation, dispersal, and reformation are very much on his mind. O'Neill planned a huge eleven-play cycle on the history of an American family from colonial times to the present. It was entitled: "A Tale of Possessors Self-Dispossessed." Six of the plays in the cycle were actually written. Shortly before he died, O'Neill destroyed them all, except for *A Touch of the Poet* (1957) and an unfinished version of *More Stately Mansions* (1962), which he overlooked. " 'He could tear only a few pages at a time, because of his tremor,' Carlotta said. 'So I helped him. We tore up all the manuscripts together bit by bit. It took hours. After a pile of torn pages had collected, I'd throw them into the fire. It was awful. It was like tearing up children.' " [43]

A cyclic quality informs other plays as well, such as *A Moon for the Misbegotten* (1953), which is better seen as providing an eligiac ending for *Long Day's Journey into Night* (1956) than as a play standing on its own merits. In these long tales of family life which come after the elaborate experiments and symbols of his middle period, O'Neill is once again presenting his vision of family in a realistic style: freedom has not led us out of family strife, and elements of both freedom and security agitate each other. *Ah, Wilderness!* (1933) is an attempt to escape from this dilemma by asserting the possibility of order through family goodness. It is O'Neill's other dream of family life.

Ah, Wilderness! is untypical of O'Neill. Instead of bitterness or harshness, it offers a steady glow of love and gentle laughter. In the movie ads they would call it "Warm and Wonderful." John Henry Raleigh typifies it as a middle-class idyll: "For everything is finally solidly encased in a thick, warm, bourgeois domesticity ...." [44] The tone is pure nostalgia. There are old jokes, old songs, and the good old Fourth of July celebration during which much of the action takes place. [45] Verses from *The Rubaiyat of Omar Khayyam,* which several characters quote, add just the right touch of the exotic, the far away and innocently scandalous. All the poetry—FitzGerald, Swinburne, Wilde—is an exercise in romantic memory on the part of the characters as the play is on the part of the author (the action is set in 1906). The title itself, in which the quote from the *Rubaiyat* is changed from the dramatic "Oh" to the reflective "Ah," is the best indicator of the play's tone; it is a play of reflection, of memory and nostalgia. The movement of the play is back into the past; the energy for this movement comes from an intense longing for the innocent world of the play and for the loving, harmonious family group which is at the center of the world.

In *Ah, Wilderness!*, O'Neill tells a simple story about the Miller family, who live "in a large small-town in Connecticut," and about the "rebelling" son Richard, a high school senior who spouts scandalous poetry and avant-garde ideas about life, love, and property. This worries his family, and particularly the father of his girl friend Muriel, to whom Richard sends love notes full of Swinburne. Forbidden by Muriel's father from seeing her, Richard decides love is a hollow mockery and goes off to live a life of dissipation; he has his first drink and meets his first prostitute. But Muriel defies her father, meets Richard secretly on a moonlit beach, and everyone is back to normal at the end.

If the story sounds innocent enough, the dramatization makes it even more so. A good example of just what issues are being raised in the play comes in the first act when David McComber, Muriel's father and the epitome of stiff-necked New England conscience, charges Richard "With being dissolute and blasphemous—with deliberately attempting to corrupt the morals of my young daughter, Muriel." Nat Miller, Richard's father, answers him:

> Why, you damned old fool! Can't you see Richard's
> only a fool kid who's just at the stage when he's out to
> rebel against all authority, and so he grabs at everything
> radical to read and wants to pass it on to his elders and
> his girl and boy friends to show off what a young hel-
> lion he is! Why at heart you'd find Richard is just as
> innocent and as big a kid as Muriel is! [46]

From this speech on there is never any question as to who is in control and whose values will be affirmed. O'Neill drives the point home a minute later:

> RICHARD *(impressed—with dignity):* I won't lie, Pa.
>
> MILLER: Have you been trying to have something to do with Muriel—something you shouldn't—you know what I mean.
>
> RICHARD *(stares at him for a moment, as if he couldn't comprehend—then, as he does, a look of shocked indignation comes over his face):* No! What do you think I am, Pa? I never would! She's not that kind! Why, I—I love her! I'm going to marry her—after I get out of college! She said she would! We're engaged![47]

Richard, essentially good and innocent, will pass through "the stage" of his rebellion without a mark. In fact, it improves his moral character, as we learn later. Too embarrassed to go with the prostitute, he even decides that getting tipsy "wasn't any fun. It didn't make me happy and funny like it does Uncle Sid—."[48] Nat Miller is the ideal of fatherly wisdom. He knows just how far to let Richard go, when to curb him and when not to. But Richard, as we have seen, does not really need much curbing and Nat Miller's idea of discipline consists of pretending to Richard that he will not be allowed to go to college. Decency, honesty, love, authority, and the status quo are the characteristics of the Richard-Nat relationship, and their relationship is the anchor for the ethic of the play.

A good example of how this ethic works can be seen in the major subplot concerning Aunt Lily and Uncle Sid. They have loved each other for sixteen years, but Lily will not marry Sid because he drinks. Here are the ingredients for the kind of relationship we expect from O'Neill. Indeed, in *Diff'rent* (1920), an early one-act, O'Neill had written of the disastrous psychological effects of a similar refusal to accept human imperfection in a loved one. In *Ah, Wilderness!,* however, there is no corrosion and no destruction. The problems of Lily and Sid are, the play suggests, painful ones, but all problems of life can be minimized and overcome when they are placed in the context of family love. Lily and Sid can function because they have a place in the family and contribute to its life: Sid is the humorist, and Lily is a companion for Mrs. Miller. They each depend on the family to fulfill essential needs; for Sid, who needs protection from his own irresponsibility, it allows a quasi-childhood, and for Lily, who loves children, it allows a quasi-motherhood. Everyone gives and gets in the Miller family, and the medium of the exchange is love. The total result is harmony, solidarity, loyalty, and consensus. It is an ideal of domestic mutuality.

In *Ah, Wilderness!,* O'Neill presents the Miller family as a positive good. He suggests it has qualities both of the family of freedom and of the family of security. In fact, the Miller family manages an harmonious balance between them. First of all, O'Neill has taken care to show this family as opening out and connected to its community. Though it is cohesive, it is not isolated. Outsiders come into the house, and twice the action moves outside the house, a seemingly minor point until one realizes how much domestic drama in America never gets beyond the front porch. For example, the Millers spend most of the day away from the house in a community celebration. They have a consciousness of a world beyond their own family, a world which, moreover, is made up largely of families similar to themselves. For once, the family is neither isolated nor turned in upon itself.

While ties with the outer world survive, so does the ordered structure of the family of security. There is no atomization, but a series of relationships of interdependency which stem from the father. Nat Miller establishes the values of the play in his relationship with his son, for he sets the outer limits of order beyond which the action will not progress. Richard's rebellion, carefully enclosed within these limits, is, or course, no rebellion at all. The bourgeois world was never safer than when Richard seemed to reject it. As with Lily and Sid, Richard's weaknesses are carefully enclosed within the larger family group.

Despite the presence of order and authority in the family, O'Neill suggests that the Millers exist as naturally and spontaneously as the family of freedom, for in the world of his play, the

Millers are essentially innocent and therefore good. Thus authority and order never have to be invoked: everyone acts as he ought to. The few spots on the human character are faults easily remedied by the general good. If Sid and Lily only love and do not marry, that is enough, for we can be sure that Richard and Muriel will both love and marry. The assertion of self never conflicts with order, nor does mutuality impinge on freedom. The cycle of family destruction as necessary to create a new family does not operate. Instead O'Neill creates "the home," the place of natural harmony where inwardness and outwardness balance. Through the special goodness of the home, O'Neill is able to affirm the possibility of spontaneous affections *and* family stability. He is able to avoid the arbitrariness of hierarchical order *and* the lonely competitiveness of the individual ego. The innocent Miller home is O'Neill's escape from the family dilemma of freedom and security wherein he claims the advantages of both and the disadvantages of neither.

When O'Neill wrote *Ah, Wilderness!,* he was looking back—and asking the audience to look back—to a time of innocence, when family life had been good and full of love. In some moods he felt this to be a true picture: "To me, the America which was (and is) the real America found its unique expression in such middle-class families as the Millers...."[49] The phrasing is a bit ambiguous. It may mean that the past world of the Miller family has never since been excelled. Or perhaps O'Neill felt his contemporary America was still characterized by such families. In either case, the Millers are the defining ideal.

It is important to read this affirmation in light of the tone of the play. The nostalgia of *Ah, Wilderness!* combines a sense of loss with a wishful feeling for the harmony of home. O'Neill's definition of America and its harmonious family is more of a wish—this is how things ought to be. Assuming an innocent world, O'Neill could side-step questions of order, authority, and power; he could accept the bourgeois dream of home and, indeed, glory in it. When O'Neill felt compelled to portray that family without its innocence—as he usually did—he had no way to reconcile order with natural, spontaneous love. He gave fullest expression to the tragic conflict in *Long Day's Journey into Night,* which sums up O'Neill's family vision. It is his finest achievement, in which he powerfully compresses the struggles of family life into a single, sustained, unresolved dramatic action.

The action of *Long Day's Journey* takes place in the summer home of the Tyrone family on a single day in August, 1912. The four acts of the play begin at family gathering times—breakfast, lunch, dinner, and bedtime—and they chronicle the story of the four Tyrones. We learn each person's history: the two sons, Jamie, who is a drunken failure, and Edmund, isolated, but with the dreams of a poet; the father, James, an aging actor who might have been great if he had not been penurious; and the mother, Mary, who hides from the world by taking morphine. The principal events are the discovery that Edmund has tuberculosis and that Mary, home from the sanitarium, is on drugs again.

Neither the world nor the characters of *Long Day's Journey* bear any strong resemblance to those of *Ah, Wilderness!,* and yet there is a remarkable correspondence in the materials out of which O'Neill constructed the two plays. Curiously, the stage sets of both living rooms are nearly identical, with only a few minor pieces of furniture to distinguish them. Thus the two families act out their very different lives in the same room. Many of the same books are read by both the Millers and the Tyrones, though the latter have more books and, as befitting James's profession, more are plays. Both Richard and Edmund quote poetry of a morbid turn and hint at holding radical political views. In both plays there is an inefficient Irish servant girl. The plays duplicate, but with different emphasis, certain situations. Clint, a friend of Richard's brother, worries about corrupting Richard by taking him to a bar with loose women. Jamie, Edmund's older brother, has introduced Edmund to liquor and prostitutes, a fact which becomes the specific example of Jamie's general corrupting effect. In the initial description of Richard there is a touch of the isolation yet interconnection which dominates the Tyrone relationships; and in the Lily-Sid subplot is discernible the emotional pattern of failure-accusation-guilt-forgiveness which animates the Tyrone relationships.

The similarity between the two plays helps to define their differences, which can be understood in relation to the family images of security and freedom. In *Long Day's Journey* the family is cut off from the world and turned in upon itself, with no re-sources or relations beyond it. There is equality of status, but where a spontaneous and tender affection ought to develop, O'Neill presents agony, alienation, and disintegration. The egalitarianism of the Tyrones does not mean natural harmony among individuals, but constant collision of egos.

O'Neill takes special pains to isolate the Tyrones, and their story is the most purely presented of any of his dramas. All the action takes place in one room on one day. The family is small, with two parents and two children. Contact with the outside world is spare and the minimum that a play in the realistic mode will allow. With the exception of Cathleen, the servant, we see no one but the Tyrones, and Cathleen's appearance is used to accentuate Mary Tyrone's loneliness. When the Tyrones go off-stage and out into the world, it is a foray into an antagonistic environment: Mary goes to purchase her drug, and Edmund to learn he has tuber-culosis; Jamie leaves to drink and whore, and James to be bilked of money. Both Jamie and James have pretensions toward social respectability, but it is a game to fool outsiders. The humor of the Shaughnessy story, in which one of the Tyrone tenants outdoes a millionaire, also depends on this sense of being an outsider. And, finally, the phone call which the Tyrones receive is an ominous and dreaded one.

Not only is the Tyrone family isolated from the exterior world, but isolation is the keynote of their relations with one anoth-er. They seldom communicate; rather they impinge on each other's loneliness. The same pretense exists between father and son as between the family and the outside world. After Jamie waters the whiskey bottle, Edmund says: "You don't think it will fool him, do you?" Jamie replies: "Maybe not, but he can't prove it."[50] Here is a bitter game which is the antithesis of mutuality.

Suspicion and pretense is a major mode of encounter for the characters. A moment after the whiskey-watering episode, Jamie and Edmund, apparently the closest persons in the family, are involved in verbal hide-and-seek, Jamie suspecting his mother's actions and Edmund pretending he thinks them innocent. This kind of encounter goes on among all of the men, and in a larger way between the men and Mary as her drug-taking becomes increasingly evident. Although they all know that Mary is back on morphine by the end of Act Two, they continue to pretend that they are only suspicious. It is not until the fourth act that suspicion gives way to confrontation. The first note is sounded as Edmund and James play cards:

> EDMUND: She's coming downstairs.
> TYRONE *(hurriedly):* We'll play our game. Pretend not
> to notice and she'll soon go up again. [51]

When she does come down, Jamie introduces her as in a play: "The Mad Scene. Enter Ophelia!" This time she cannot be ignored, for her own pretense has become momentarily unshakable. She has slipped back into the world of fantasy where she not only remembers but relives the innocence of her youth and the romance of her courtship and wedding. Her isolation has become complete, and it stands as the symbol of what is true of all of them.

The emotional dialectic of *Long Day's Journey* is a recurring pattern of charge and countercharge, of wounding and being wounded, of striking back followed by guilt, remorse, and recrimination. There is in the Tyrone family no structure, no order, to mitigate this pattern as there was in the Miller home. Nor is there authority or power to destroy in order to free one's self as there was in the Cabot house. James's attempts to act like a father are either hollow and ludicrous or proceed out of wrath and are immediately withdrawn. [52] Here is an egalitarian family where each member participates equally in the pattern of isolation, sin, and guilt. Between any two members the same basic relationship exists, though the occasions for it differ. The following exchange takes place early in the play and establishes this pattern:

> EDMUND: Yes, you certainly look grand, Mama. *(She
> is reassured and smiles at him lovingly. He winks
> with a kidding grin.)* I'll back you up about Papa's
> snoring. Gosh, what a racket!

JAMIE: I heard him, too. *(He quotes, putting on a ham-actor manner.)* "The Moor, I know his trumpet." *(His mother and brother laugh.)*

TYRONE: *(Scathingly.):* If it takes my snoring to make you remember Shakespeare instead of the dope sheet on the ponies, I hope I'll keep on with it.

MARY: Now James! You mustn't be so touchy. *(Jamie shrugs his shoulders and sits down in the chair on her right.)*

EDMUND: *(Irritably.):* Yes, for Pete's sake, Papa! The first thing after breakfast! Give it a rest, can't you? *(He slumps down in the chair at left of table next to his brother. His father ignores him.)*

MARY *(Reprovingly.):* Your father wasn't finding fault with you. You don't have to always take Jamie's part. You'd think you were the one ten years older.

JAMIE *(Boredly.):* What's all the fuss about? Let's forget it.

TYRONE *(Contemptuously.):* Yes forget! Forget everything and face nothing! It's a convenient philosophy if you've no ambition in life except to—[53]

They spring to each other's defense in a rapidly shifting pattern of accusation and alliance. Furthermore, this exchange occurs between first suspicions (and Mary's evasions) concerning morphine, and the Shaughnessy story, which relieves the tensions of the first family wrangle but establishes hostility between the family and the outside world. Thus, both within and among the first three movements of the action, O'Neill has set up the patterns of suspicion, accusation, and isolation which are basic to the play.

The texture of the play is rich in simultaneous levels of action which embody variations and permutations of its patterns. The fourth major unit of action in Act One—the encounter between Jamie and Tyrone—develops themes and attitudes lightly introduced in the first three units. Yet in contrast to these units it is a scene of disclosure in which we are shown the feelings both men have kept hidden. Gestures of revelation are presented, and we become aware of pretense in the preceding action. The uneasiness which has flickered across the surface of the first units is now shown to be hidden suspicion. In this way a rhythm of pretense and revelation is established which is subsequently embodied in the major encounters of the play. The pretense often revolves around Mary but is not exclusively related to her presence on stage. Underlying feelings of many sorts erupt despite attempts to keep them from view. Indeed, the attempts become more desperate and less successful as the play goes on, and the encounters between characters fluctuate between ferocious denial and increasing nakedness of feeling. This is a play in which a direct encounter is always suggestive of an indirect one, each theme a variation of the others.

The initial revelation of this fourth unit is that Edmund may have tuberculosis; the ensuing reaction to Jamie's stating what he and his father have suspected is one of pity. But pity quickly gives way to the primary mode of this encounter—accusation. The fourth unit is structured as an agon, or debate, over who is to blame. Jamie begins: he charges Tyrone with being a skinflint. After his attack has run its course, he is put on the defensive by Tyrone, who counters with the statement that Jamie is a wastrel. Both attacks have an effect. Each man's defense is weak since each recognizes a truth in what the other says. The alternation of dominant and subordinate energies is then repeated: Jamie accuses Tyrone of writing Edmund off, and Tyrone says Jamie's drunken ways helped weaken Edmund's health. After this reprise, the cyclic debate begins a third time but with a complex variation. Tyrone, in criticizing Jamie's ways, defends Edmund's bohemian past, which he has previously condemned; and Jamie, in his own defense, begins to suggest that Edmund's case is hopeless, which brings him to the very attitude he earlier has accused his father of holding. Thus the structure of accusation is repeated and developed to the point where it begins to reveal that each *j'accuse* is also a self-accusation, each act of striking out at another is a punishment by and for the divided and guilty self.

This intricate debate is operating on other levels as well. The tension between the two men is interrupted by a reference to Mary's illness, and with the mention of her name there is a pause in the conflict as the love between the two men surfaces through the common love they have for her. This, too, is to be a characteristic rhythm in the play. For if *Long Day's Journey* is a play about family hatred, it is also about love. Without the strong pull of love to bring them back together, the Tyrone family would quickly disintegrate. Their love is a persistent force, though brief admissions of it come only between declarations of hatred. There is a balance of love and hate in the Tyrone family, a constant equalization of pain. The raw emotions of the Tryones hold them together and apart. Freedom from authority and order means for them the constant battle of self against others.

Despite their love for Mary and each other—or perhaps because of it—the subject of Mary's illness is a hard one for the two men to face at this point. Though they approach open acknowledgment to each other of their suspicions, they also fend each other off. They never name her illness for us as they do Edmund's. The effect O'Neill creates is of an additional secret hidden and in need of revelation, of still another layer of fear and guilt to be discerned beneath the previous one. And he increases the density of the action by returning the debate to its starting point. The same accusations as to the blame for Edmund's illness now emerge with regard to Mary's, only to be cut short by her entrance and the air of mundane conversation both men feign.

The cyclical movement of the action in this unit—and in the play as a whole—has a cumulative force, for O'Neill's repetitiousness in *Long Day's Journey* is artfully done. In this play he designs structures of dramatic action by which the play moves forward without getting anyplace. The accretion of gestures and images gives the effect of Chinese boxes. After the simple introductory movements of the first three units, establishing large rhythms for the audience, O'Neill begins to vary and modulate the forces at work, creating an increasingly intricate pattern out of which will grow the subsequent action. Looked at closely, the repetition in *Long Day's Journey* is never exact (this is not so true in his other plays). The circumstances which call forth a familiar statement or action usually differ. Or one character will adopt the weapons of another, in effect creating a web of obsessions, a general air of accusation in which all participate.

Furthermore, the multiplicity of blame and the continually shifting blame tend to neutralize each other. No one is at fault because, although blame is one of the chief topics of argument, the play does not allow us to take sides or to determine who is right. Perhaps there is a tendency, early in the play, to side against Tyrone, but by the second act we see that such a judgment is too simple; in fact, it is not possible. For example, Mary makes a series of accusations in Act Two, scene two: her drug habit is Tyrone's fault for having chosen an inexpensive doctor to treat her; it is Jamie's fault for communicating a fatal disease to the baby Eugene; it is Edmund's fault for giving her pain at his birth. She leaves out her own complicity—that she takes the drug because she likes its effect. In fact, she has so many versions of blame that no one can be the true one. So it is with all the Tyrones.

Finally, it should be said that the repetition in *Long Day's Journey* evokes a sense of endlessness to the actions of this family. The attacks are old games. As the play goes on perhaps the greatest pain we see in the lives of these characters is not in the cruel remarks made—though each has a devastating instinct for the weaknesses of the others—but in the terrible fact of these cruelties having been said before. The Tyrones endlessly play roles which they do and do not wish to play. In this sense, as Mary says, the past is repeated in the present. What happened is always going on again.

Even here, though, we must be careful to notice the linearity of the action. It moves forward toward revelations: Act Two confirms the fact of Edmund's tuberculosis, and Mary's drug habit is named; Act Three shows her falling under the drug's effect; and in Act Four each character shows or is exposed to some new truth: Edmund tells of his transcendental experiences of belonging and of his desire for the loss of self; he genuinely listens to his father's tale of youthful poverty and learns to understand Tyrone's penuriousness; Tyrone admits that his fear of poverty has ruined his talent for acting and so his life; Jamie warns Edmund that his brotherly love is mixed with jealousy and hate; and Mary appears at the end as shockingly lost in her fog of drugs as she can make herself. These moments are revelations of motives implicit from the beginning for each character, the emergence of the sub-text into the text at last. Yet nothing has changed and only night (or death) ends such a day.

I have said that *Long Day's Journey* is a play about love as much as hate. In a similar sense it seems a play about people who must face reality as much as it is about people who live in a world of dreams and illusions. The Tyrones would like to hide in this world. They try to maintain pretenses, but no escape from the reality of what they feel and what they are is possible. All dodges, games, escapes, and chemical anodynes are temporary and break down. Mary Tyrone, who might appear to be the character least in touch with reality, in fact illustrates the pervasive presence of reality in her actions. One pretense she tries to erect early in the play is that Edmund's illness is a summer cold; another is that she has not begun taking morphine. As the play proceeds she is less and less able to maintain either fiction though more and more desperate to do so.

The increasingly abrupt fluctuations in Mary's personality indicate the fragility of her pretenses as she shifts her attention from the present to the past and from caring to detachment. Throughout the second act and even more so in the third, she approaches the point of admitting what is agitating her, what she fears and what she feels guilty about. Each tentative admission is marked by a more transparent and obvious attempt to cover up. Pretense here is not fooling anyone, least of all the pretender. In fact, all the Tyrones know what they are doing and never escape themselves. Escape is a longing, the ultimate unrealizable dream. Escape is itself a kind of pretense. Even at the end when Mary seems lost in the drug, her self-consciousness about what she is doing does not disappear. And, of course, tomorrow she will awaken without the buffer of morphine; she will be in the present not in her dream of a childhood past; she will have to face herself the way the other members of the family do in the final dramatic image of the play.

One of the chief dreams which permeates the play has to do with the idea of a home. The word "home" echoes and reechoes in *Long Day's Journey*. A respite from the burdensome isolation of the family of freedom is longed for by the characters. They want security without structure. Home is their intangible yearning to be done with the dilemmas of family life. Mary says of her husband:

> He doesn't understand a home. He doesn't feel at home
> in it. And yet, he wants a home. He's even proud of
> having this shabby place. He loves it here. [54]

In his life as an actor James Tyrone has become an extreme example of the peripatetic American, always on the move, restless and rootless, longing for a social permanence he cannot accept. [55]

The sons, Jamie and Edmund, never articulate a desire for a home; they are cut loose from even this hope. Yet so pervasive is Mary's longing for a home, and so poignant is the anguish she feels, her emotion encompasses the entire family. The home becomes a principal symbol for what is lost, missing, and yearned for. It is a place of rest, of freedom and harmony—exactly what the Tyrones do not have. The ironic distance between what is dreamed and what is real sets the tone for the life of the Tyrone family.

In Mary's mind the lack of a home was the cause of her third son's death, of her thwarted career as a pianist, and of the misery which has attended her marriage. Worst of all is the loss of human contact:

> In a real home one is never lonely. You forget I know
> from experience what a home is like. I gave up one to
> marry you—my father's home. [56]

Later, in a remarkable sequence in the third act when Mary is left alone with only the servant girl, O'Neill weaves together the motif of home with that of the fog. [57] The isolating fog, like the dream of innocent mutuality in the home, is an anodyne for pain. It shuts out the world as does the drug she takes, but the peace which this kind of withdrawal affords is only momentary and has its own destructive terrors.

A more soothing escape is the childhood home, which is contrasted with the present and imagined as a place of innocence and harmony where human pain was dissolved in a general goodness. What Mary longs for is the world of *Ah, Wilderness!* and the home of Nat Miller. This is her view of what a home should be, and when, early in the play, she admires the Chatfield family, it is because she thinks of them in these terms; they have "decent, presentable homes" and are "not cut off from everyone."[58] But even before James tells us of the reality of Mary's childhood—her father was a drunkard, and her musical talent was minor[59]—we sense that it is all a dream, a touching, pathetic fiction through which Mary seeks refuge from the terrible agony and isolation of her real family life. In her devotion to the dream, she tries increasingly to remove herself from human contact until, at the end, she wishes to be lost to everyone.

There is no innocence in the Tyrone family, and there is no natural check on the passions of each family member as there is in the Nat Miller family. The innocent bourgeois home of *Ah, Wilderness!* provides implicit limits of conduct which are ingrained on private character. These limits do not exist for the Tyrones, each of whom struggles with his own loves and hates, almost at random (though not without form), attracting and repelling those around him. There are, in *Long Day's Journey,* no outward social limits of authority against which the characters can measure themselves and struggle, for the essence of O'Neill's tragic art is the denial of any such limits. The Tyrones' struggle is private. They achieve dignity because, without accepting outward bonds, they refuse to accept their painful isolation as final. None of them, even the cynical Jamie, ever fully does so. They struggle for mutuality even through pathetic dreams of childhood innocence, as in Mary's case, or mystical notions of transcendence, as in Edmund's.[60] They have what O'Neill calls a "hopeless hope." And though harmony and peace are an illusion, O'Neill sees their struggles not as pathetic and foolish, but as achieving strength and dimension.

O'Neill's vision of the human condition in *Long Day's Journey* is as extremely individualistic as it can be. His dramatic problem was how to give form to this vision without implying social order. His solution was to have the characters caught in a series of emotional conflicts which are never resolved but are constantly recurring. The Tyrones have this in common with the soap opera: disintegration is never complete; and so, short of death, there is never any clearing away of obstacles. Unlike the soap opera, there is a complex structure of action which makes each encounter a defining one rather than simply the raw material of longing and anxiety. In this way O'Neill pushes his individualism—the atomistic isolation of his characters—to its furthest anarchical limits. The characters, who maintain their extreme isolation, embrace the constantly disintegrating family which provides the major ordering structure in their world. By this paradox O'Neill gives aesthetic form to his vision of family life.

What is it, then, that links the families of Ephraim Cabot, Ezra Mannon, Nat Miller, and James Tyrone? Do their separate worlds have anything in common? They do, for they all preclude any conception of creative order, creative power, or creative authority beyond the nuclear family. The choice between security and spontaneity has to be made within this limit. In *Desire Under the Elms* neither mutuality nor self-assertion brings the harmony that is expected for each is destructive. Yet O'Neill is committed to both. As to the mutuality of the family of security, he surrenders himself completely to the bourgeois world of *Ah, Wilderness!* by asserting its innocence; or, as to the freedom from order which leads to family harmony, he rejects the social context entirely and in *Long Day's Journey* bases his drama on the heroism of individuals who struggle with the impossibility of their isolated existence. In all cases, he expressed himself in terms of family relationships. The Cabot and Mannon families embody the cycle of futile escape from family. Yet the orderly Nat Miller family stands not for social renewal, regeneration, and creativity, but as a symbol for the status quo rendered as the innocent home, which O'Neill embraces passively and perversely. [61] The Tyrones, on the other hand, are symbolically the quintessence of family atomism. The differences in these plays are in the shifting mix of freedom and security of the family: the degree to which family structure disintegrates renders it incapable of redeeming the individual, yet without innocence this structure is fatally confining.

The elements of O'Neill's family drama persist throughout his career. The warmth and structure of the family of security lures his people. But they are also driven by the selfhood of the family of freedom which is rendered as an agitated collision of egos. This dichotomy is fundamental to O'Neill's images of family life. In them, O'Neill tests the possibilities of both family models. He proves the necessity of authority and security at one point and the necessity of freedom and loneliness at another. He even presents the special conditions of innocence under which both would be possible. In doing so he explores the full range of these family possibilities in their American expression.[62] The extent of his accomplishment is such that, in effect, he has worked out the major conventions of American drama which our playwrights have reacted to ever since. In other words, O'Neill established the baseline of serious American drama, and its traditions and conventions are most fully embodied in his family plays. The degree to which this is true can be seen next by examining the family plays of our other premier dramatists—Arthur Miller and Tennessee Williams.

NOTES

1. David R. Mace, "Personality Expression and Subordination in Marriage," *Marriage and Family Living,* 15 (Aug. 1953), 207.

2. Arnold W. Green, "The Middle Class Male Child and Neurosis," *American Sociological Review,* 11 (Feb. 1946), 41.

3. Arthur and Barbara Gelb, *O'Neill* (New York, 1974); Louis Shaeffer, *O'Neill: Son and Playwright* (Boston, 1968); Louis Shaeffer, *O'Neill: Son and Artist* (Boston, 1973).

4. "The attacks that were leveled at apartment hotels were almost precisely those that had bombarded the boarding house for so many years. The voices of those who looked upon them as destroyers of the American home, pamperers of young wives and spoilers of children, echoed the voices of those ... who decried the boarding house many decades before." Russell Lynes, *Domesticated Americans* (New York, 1963), p. 52.

5. Gelb, *O'Neill,* p. 939.

6. Ibid., p. 934.

7. Ibid., pp. 379, 538, 938.

8. I am referring to O'Neill's celebrated remark to Joseph Wood Krutch: "Most modern plays are concerned with the relation between man and man, but that does not interest me at all. I am interested only in the relation between man and God." Quoted in Joseph Wood Krutch, "Introduction" to Eugene O'Neill, *Nine Plays by Eugene O'Neill* (New York, 1943), p. xvii.

9. To date, the fullest treatment of O'Neill and domesticity has been John Henry Raleigh, *The Plays of Eugene O'Neill* (Carbondale, Ill., 1965), pp. 118-143. His conclusion is very different from mine: "In a general way O'Neill's picture of marriage evolves from the early plays, where it is usually pictured as an unmitigated disaster, through a middle period where it is a conflict between idealism and realism, to the final period where it tends to be creative and positive, though not without its stresses and strains." p. 130.

10. Both quotations are from Barrett H. Clark, *Eugene O'Neill: The Man and His Plays* (New York, 1947), p. 78, and note 1.

11. Eugene O'Neill, *All God's Chillun Got Wings* in *The Plays of Eugene O'Neill* (New York, 1951), II, 342—hereafter all volumes in this edition will be cited as *Plays*. For a brilliant discussion of O'Neill's stance see Francis Fergusson, "Melodramatist," in *O'Neill and His Plays,* ed. Oscar Cargill et al. (New York, 1961), pp. 274-276.

12. Eugene O'Neill, *Welded* in *Plays,* II, 447-448.

13. Ibid., p. 448.

14. Ibid., p. 488.

15. Ibid., p. 489.

16. Gelb, *O'Neill,* pp. 539, 761-762. Raleigh tries a "Jungian" interpretation of the two in Raleigh, *Plays of O'Neill,* note 18, pp. 296-297.

17. Raleigh, *Plays of O'Neill,* pp. 30-33, 53.

18. Eugene O'Neill, *Desire Under the Elms* in *Plays,* I, 226.

19. Ibid., p. 238.

20. Ibid., pp. 232-233.

21. Ibid., p. 206.

22. Ibid., p. 229.

23. Ibid., p. 267.

24. Ibid., p. 236.

25. Ibid., p. 234.

26. Ibid., p. 258.

27. Ibid., "General setting," p. 202.

28. The distinction between "victim" and "hero" which I am utilizing here is Raymond Williams's. For him it characterizes an historical shift from nineteenth- to twentieth-century tragedy. I am using it in a slightly different way as a critical concept to apply to modes (or a mode) of action in which a character is caught between otherness and self, that is, between the family of security and the family of freedom. Williams calls the drama of O'Neill and of Tennessee Williams "private tragedy" and that of Arthur Miller "liberal tragedy"; see *Modern Tragedy* (Stanford, Calif., 1966), pp. 87-120. But all three writers portray men as family victims in some sense.

29. O'Neill, *Desire,* p. 269.

30. Ibid.

31. *Lazarus Laughed* and *Marco Millions,* which are of this period but are not family plays, draw on remote historical figures for their protagonists.

32. The Mannons present themselves to their public world as an ordered, hierarchical family of security, but our view of their private life shows a war between the impulses associated with this image and those associated with the family of

freedom. And yet, incest seems to symbolize the perversion of both models, as if the two converged at this point. Mutuality leads to a dangerous closeness and spontaneity to a dangerous freedom. In chapter 5, I make a similar interpretation of the incest theme in Arthur Miller's *A View from the Bridge.*

33. Eugene O'Neill, *Mourning Becomes Electra* in *Plays,* II, 140.

34. Ibid., p. 142.

35. Ibid., p. 147.

36. Ibid., p. 167.

37. Ibid., pp. 115-116.

38. O'Neill makes this point explicit in the stage directions: "By the very act of disowning the Mannons she had returned to the fold...." Ibid., p. 168.

39. Ibid., p. 173.

40. Ibid., p. 178.

41. "On the whole, however, and especially in the late plays, he [O'Neill] is the celebrator of the values of wedded love, as well as the analyst of its complications. Almost alone among modern writers he presents marriages which are believable, durable, and positive, without being idealized and romanticized." Raleigh, *Plays of O'Neill,* p. 130. What Raleigh sees in O'Neill when he calls him the "celebrator of wedded love" is the stripping away of all externals to reveal the bedrock functioning of family relationships. That these are "durable" is without question, for the rhythms of love and hate are carried by an unending perpetual action, which is meant to imply the universal condition. But that these relations are in the main "positive" seems to me mistaken.

42. The unfinished manuscript of *More Stately Mansions* shows the use of the interior/exterior monologue in Act II, iii. *The Iceman Cometh* (1946), not a family play, has a touch of expressionistic choral effect in its final scene.

43. Gelb, *O'Neill,* p. 938.

44. Raleigh, *Plays of O'Neill,* p. 81.

45. For an exhaustive account of how much nostalgia the play has, see Raleigh, *Plays of O'Neill,* pp. 77-83.

46. Eugene O'Neill, *Ah, Wilderness!* in *Plays,* II, 202.

47. Ibid., pp. 206-207.

48. Ibid., p. 270.

49. Quoted in Raleigh, *Plays of O'Neill,* p. 83.

50. Eugene O'Neill, *Long Day's Journey into Night* (New Haven, Conn., 1956), p. 54.

51. Ibid., p. 139.

52. E.g., ibid., pp. 127-128.

53. Ibid., p. 21.

54. Ibid., p. 61. For other indications of James's views, see ibid., pp. 36, 72, 73, 75, 110-111, 141, 146.

55. For an account of the relation between hotel and boarding house life and the American family see Calhoun, *Social History,* III, chapter 9, esp. pp. 179-181.

56. O'Neill, *Journey,* p. 72.

57. Ibid., pp. 97-112.

58. Ibid., p. 44.

59. Ibid., pp. 137-138.

60. Ibid., pp. 153-154. Edmund's experiences of transcendence are similar to those of Ishmael in the crow's-nest, which Melville warns against. In the context of O'Neill's world they represent an attempt to turn outward from the self. O'Neill's attitude toward Edmund's yearnings seems less critical than his attitude toward Mary's dream of family innocence.

61. Doris Alexander has written perceptively on the paradox of O'Neill's social views, though she offers no explanation for the incongruity. "O'Neill could never connect the negative concept of social criticism with the positive concept of love for others.... When he sought love, he could see it only in the context of total acceptance, conformity to the very status quo he despised." "Eugene O'Neill as Social Critic," *American Quarterly,* 6 (Winter 1954), 361.

62. John Henry Raleigh asserts that there are many Irish qualities in O'Neill families: "Excessively familial; noncommunal; sexually chaste; turbulent; drunken; alternately and simultaneously sentimental and ironical about love; pathologically obsessed with betrayal; religious-blasphemous; loquacious"—he adds a tenth trait, "a tendency ... for ... young men to remain at home with their father and mother. In short, here is an abstract picture of the Tyrone family...." "O'Neill's *Long Day's Journey into Night* and New England Irish-Catholicism," in *O'Neill: A Collection of Critical Essays,* ed. John Gassner (Englewood Cliffs, N.J. 1964), p. 128.

Other O'Neill families can be found to dispute the ten traits. And, more important for my argument, traditional Irish family culture is communal and here O'Neill's "Americanism" shows plainly. See e.g., Alexander J. Humphrey, S.J., "The Family in Ireland," in *Comparative Family Systems,* ed. M.F. Nimkoff (Boston, 1965), p. 241 ff., for a discussion of the importance of communal "friendliness"; this trait is now disappearing in urban, industrial areas. Also, as Raleigh admits, the Irish family has a large kin network, which O'Neill's families lack. Thirdly, as I will try to show, Arthur Miller (Jewish family?) and Tennessee Williams (Southern family?) share a habit of mind with O'Neill which is not simply Irish. Finally, O'Neill's family plays have drawn forth a large response on the part of a more than Irish public here in America (as well as in Sweden). For these reasons I disagree with Raleigh's claim that: "It would be no exaggeration to say that a straight line can be drawn from the primitive forests of antique Ireland to the haunted New London, Connecticut, residence of the Tyrone family in the twentieth century." Raleigh, "O'Neill's *Long Day's Journey,*" p. 122.

Perhaps the best way to put the matter is to say, following William Goode, that because of industrialism the West shares characteristics of a nuclear family pattern, of which America is the most extreme development. I would add that only those Irish traits which fit American dreams and anxieties about the nuclear family structure are important to O'Neill.

4

REACTIONS I: FAMILY AND SOCIETY IN ARTHUR MILLER

> *The new view is that the higher and more obligatory relation is to society rather than to the family; the family goes back to the age of savagery while the state belongs to the age of civilization. The modern individual is a world citizen, served by the world, and home interests can no longer be supreme.*
>
> Arthur W. Calhoun[1]

In the drama of O'Neill we can see the challenge which the changing family structure presented to notions of the natural harmony of self-sufficient individuals as well as to the ideal warmth and nurture of a self-enclosed family hierarchy. O'Neill tried both the family of security and the family of freedom and found them wanting. He could not imagine any support or melioration of isolated man's condition which would come from outside the family. He followed the logic of his denial of creative order to its conclusion, sparing neither himself nor his characters the pain of that logic. And in *Long Day's Journey into Night* he reached the height of his aesthetic achievement in creating a dramatic action which embodied with crushing sincerity his vision of endless family isolation.

O'Neill seemed to equate the drama of family life with the universal condition of human nature. Arthur Miller represents an attempt to move out of that deadlocked cosmic rule by relating the individual and his family to society. Miller did not abandon the realistic family drama, but the extremes to which O'Neill had taken it were incompatible with what Miller had to say. He attempted to turn the connections and energies of the family situation outward, to show a clash between the private loyalties of the household and the public responsibilities of living in society. He tried, in effect, to rescue domestic drama from the logic of O'Neill's vision.

A clue as to how he went about that task can be seen in an essay Miller wrote in 1956 entitled, "The Family in Modern Drama." Miller argues that "the magnetic force of the family relationship within the play" tends to result in the realistic mode, while "the pressure which evokes in a genuine, unforced way the unrealistic [sic] mode is the social relationship within the play."[2] Family plays—which are naturally realistic, then—deal with a much different area of life than do social plays—which are naturally "symbolistic," or, to use the more common term in modern drama, expressionistic. Here Miller accepts as a fundamental stylistic premise the self-enclosure of family experience. According to Miller, family plays touch upon our deepest private feelings, while social plays deal with our conscious understanding of the public world. The "primary pressures" of family and society, producing our two main dramatic styles of realism and expressionism, reflect the wide split in modern life between private (family) life and public (social) life, according to Miller.

As a way of understanding and healing this split, Miller formulates the question: "How may a man make of the outside world a home?"[3] Especially in modern plays, says Miller, the movement out of the family circle lifts the play from the particular case to the general and universal one. This is true because the alienation we all feel is based not only on a sense of our dissatisfaction with our place in society, but also on the remembered sense of "the safety, the surroundings of love, the ease of soul, the sense of identity and honor which, evidently, all men have connected in their memories with the idea of the family."[4]

Miller is not writing directly about his own plays here, but what he has to say about modern drama in general reveals the fundamental importance that the family holds for him. And we have seen the term "home" before—in O'Neill, who understood the assumptions it entailed, and in the soap opera, where the point was not to understand them. In both, "home" represented an escape from family dilemmas into a world of innocent domestic love. Miller uses the term to suggest a personal longing which, he feels, must be turned into a social, rather than familial, reality.

The important question is how to remake society in terms of the values we associate with this past experience of home. This question appears as the theme of social responsibility in his first major play, *All My Sons* (1947). But in exploring this theme, Miller is also attracted to the dramatic clash between family life and individual integrity. Most of his plays contain some mix of these two impulses: one related to the question of making the world into a home; and the other, and I think deeper, impulse to show the struggle of the individual escaping from the family. The artistic success of his plays can be measured in large part by his skill in keeping the two in balance and even interrelated, as he does best in *Death of a Salesman* (1949).

In his career as a whole, there is an increasing tendency to move away from the question of making the outside world into a home. Instead, social responsibility is associated with the drama of being true to yourself in the face of domestic claims. Not until *The Price* (1968), however, does Miller focus on these claims apart from the question of social responsibility. Then he begins to look at the complexities and contradictions implicit in his ideal of "home": "safety," "surroundings of love," and "ease of soul" are not in *The Price* as compatible with "identity and honor" as the rhetoric of his earlier definition implied. What I am suggesting is that, despite his attempt to move his plays into a larger social context, Miller has had difficulty in dramatizing subjects other than the individual consciousness concerned for its own integrity and adjustment to family. At least this is at the core of his dramatic imagination in a way that shows how obsessive family experience is to our playwrights, even one who attempts as skillfully as Miller does to enlarge the subject of our drama. It is a problem for him beginning with his first play.

The story Miller tells in *All My Sons* concerns Joe Keller and the discovery that he shipped defective cylinder heads from his aircraft engine factory during World War II. The entire structure and movement of the play is aimed at this revelation and at Joe's belated recognition of the responsibility which he bears for his act. Miller has constructed a situation in which the nearly sensational social consequences of an act are easily and clearly identified. He dramatizes this strong situation by depicting the pressures of the Keller family relationships which drive the action toward revelation. The reaction of the two sons, Chris and Larry, to their father's crime generates the play's climax. As Dennis Welland has put it: "What concerns Miller here ... is the impinging of the public issue on the private conscience and the domestic circle of the family."[5]

All My Sons takes place entirely in the Keller's back yard, which we quickly see is a center of neighborhood activity with a constant stream of friends moving in and out. Thus the action is set in a half-public, half-private environment, one where the warmth, ease and love of family life is extended to encompass a larger area of society. In turn, the neighbors know and have sympathy for the problems of the Keller family. Here, then, is a family which seems to connect with the outer world.

It is worthwhile to examine the method Miller has used to tell the story of the Kellers. I have already noted that the play is aimed at a single revelation and recognition. Miller builds toward this crisis by starting out with a different story, a rather complicated domestic crisis concerning Chris's desire to marry Ann Deever. Kate Keller refuses to recognize that her son Larry, missing in action three years earlier, is dead and that his fiancée Ann is therefore free to marry. In the midst of this family difficulty, a different subject begins to take shape during the long first act, one which at first is apparently a gratuitous complication of the approaching crisis of marriage. Ann's father had been Joe Keller's partner in their wartime factory and was convicted for shipping faulty airplane parts, a charge of which Joe was cleared. Here is the first hint of the ethic which is to dominate the play—antisocial action by the individual produces horrifying public consequences which in turn react on the individual. The realization that twenty-one pilots died as a result of the defective equipment has turned neighbors and his children against Steve Deever. As Joe Keller pleads for sympathy for his former partner, Chris and Ann pronounce their judgments on him.

> ANN, *a little shamed, but determined:* No, I've *never* written to him. Neither has my brother. *To Chris:* Say, do you feel this way [as your father does], too?
> CHRIS: He murdered twenty-one pilots. [6]

At first this censure is applied at a distance, as it were, to a person we do not see whose story seems only tangentially related to the gathering crisis in family relations. Chris threatens to leave the family business rather than give up Ann, and Kate seems inflexibly determined to deny Larry's death. But in the second act the theme of social responsibility becomes more directly a part of the domestic crisis with the arrival of George, Ann's brother. George has now come to believe his father's denial of guilt. He accuses Joe of being responsible for shipping faulty equipment; and he attempts to dissuade Ann from her marriage. His attack fails to move anyone except Kate. Driven to desperation by the determination of Ann and Chris to marry, she reveals that George's charge is true:

> MOTHER...*To Chris, but not facing them:* Your brother's alive, darling, because if he's dead, your father killed him. Do you understand me now? As long as you live, that boy is alive. God does not let a son be killed by his father. Now you see, don't you? Now you see. [7]

Here Miller neatly brings his social ethic and his family situation together. For Kate the engagement of Chris and Ann means an admission of Larry's death, an admission which in her mind brings the consequences of her husband's act to bear on his own family. Joe is able to avoid this dilemma because his shrewd, practical outlook assures him his son never piloted a P-40 airplane. But Kate, a half-mystic, makes a symbolic connection between her son's death as a pilot and the deaths of those who actually flew P-40's. Despite her inability to hold any values other than family preservation and solidarity, despite her lack of understanding of the larger moral import of what her husband has done, she senses intuitively that her husband's act and her son's death bear some relation to each other.

In the structure of the play's dramatic action, as the domestic crisis comes to a head it brings with it a revelation of the consequences of a previous antisocial action. Each succeeding act of *All My Sons* is drastically shorter than the last, has sharper and more compact conflicts, and brings us closer to the crucial revelations. What Miller is saying is that one cannot escape into the family from the social consequences of one's actions. In *All My Sons* the family is part of a larger world and the structure of the dramatic action is designed to drive this lesson home.

Miller is not content with this revelation; the assertion of the family's connection with the outer world does not satisfy the question of moral responsibility, nor does it resolve the tensions set up in the Joe-Chris relationship. In the first acts Joe is a remarkably passive character, considering the fact that he is central to the whole argument of the play. This is part of Miller's strategy, for he wishes to show that Joe is incapable of recognizing the consequences of his decision,[8] and he wishes to heighten through contrast the drama of Joe's final action, his suicide. But in addition to these reasons of characterization and dramaturgy is the fact that Joe cannot see beyond his family and so has no sense of the crisis which is gathering about him. And when he is confronted by Chris, he is unable to admit his social responsibility because he does not think he has one. He justifies his actions in terms of his family:

Chris, I did it for you, it was a chance and I took it for

you. I'm sixty-one years old, when would I have another chance to make something for you? Sixty-one years
old you don't get another chance, do ya? [9]

Joe's role in the business world has no other meaning for him than
as a provider for his family. He cannot see the consequences of
his action in any other way. After his break with his son, Joe becomes antagonistic toward his neighbors and turns to Kate, whose
great maternal warmth has always held the family together. "I
thought I had a family here. What happened to my family?" [10]
Joe's highest, and indeed single, loyalty is to the family.

Chris believes in a loyalty that transcends the family, but he
is unable to act on that belief until the final revelation, the disclosure of Larry's suicide in expiation of his father's sin. Chris is
unwilling to act against his father since Joe's corruption has revealed the corruption of the whole business society, but Larry's
letter convinces him of the necessity for action. It also convinces
Joe, who can now begin to see his own responsibility:

Sure, he was my son. But I think to him they were all
my sons. And I guess they were, I guess they were. [11]

Yet Joe is able to admit this only in retrospect, in his memory of a
past action. He still cannot see it as the basis for a moral life, and
so he kills himself as he said he would:

I'm his father and he's my son, and if there's something
bigger than that I'll put a bullet in my head. [12]

In *All My Sons* Miller establishes the family as intimately
connected with society, and he is brutally critical of the impulse
to withdraw into the family. When loyalties to family and to society
come into conflict, as they do in the Chris-Joe relationship, he

demonstrates the necessity for family relationships to give way to a larger social responsibility.

The Keller family is one which disintegrates completely, yet out of this chaos Miller is attempting to bring his self-conscious character, Chris, into a moral and so human relationship with the world. Presumably, it is also supposed to be a "life-giving" relationship, to use Dennis Welland's term. [13] But *All My Sons* does not clearly define this new alternative. The morality of the play is measured by Larry's suicide, which is meant to be a symbol of ultimate commitment to one's social responsibilities. But it is life-giving only if one insists on the pun. Its dramatic effect is to save Chris's integrity by providing a model of extreme personal integrity for him to follow. Because commitment to one's individual integrity is a loyalty apart from family ties, Larry's suicide is associated with questions of social responsibility. He stands against wartime profiteering, which Joe justifies in terms of family prosperity. And Chris is motivated to take his father to the police by Larry's gesture. Still, Larry is a character we never see, one who does not appear in dramatic action before us, and our sense of the meaning of his life and death depends solely on a short suicide note. As a result, its revelation is more theatrical than dramatic.

More to the point, Chris needs such a model to follow because the society he lives in is, he feels, a false and corrupt one when compared to the wartime self-sacrifice he has seen. Banal common sense and immoral compromise must not win out as the neighbor, Jim Bayliss, wrongly predicts they will. Chris struggles to keep his "star of honesty." He is as involved with saving his individual soul as he is with gestures of social commitment. Larry's suicide, like the sacrifice of the soldiers for each other, is meant to provide Chris with a model which affirms a moral order larger than the family. It is intended as the dramatic counterbalance to Joe's suicide to establish the social theme Miller wishes to convey. But what is left dramatically inert is how Chris is to act after all this self-destruction. In the world of the play there is precious little room between innocence and death. One does not make the world a home by suicide.

Miller tries in *All My Sons* to use the family drama to illustrate the moral necessity of recognizing a human community beyond the family. He is not entirely successful. He establishes, through a highly crafted dramatic structure, the relentless destruction of the Keller family as the price they pay for refusing to recognize social responsibilities. This is the play's chief artistic success. But large elements of his theme of social responsibility remain only partly and indirectly realized in the action, for he is unable to define the way in which one was to *live* after the obstacle of family loyalty is removed. *All My Sons,* with its primary emphasis on the realistic psychology of familial relations, finally traps Miller within them. Once the Keller family relations are broken, he has no other dramatic materials to put in their place. Faced with the conundrum of the democratic family's isolation which Tocqueville had recognized and O'Neill had dramatized, Miller reaches outside the realistic style in his next play. What he retains of the materials and style of domestic drama is as important as what he discards.

Death of a Salesman develops many of the situations and issues of *All My Sons* but does so with different emphases. Miller is still attempting to define and examine the problems of the social order and the individual, and he again uses family relations, particularly the father-son relationship. Here, too, is a son who loves his father deeply, but is disillusioned by him. Out of this disillusionment comes the disintegration of the family, and the family crisis is again meant to stand for the need to readjust one's relation to the outer world. However, Miller is less interested in the social consequences of this family's acts than he was in the Kellers's. In *Salesman,* the question of social responsibility becomes that of a social victim, who may be partly responsible for his own plight but who is not charged with injuring or betraying the world outside the family. Moreover, here is no heroic act of suicide to redeem society (as Larry's was meant to be), or act of self-punishment (as Joe's was), but a desperately misguided suicide to redeem family. The Lomans do not fall apart because they are antisocial, but because they are, in a sense, too socialized, too uncritically accepting of the false ethic of material success.

The story of Willy Loman is too well known to need more than the briefest retelling. A salesman who can no longer sell,

Willy is sixty years old and on the verge of collapse. His favorite son, Biff, has returned home penniless once again and, in the face of his father's breakdown, promises to try one more grandiose scheme to become the "magnificent" success they have all dreamed he was destined to be. Increasingly immersed in his memories and guilts about the past, Willy loses his job at the same time that Biff gives up his pipe dream of instant achievement. Willy is unable to survive the failure of his life and kills himself to provide insurance money for his family, particularly Biff.

It is usual to consider the ethic of the play as an indictment of the falsity of contemporary values and institutions. Clearly, Willy is cheated by life and duped by society in matters large and small. To begin with, there are the minor breakdowns of cars and refrigerators which punctuate the action and give the play an added comic texture, though Linda's little notebook of expenses and debts is no laughing matter. The mortgage payments tick away like a time bomb under the house (Willy's suicide provides money for the last installment) in the endless scramble of the Lomans to keep up with their lives. More directly, Willy is a victim in that he is used and discarded by the business he works for when he is no longer effective. Trapped in his boss's office with a tape recorder gone mad, Willy is unable to cope with the circumstances of a ruthless mechanical civilization. He is fired still insisting on the personal ties he feels ought to give him some rights with the company.

Willy is also a victim of the culture's sterility. The inane repetition of "facts" by the tape-recorded children's voices in the scene just mentioned, along with the deadly clichés of his boss—"business is business"—are contrasted with Willy's own creative instincts, his skills as a carpenter and gardener. Here, too, the texture of the play is richly detailed as Willy's house is crowded by highrise apartment buildings, and the soil is barren, cut off from the sun. Willy's dream is of a pastoral family life in the suburbs, a modernized version of Crèvecoeur's easy family civility. Moreover, Willy's father is described as an artisan, a flute maker whose skills made him free and independent of the wage economy in contrast to Willy's life as a wage slave. However, this pioneer spirit may be seen as covertly ominous as well. It is related to the vicious instincts of Willy's brother Ben, who is a frontiersman of sorts. And his father's transient ways mean that Willy was cut off from his own family as a child.

The most pervasive way in which Willy is victimized is by the success ethic. In his dreams for his son as a football star and big-time businessman, and in his own allegiance to the story of David Singleman, the premier salesman, Willy risks everything on making it to the top. When he cannot do so, Biff must.

This last point involves a complication, one which enriches the play immensely, for Willy is not simply a victim of a success-mongering culture. Miller wishes us to see, also, that Willy accepts the success value too easily and completely. The play suggests that, along with our pity for Willy, we take a critical attitude. In the structure of the dramatic action Biff's story is juxtaposed against his father's to provide a major comment on Willy's life. We judge Willy, in part, by seeing how Biff acts when facing the same temptations. Biff, too, is infected with Willy's dreams of success, and even when he discovers his father is not a god, he continues to judge himself in Willy's terms. Finally, when Biff goes to an old employer for a loan, the absurdity of his life comes home to him.

> How the hell did I ever get the idea I was a salesman there? I even believed myself that I'd been a salesman for him! And then he gave me one look and—I realized what a ridiculous lie my whole life had been! We've been talking in a dream for fifteen years. I was a shipping clerk. [14]

But when Biff confronts Willy with the truth about themselves, Willy will not accept it, even while he finally recognizes Biff's love for him:

> WILLY: Oh, Biff! *Staring wildly:* He cried! Cried to me. *He is choking with his love, and now cries out*

his promise: That boy—that boy is going to be magnificent![15]

Willy translates his love for Biff into the terms of the success dream and kills himself to give Biff the insurance money to start a business. Willy's act has a terrible vitality about it, but it is also a terrible mistake. He has attempted to reaffirm the meaning of his life, the ethic of success, but the ethic is a false one. As one critic has put it: "He brings tragedy down on himself, not by opposing the lie, but by living it."[16]

Another way Miller provides a critical context for Willy's actions is by the use of expressionism. Miller had felt boxed in by the realistic mode of *All My Sons,* a problem he identified as having its locus in the use of time.[17] In *Death of a Salesman* he began to use expressionist elements, not to attack or deny the reality of our perceptions of the world, but to enlarge upon the strict probabilities of the mundane. Unlike O'Neill, who moved away from expressionism and rejected it in his best work, Miller moved toward a special sort of acceptance of it in his finest achievement. He used expressionism in a way that allowed him to retain the family subject matter which, in his own terms, implied realistic treatment. By telling the play partially from Willy's point of view, Miller extends his examination of the Loman family to scenes which project the interior of Willy's mind. (Miller subtitled the play, "Certain Private Conversations in Two Acts and a Requiem.") Willy's memory scenes come closer and closer to a revelation of his deepest motives, a structural pattern common to realistic plays which aim at showing *why* a character acts the way he does. These scenes give us another way of evaluating Willy's behavior within the realistic family world. Through the breakdown of the normal time sequence which accompanies Willy's memories and hallucinations, we have dramatic contrasts calculated to call Willy's actions, past and present, into account. His philandering and his encouragement of Biff's stealing are two of the more obvious examples. In addition, Willy is given to speaking in contradictions:

WILLY: Oh, I'll knock 'em dead next week. I'll go to

> Hartford, I'm very well liked in Hartford. You
> know, the trouble is, Linda, people don't seem to
> take to me. [18]

Such abrupt reversals are meant to be more than a sign of a wandering mind, which is what they seem in terms of realistic psychology. They have a mordant comedy to them and keep us at a certain distance from Willy, watching and evaluating him.

The character of Ben, Willy's brother, appears only in the expressionistic scenes. It could be argued that most of Ben's scenes are memories of real conversations between him and Willy. But they have an hallucinatory edge as well. Ben's strangeness is enhanced by his sudden entrances and exits, and by the leitmotif repetition of his maxim of life: "When I was seventeen I walked into the jungle, and when I was twenty-one I walked out. And by God I was rich." By his final appearance, when he and Willy discuss suicide, Ben is no longer a memory, but now clearly a figment of Willy's desperate imagination.

Willy clings to the idea of Ben as the personification of success, but he does not hear what Ben is telling him about success. Willy thinks it is a matter of being liked; his true ideal is David Singleman:

> He was eighty-four years old, and he'd drummed merchandise in thirty-one states. And old Dave, he'd go up
> to his room, y'understand, put on his green velvet
> slippers—I'll never forget—and pick up his phone and
> call the buyers, and without ever leaving his room, at
> the age of eighty-four, he made his living. And when I
> saw that, I realized that selling was the greatest career
> a man could want. Cause what could be more satisfying
> than to be able to go, at the age of eighty-four, into
> twenty or thirty different cities, and pick up a phone,
> and be remembered and loved and helped by so many
> different people? Do you know? when he died—and by
> the way he died the death of a salesman, in his green

velvet slippers in the smoker of the New York, New Haven and Hartford, going into Boston—when he died, hundreds of salesmen and buyers were at his funeral. Things were sad on a lotta trains for months after that.[19]

But Singleman is the exception, as one of the meanings of his name suggests. Even while Willy tells this story, he is being fired. The harsh rule is Ben: success comes through vicious competition in the "jungle" of a materialistic civilization. Ben says this, and he shows it to us early in the play in his first scene:

BEN, *To Biff:* Hit that, boy—hard as you can. *He pounds his stomach.*

BIFF: Oh, no, sir!

BEN, *taking a boxing stance:* Come on, get to me! *He laughs.*

WILLY: Go to it, Biff! Go ahead, show him!

BIFF: Okay! *He cocks his fists and starts in.*

LINDA, *to Willy:* Why must he fight, dear?

BEN, *sparring with Biff:* Good boy! Good boy!

WILLY: How's that, Ben, huh?

HAPPY: Give him the left, Biff!

LINDA: Why are you fighting?

BEN: Good boy! *Suddenly comes in, trips Biff, and stands over him, the point of his umbrella over Biff's eye.*

LINDA: Look out, Biff!

BIFF: Gee!

BEN, *patting Biff's knee:* Never fight fair with a stranger, boy. You'll never get out of the jungle that way.[20]

The dramatic effect of this moment is very strong. The steel point of the umbrella barely restrained from puncturing the soft, vulner-

able eyeball is an inspired choice of gestures by Miller to show us
from the outset Ben's evil and rapacious nature. Even Linda senses
the horror, and she refuses Ben's hand immediately after. But
Willy never does perceive Ben's destructive nature and the success
he represents. Ben's appearances throughout the play are reminders
of Willy's delusions about success, and reinforce Biff's rejection
of that ideal.

Death of a Salesman is a criticism of society for using Willy
and failing to provide him with outlets for his creativity—symbolized by his gardening and his carpentry—but, also, it is a criticism of Willy for accepting society on its own terms. Willy's sin is
the lack of self-consciousness, the lack of critical knowledge; it is
the sin of not keeping his inner life inviolable. Biff learns to do so;
he reconciles himself to the truth of his father and still loves him,
just as he accepts the truth about himself. Biff shows us what is
wrong with Willy's life by refusing to live it. To complete the pattern, in one of the many parallels and inversions that make the
play resonant, it is Hap, Biff's younger brother, who in the funeral
scene reaffirms Willy's success dream. And Hap, the insincere
playboy bachelor, is a compulsive destroyer of families.

Death of a Salesman, then, contains an impulse toward a
critical judgment of Willy Loman as well as of American society.
But it should be emphasized that this judgment is secondary to the
main effect of the play. The critical context never controls the
play or dominates our view of Willy. At best it shows the potential
for the sort of "toughness" Miller wanted in his plays (and in
modern drama), but knew he failed to achieve. [21] Miller is too good
at making us empathize. We feel the full weight of the pressures
against Willy; we pity him as victim; and we are emotionally attracted to him by the desperate energy with which he pursues the
ideal that destroys him.

The design of the sequence of actions is such that our criticism
of Willy's past gives way to our intense awareness of his present
pain. While Willy is, in his memory, reliving his deepest guilt,
which is the past betrayal of his family with another woman, he is
deserted by his sons in the present. There might be a certain ironic
justice in this for Willy—since they go off chasing women. But
Linda's bitter denunciation of them in the next scene subordinates

any such perception to our feeling that Willy's needs are much greater than his errors. Willy's life is one of poetic *in*justice. Or again, in the Requiem Linda's touching bewilderment is allowed to dominate the mood. The critical, distanced tone which Miller begins to establish through Biff's judgment on his father's life as he rejects Hap's and Charley's evaluations is undercut by Linda's final lonely speech and its implicit appeal for Willy, the victim. As Miller put it, "*Salesman* was written in a mood of friendly partnership with the audience."[22]

A good deal of the play's formal novelty and structural ingenuity is aimed at moving the audience to an emotional attachment to Willy, then to a critical wariness, and back again. It assures that we will love Willy and reject his life, just as Biff does. In this way, Miller can bring together—more successfully than he did in *All My Sons*—his interest in the individual escaping from the family and his pursuit of the larger question of making the world a home. In the earlier play Larry's suicide was intended to have a positive social meaning, but its actual dramatic effect was unclear. Ostensibly, it was to represent a commitment to a higher ethic than the family, but this ethic appeared to be as much individual as social. In *Death of a Salesman* this difficulty is minimized, for the question of direct social repercussions is never raised. Willy does not hurt others in the community with his life and his death, only himself and his family. In a sense, Willy is irrelevant to his society, and this is seen in the final dramatic image when no one but the family and Charley come to the bleak funeral. Also, Biff has no war experience of sacrifice for others, as Chris has, which would force him to face the problem of living justly. Redeeming yourself rather than society is the most that is asked for in the world of the Lomans. Social responsibility comes to be seen as the recognition and rejection of false social values.

The core of Miller's dramatic design is that he unites his condemnation of the society that destroys Willy to Biff's struggle with his family. Biff learns to be himself by rejecting the success ethic, which means rejecting the family structure as well. He loves his father; but even before Willy's death, Biff decides he must leave the family forever. Willy is not able to find such self-knowledge because he believes too fully in the success values and makes them the terms of his family love. By giving us the full measure of Willy's pain, while linking Biff's maturity to a rejection of both family and false society, Miller creates a powerful, intricate dramatic action. He puts the struggle with the family at the service of social responsibility (defined as self-knowledge); its energies provide the tension and release which underpin the drama of Willy's downfall.

The fusion of individual, family, and society has not been equaled in Miller's subsequent plays. In *Death of a Salesman* he managed to convey—through the interrelationship of its impingement on Willy and its rejection by Biff—more of a sense of social experience than he has since. If we look at his next plays in terms of making the world a home, as attempts to extend the family drama to the points at which it touches on social responsibility, we see that Miller is apt to blur distinctions. Public and private experience are compounded in a way that makes them nearly synonymous. Leonard Moss notes this has not been to the benefit of Miller's art, for it often results in Miller's "ascribing a spurious public significance to private experience."[23] In *The Crucible* (1953), for example, the issue of public hysteria over witchcraft gives way to that of the private honesty of John Proctor. Proctor's triumph at the play's end in refusing to betray his integrity is, in turn, supposed to cure the social hysteria.[24] Here we have a prime example of how the inner life of the individual is the touchstone for the social comment of the play as if individual redemption meant social redemption. Miller simply asserts that this healing takes place in a footnote to the play; the dramatic action does not show it at all. What it does show most convincingly is that the family is at the basis of Proctor's struggles. Proctor's chief sin is a domestic one. Unhappily married to a cold woman, he has committed adultery with a young girl, who exploits the witchcraft hysteria in an attempt to win him back. By establishing his personal integrity, he finally heals the breach in his marriage; a genuine mature love is now possible between him and his wife, though he must die to confirm that possibility. Family life is private only in relation to the outer world. By the end of the play we see that the truly private areas are those of individual motive and self-judgment.

The core relationship, and the source of the play's strength, is the Proctor-Elizabeth relationship. In learning to forgive himself for his adultery, Proctor discovers the strength to maintain his integrity in the face of death. He will not confess to witchcraft when confession will save his life. The success of this play, as with *All My Sons,* rests on the carefully controlled rising tensions within each act and from act to act. In addition, its climax is an extended reversal of Proctor's attitudes which is absolutely convincing in terms of character development. As long as we are concerned with Proctor's realistic psychology, we are compelled by the drama of self-discovery enacted as Proctor finds, to his joyous amazement, that he is capable of good. He defies the judge:

> You have made your magic now, for now I think I see
> some shred of goodness in John Proctor. Not enough
> to weave a banner with, but white enough to keep it
> from such dogs. [25]

And in a rich counterpoint to Proctor's development, Elizabeth learns that she is capable of evil. Her virtue was a vice, for she lacked love: "It needs a cold wife to prompt lechery." [26]

This is nearly an affirmation of the family. Nearly, but not quite. Proctor must die to establish the basis of their love—his integrity—and, in fact, the family must be destroyed. Elizabeth has learned love rather than judgment; but judgment is still the issue—self-judgment, for Proctor must stand alone. The family relationship is of no help here, a fact Miller dramatizes by Elizabeth's painful battle not to give way to her desire to share Proctor's decision. Her epitaph for her husband is: "He have his goodness now. God forbid I take it from him!" [27] Miller has difficulty, as do most American playwrights, in seeing the family as a source of strength for his characters; but when he shows it as a struggle of conflicting relationships, it is a source of strength for his dramatic art.

Miller compels our admiration for his heroes through their dedicated allegiance to themselves when pitted against a destructive family or a false society (or both). But what happens when the fanatic drive of the hero comes up against the healthy family and the true society? Then we border on pathology, which is the case in *A View from the Bridge* (1956), where the main character, Eddie Carbone, betrays his family—and so its ancient Sicilian community law—because of his incestuous love for his niece.[28] In *A View from the Bridge* the theme of social responsibility has been drastically recast by Miller. The question of making the world a home becomes irrelevant since the Sicilian community and the family are not separate institutions alienated from each other. The world is a home, but Eddie still does not belong. In other words, Miller has dramatized the antisocial implications of one of his most fundamental values, personal integrity. It is to his great credit that his artistic honesty did not allow him to sidestep this question. Both Eddie Carbone and John Proctor cry out that they want their name. But in *A View from the Bridge* Miller recognizes that being true to yourself does not always align you with the forces of right against the false society or the meddlesome family. Eddie is not right, his society is not false, and his family does not suffocate him. What is striking is how, nonetheless, his commitment to his own desires is meant to make us feel tame, only half alive as it were. Miller is fascinated by such integrity. Eddie really lived, if badly.

Miller is relatively successful in *A View from the Bridge* because he allows himself a special dispensation: the Sicilian code which pervades the family life links it to the values of the larger community. Only by establishing this special—in American drama—family ethos can Miller slip easily from the private to the public spheres of experience. And even here it is only by constantly reminding ourselves of the special community-family relationship that we can modify the fundamental impression of a man rebelling, perversely, against family order, rebelling against an authority which he, above all others, should enforce. Marco, who denounces Eddie in public thus precipitating the final action, is, significantly, part of the family. He establishes those limits beyond which Eddie knows he must not go. Marco prefigures this function early in the play by warning Eddie not to bully his brother, Eddie's rival.

The drama of escaping from the family has, then, a different emphasis in this play. Eddie's motive of incest is the debasement of the family of security. The family's destructive closeness is what he will not give up, and the reason for his conflict with the world. In another sense he is giving way to the urge for a perverse family of freedom in which he could love as he chooses. Miller employs a choral figure, the lawyer Alfieri, whose commentary attempts to bridge the gap between the private impulses and the public actions of Eddie. But as Moss notes:

> Alfieri elevates an abnormal emotional condition to a metaphysical plane where it is seen as legendary, objective, predictable, and sacred—even though Eddie's behavior reveals it to be idiosyncratic, subjective, erratic, and shameful. [29]

Neurosis comes to equal myth; Alfieri functions not to connect public and private life so much as to widen the personal inner state of Eddie to a point where both areas are accounted for and explained as one. Eddie's motive goes from private obsession to the demand for public apology. Despite Alfieri's last speech, which invites us to see Eddie's drama as awesome because it shows he was a man who let himself be "wholly known," Eddie never admits to himself what he really wants. And so the public gesture he asks for from Marco is in danger of seeming irrelevant, or a mad rationalization, rather than the plea of a man who has faced the essence of his being in his social identity.

Eddie, in fact, wants his esteem not from others as he claims but from himself. His concern with the public accusation that he has betrayed his rival to the immigration authorities changes the focus of the play from a domestic struggle to a confrontation between the individual and the code of his community. But it is Eddie's integrity that is really at issue, just as it is Proctor's. Whereas we are meant to accept Proctor's act as social in that it will cure the hysteria of Salem, here we are meant to see Eddie's lost integrity as socially significant in that it violates the code of Sicilian loyalty (not, of course, in that it violates the code of law). In both plays the family struggle is used ambiguously, first as the source of private dilemma and then as the touchstone of public (and so social) significance.

A similar pattern can be seen in *After the Fall* (1964), Miller's long, rambling, psychoanalytic montage of lost innocence, betrayal, and offers of love. The play takes place entirely in the mind of the protagonist, Quentin, and so is the most expressionistic of Miller's works. Here the family has been reduced to Quentin's memories of his love-marriage relationship to each of the three women in his life. And the struggle between the individual and society has shrunk to the thrashings of debate between the inner (psychological) and outer (social) roles of one character.

"I am bewildered by the death of love and my responsibility for it," says Quentin, [30] because love for him means loss of ego, the ultimately intolerable state to Miller's heroes. He cannot live with his first wife because he fears such a loss, and he finds he cannot live with his second wife after he tries disastrously to tolerate the loss through limitless love. It is only with Holga, his third woman, that he moves toward love through a recognition of his own capacity for evil selfishness, a recognition that comes with his discovering his own psychic identity. If he can forgive himself his own persistent survival when others have been destroyed, then love will become, at last, a possibility.

Again, there is no dramatic enactment of the solution. How Quentin is going to manage with Holga is patently unclear. We have only a low-keyed hope that he will. At first, Quentin's guilt over his ego is based on the false expectation of a dissolving family love, on the expectation that the family of security will save him. When he conquers that expectation, we are meant to believe he is now self-reliantly prepared to create a family through self-forgiveness, a rather Freudian version of the democratic family of freedom. Walking past the embodied memories of his past families on stage, Quentin holds his hand out toward Holga, but we do not see them touch. Quentin's capacity to build family order out of self-forgiveness has yet to be tested, as Miller knows.

As in *The Crucible* the family is close to being affirmed thematically, but Miller cannot quite bring himself to dramatizing it. But then, this is a problem with the entire play. It seems more like a novel than a piece for the theater. *The Crucible* also took us right up to the capacity for domestic love and, with the help of its tight construction and sharply defined character psychology, it was dramatically vivid. In *After the Fall* the family struggle and the characters are conceived of as narrated states of being rather than in terms of gestures and actions.

The Crucible, A View from the Bridge, and *After the Fall* belong to a second phase in Miller's career with regard to the family.[31] Having explored the connections between social responsibility, the family, and the individual in his first two plays, Miller began to modify the terms by which he tried to turn the family drama outward. Rather than a direct evocation of contemporary society, Miller attempted to relate the family and the individual psyche—as he sees it, so closely and prerationally formed by family—to some larger force, whether of history or of psychological impulse. Indeed, the latter interest led him into the paradox that in *After the Fall* total subjectivity, the individual consciousness, replaced the "larger" world. The expressionism of *After the Fall* became a retreat from the conditions of myth and of history with which he attempted to universalize his domestic psychology in *The Crucible* and *A View from the Bridge.* It may be that Miller felt he had arrived at a dead end in this approach to exploring the drama of family life. Certainly exploring the private psyche did not trigger his dramatic imagination the way it has that of his contemporary, Tennessee Williams. Whatever the case, in his next family play Miller focused on the subject with which he began his career, and which has provided him with his most successful material: the realistically presented family with its anxieties and contradictions. This is the world of *The Price* (1968).

In *The Price* Miller is looking more closely than before into the ambiguities contained in our memory of home: "safety, the surroundings of love, the ease of soul, the sense of identity and honor...."[32] As I have already suggested, this series implies the equality and harmony of its elements. But the first three are, in fact, in conflict with the last two in Miller's plays, as they are in O'Neill's. What is the nature of that home which the world is to be made into? In *The Price* Miller shows it to be full of (familiar) contradictions, and he has embraced the contradictions and raised them to the status of doctrine, a statement on the "human condition," as it were. Like O'Neill, Miller has come back to the dramatic style of his earliest work, though he had never ventured as far into expressionism as O'Neill. And like O'Neill, he establishes a human predicament imbedded in the domestic crisis which is fundamentally without resolution. I am tempted to say that Miller brought his drama full circle in *The Price,* back to where O'Neill left it in *Long Day's Journey into Night.* But that is only partly true. The dilemma is familiar but the stance is somewhat new. O'Neill had raised his predicaments, through his intensity and his sincerity, to the energy level of tragedy. Miller, always more cool, more flat, more analytical, has presented his domestic crisis with a careful irony. He uses laughter (in the play, not in the audience) as a guard against sentiment and vulgarity, rather than as a solvent for his characters' troubles.

The Price has an aura of looking back, of taking stock, and even of nostalgia. A brownstone in New York is about to be torn down and the apartment in which the story takes place is a concentration of the domestic paraphernalia of a family's lifetime, "the chaos of ten rooms of furniture squeezed into this one."[33] The set is filled with the stuff of yesteryear—outmoded furniture, mementoes of the past, a broken oar, a harp, a crystal chandelier. It is all an anachronism, a faded memory of something now out of date. "It is difficult to decide if the stuff is impressive or merely over-heavy and ugly."[34] Miller never does decide and that, as he intends it, is the point of his play.

The opening scene of *The Price* is simply and skillfully done. We are introduced first to a middle-aged policeman, Victor Franz, and then to his wife, Esther. They have come to dispose of the Franz family possessions stored in this apartment for the last several years. Quickly we learn that Esther drinks too much, the Victor resents her pushing him and implying that he cannot handle the business of setting a price for the furniture. Esther wants the status of something better than a policeman's life; she feels that she and Victor have undervalued themselves. Victor is unable to decide about his future; apparently immobilized by the passage of time, he cannot really believe that he is what he has done.

But from the moment of Victor's entrance, when he sheds the social identity of his gun, we are also made to feel the magnetic pull of the memory of family on these characters. The play hints at the subjective mode without ever lapsing into it, and herein lies Miller's particular effect. We are not certain if we are fully in the present or moving slightly back into the past. When Victor plays an old phonograph record, his laughter merges with that of the recording and the first voices of the play bring together past and present.

The action of the first half of Act One consists of the dynamic ebb and flow of the past catching Victor and Esther, and their attempts to shake loose from it and deal with present concerns. Until the entrance of ninety-year-old Gregory Solomon, the appraiser, memory pulls against the material concerns of the present in the minds of Victor and Esther. They both hunger for the family days they knew in the apartment. It was a time of vitality. Things had "style," people laughed then, wonderfully, even if it was to the accompaniment of records. Everyone was "friendlier." The present is full of impermanence, which Esther finds "rotten" and "infuriating." Against this pull of nostalgia, however, Miller shows them to be equally committed to getting the job of life done now in an adult, fairly satisfactory fashion. Braced for an unpleasant experience, they look forward to the evening's celebration after.

The tug between the dislocation of the present and the vitality of the past is made manifest with Solomon's arrival. He is the voice of the past in the business of determining present realities. Solomon's extraordinarily vigorous ninety years are themselves a kind of impingement of the past on the present; and he, too, has his memories of family toward which he drifts on occasion. Moreover, his character is old to the theater. Solomon is a stage Jew, that persistent racial stereotype, which, on the American stage, came out of the vaudeville theater of the nineteenth century, a fact Solomon himself emphasizes in his own fond memories of the comedy team of Gallagher and Shean.[35] Shrewd, witty, wise to the ways of the world, Solomon, with his Yiddish accent and sharp eye for the trade, is a type from the past juxtaposed against the "contemporary" realism of Victor and Esther.

Solomon is more than a conveniently contrasting type, however; he has his own individual drama to play. Having retired from business and living alone, Solomon returns to the world because of Victor's chance phone call. He is called back to life, and his life is that of setting prices. Though reluctant and fearful, Solomon is tempted to resume this most essential life process: giving value, particularly to the past. He is hesitant, and he demands Victor's trust because he knows just how difficult it is to live:

> Let me give you a piece advice—it's not that you can't believe nothing, that's not so hard—it's that you still got to believe it. *That's* hard. And if you can't do that, my friend—you're a dead man! [36]

Solomon's is no simple faith, for he is acutely aware of the impermanence of all things in modern life, whether furniture or philosophies. He deals in the relativity of values. As he says of the furniture:

> So I'm trying to give you a modern viewpoint. Because the price of used furniture is nothing but a viewpoint, and if you wouldn't understand the viewpoint is impossible to understand the price. [37]

This relativity is dangerous, enervating. One must believe despite disbelief, decide things without really knowing what is involved, only to regret and agonize later over what your values and "viewpoint" were in the past. Knowing this, Solomon resists pricing the furniture. To do so means he is recommitted to the painful market economy of life.

Miller's introduction of such abstract themes of Time and Belief are, I think, his attempt to generalize or "universalize" his domestic situation. Though the touch is much lighter here, Solomon, like Alfieri, is supposedly a link with a larger world. We are meant to see him as establishing a connection to fundamental truths, extending the boundaries of the world of the play. But there is, in fact, nothing larger than any of the characters in the play, nothing larger than individual consciousness in conflict with the family. This is Miller's true material; perhaps it always has been. Time and Belief have no dramatic life outside of the individual's sense of lost family and his desire to come to terms with that loss.

No matter that Miller would like this search to be an evocative manifestation of a larger human condition, it leads inward rather than outward—which is why, in Act Two, the play does not move out of the family on the wings of Solomon's wisdom, but back into the family and its contradictory claims.

Act Two is a careful, balanced, and at the beginning too pat confrontation between Victor and his brother, Walter. They are opposites not just as people but as family possibilities. Walter broke with his family, refusing to let it hold him back from rising in the competitive world. He has become a rich and famous doctor (in part through running old folks' "homes," the institutional epitome of nuclear family disruption). But now he has given up the "insanity" of ambition, which ruined his own marriage and distorted his children. He returns to offer Victor his help and friendship. Victor, for his part, stayed with his father after the latter's financial failure, sacrificed a career to keep the household together, and managed to raise an admirable family. Yet he has lived his commonplace life filled with guilt and resentment over being subordinate to his brother as well as to his father. In these two characters are the two possibilities of family life asserting themselves again in our drama. Walter's story is an archetypal model of the escape from family into freedom and independence, while Victor stands for the urge to security and communality. To present these principles in a complex and dramatic debate, Miller reverses the role of each man. Walter now wishes to reestablish family ties while Victor backs away from such commitment and refuses his brother.

The brothers' views of the past are diametrically opposed. To Walter, Victor's sacrifice was fantastical. He feels Victor brought failure on himself by refusing to leave their father out of fear. Victor denies such a choice, asserts need on the father's part, and feels Walter is merely trying to salve a guilty conscience by offering friendship now. Such opposition is the basic mode of Act Two, and we are again pulled to and fro by the tug of the past on the present as Walter and Victor alternately claim our sympathy. Each in his turn seems to have the greater integrity in rearguing the meaning of the past.

This debate drives the play forward increasingly to greater self-revelation and self-awareness. After the simple opposition of conflicting views comes the revelation of the father's hidden money, which sets off a new round of blame and excuse. Victor knew of the money, but could not strip his father of his last shred of dignity by demanding it. Walter denies that the family ever was loving and together. It was always aimed at individual success and ambition, an ethic which proceeded from the father and characterized the entire family circle.

In this debate Miller has catalogued the chief sins and virtues of family life as we have thought about it. The family of security means love, warmth, protection, and mutuality, but it may depend on self-destructive sacrifice which corrodes one's vital will and independence. To flee this domestic tyranny means individuality, free will, and self-expression. Yet such freedom may rely on a brutal disregard for others which eventually isolates and crazes.

At the play's end each brother rejects the other and affirms his own evaluation of family life. Victor will not deny the meaning of his sacrifice and Walter reasserts the necessity of his independence. Victor stays, unforgiving, and Walter leaves, unrepentant. Both reiterate the substance of past family life, for the dilemma is in effect repeated even as it is being evaluated by them. The power of this play depends, finally, on our awareness of each man again assuming a role he thought no longer had meaning for him. The *agon* is an agony.

There is no final winner and the play ends unresolved. Miller emphasizes his intent in his production note:

> A fine balance of sympathy should be maintained in the playing of the roles of Victor and Walter. The actor playing Walter must not regard his attempts to win back Victor's friendship as mere manipulation....
>
> This admonition goes beyond the question of theatrics to the theme of the play. As the world now operates, the qualities of both brothers are necessary to it; surely their respective psychologies and moral values conflict at the heart of the social dilemma. The production must therefore withhold judgment in favor of presenting both men in all their humanity and from their own viewpoints.[38]

The two claims of family are elevated by Miller to our central social dilemma. Yet, paradoxically, he is now saying that we do not escape from the family into the larger world but continue to reenact our family struggles. The self-knowledge which Biff attains at the end of *Death of a Salesman* is now seen to be insufficient, for the larger world is merely the arena where we recreate the family's dilemmas—"what was forfeited to time."

We are not making the world a home; we search for a home in it, the home we remember but with its tensions made explicit. Freedom through family destruction is no longer a possible way out. Miller's dramatic aim is to present each character in his total integrity—"both men in all their humanity and from their own viewpoints"—and in this way to show the impasse between freedom and mutuality. Since both characters have integrity—since their viewpoints are equally valid—Miller treats the dilemma as ironic. With no structure greater and truer than the individual, with no formal element in the play to heal and dissolve differences, the play ends as it begins and we are left with the sound of laughter, not so much mocking life as ruefully admitting to its impossibility.

Miller is saying that we live by our family paradigms, knowing that our beliefs are illusions, and continue to do so despite ourselves. Such inconsistency may be our saving foolishness. When Solomon, alone on stage, plays The Laughing Record to close the play, his laughter blends with the phonograph's as past and present combine to mock us and, as Solomon himself well knows, to keep us going. There is a subtle question of artistry here, of the relation of form to content, for one might ask what *Miller's* saving foolishness is. Does not his stance, as reflected in the complete irony of the form of the play, contradict his thematic insistence that belief is necessary and must follow after disbelief and disillusion—in fact, after irony? How does one act in the third act?

This question aside, what is gratifying about *The Price* is the sense one has of Miller returning to the drama that he does best. Just as the play as a whole represents an artistic recovery in relation to *After the Fall,* so its movement toward rather than away from the basic family materials in Act Two represents a gathering rather than a dissipation of its energies. *The Price* gains in clarity by this concentration, though it might also be argued that it loses some power by refusing to struggle toward a third act, by giving up the question of finding a form which will reflect and project a new conception of the relationship between the individual, family, and society. *Death of a Salesman* remains the best approximation of that form.

In *Long Day's Journey into Night* the individual's struggle within the family, however doomed it might be, was the only drama of significance. At the heart of O'Neill's family ethic was a rejection of social order in favor of the entrapped individual. Freedom did not mean spontaneous harmony but the clash of unrestricted desires. Family pain was inevitable as the individual struggled against confinement and alienation. Miller's image of family struggle is much different in *Death of a Salesman.* There is an end to the Loman family, a clearing away of the obstacles to self-consciousness. Willy's fate is the terrible cost of misunderstanding one's relation to the outer world. Biff survives the family with knowledge that will help him live with himself. There is for Miller, as there was not for O'Neill, a way out of the family dilemma. The painful disintegration of the family brings with it the possibility of a new freedom and sense of identity. This struggle with the family has been typical of most of Miller's plays, and in one way or another he has wanted to end it with the hope of a new connection to the larger world. But more recently, in *The Price,* when Miller explores family relations, he seems to have given up such a hope in favor of irony. Perhaps Miller, our most social playwright, distrusts society as much as he does the family.

NOTES

1. Calhoun, *Social History,* III, 171.

2. Arthur Miller, "The Family in Modern Drama," *Atlantic Monthly,* 97 (April 1956), 35.

3. Ibid., p. 36.

4. Ibid., p. 37.

5. Dennis Welland, *Arthur Miller* (New York, 1961), p. 36. My analysis of Miller is deeply indebted to Welland's excellent book, even when I come to different or opposite conclusions.

6. Arthur Miller, *All My Sons* in *Arthur Miller's Collected Plays* (New York, 1957), p. 81. All citations to Miller's plays are from this edition unless otherwise noted.

7. Ibid., p. 114.

8. Ibid., e.g., pp. 67-68.

9. Ibid., p. 115.

10. Ibid., p. 119.

11. Ibid., p. 126.

12. Ibid., p. 120.

13. Welland, *Miller*, p. 113.

14. Arthur Miller, *Death of a Salesman*, p. 197.

15. Ibid., p. 218.

16. R. Williams, *Modern Tragedy*, p. 104.

17. Miller, "Introduction" to *Collected Plays*, p. 23.

18. Miller, *Salesman*, p. 148.

19. Ibid., p. 180.

20. Ibid., pp. 157-158.

21. Miller, "Introduction," pp. 44-46. He names Brecht as the exemplary dramatist for having moved out of the trap of emotionalism which Miller says is the weakness of modern realism.

22. Ibid., p. 47.

23. Leonard Moss, *Arthur Miller* (New York, 1967), p. 75.

24. Ibid., pp. 66-67. Moss thinks Miller erred in following his historical sources too closely: *Miller,* p. 127, note 8. In my view the difficulty is domestic and more fundamental. Miller identifies the initial impluse behind *The Crucible* as social but the final one as psychological, which for him means the individual in relation to his family. Miller, "Introduction," p. 42.

25. Arthur Miller, *The Crucible,* p. 328.

26. Ibid., p. 323.

27. Ibid., p. 329.

28. I am basing my discussion of the play on Miller's two-act, revised version, which extends the sexual implications of the earlier one-act play.

29. Moss, *Miller,* p. 70.

30. Arthur Miller, *After the Fall* (New York, 1964), p. 70.

31. Two plays by Miller—*A Memory of Two Mondays* (1955) and *An Incident at Vichy* (1965)—are not family plays and so are not pertinent to the discussion. Miller also adapted Ibsen's *An Enemy of the People* (1951) and wrote a screenplay, *The Misfits* (1961).

32. Miller, "Family in Modern Drama," p. 37.

33. Arthur Miller, *The Price* (New York, 1968), p. 4.

34. Ibid.

35. Ibid., p. 35.

36. Ibid., p. 37.

37. Ibid., p. 38.

38. "Production Note," ibid., p. 117.

5

REACTIONS II: FAMILY AND PSYCHE IN TENNESSEE WILLIAMS

> *Much psychological research has suggested the very great importance to the individual of his affective ties, established in early childhood, to other members of his family of orientation. When strong affective ties have been formed, it seems reasonable to believe that situational pressures which force their drastic modification will impose important strains upon the individual....
> We have then a situation where at the same time the inevitable importance of family ties is intensified and a necessity to become emancipated from them is imposed. This situation would seem to have a good deal to do with the fact that with us adolescence—and beyond—is, as has been frequently noted, a "difficult" period in the life cycle.*

Talcott Parsons[1]

Arthur Miller struggled to come to terms with the same family dilemma which O'Neill explored so fully. The American family had failed to achieve its natural harmony, and Miller's reaction was to search the relations between family and society for an answer. Tennessee Williams, too, has reacted to the failed family dream, but in a way opposite to Miller.[2] An inward tendency dominates his dramatic world. He asserts the painful isolation of life against which his characters violently struggle, testing the inner psychological limits of individual existence. O'Neill has rendered this impulse dramatically by trapping the individual within the family, leaving him nowhere else to go, and thrusting him into an iterating cycle of family conflict and destruction. Williams's characters are not trapped in the same way. As in Miller they leave (or are driven out of) the warring family, but the memory of family haunts them relentlessly. Escape from family does not result in a struggle to find a new order to replace family, as in Miller; it means, instead, a desperate search for some anodyne to the pain of being bereft of family.

Rather than Miller's community togetherness or O'Neill's innocent home, William's characters will settle for a moment's peace and tenderness. When even that bare victory is not possible, sex and drugs are the (unsatisfactory) substitute. Those who are defeated possess the special sensitivity needed for that contact which allows a brief moment of surcease from the torment of life. But such sensitivity makes them all the more vulnerable. The most intense expression of their need for love and an end to loneliness is the memory of family, and increasingly William's characters settle for transient groupings which are no longer really families at all.

If in Williams the ideal of family harmony is reduced to brief gestures of kindness, the family itself is an arena wherein the life forces of sex and fecundity are at war with man's spirit. This would suggest that Williams is dissatisfied with the very conditions of existence (which he symbolizes in family life and family ideal). We can go so far as to say that for Williams the family is the primary expression of organized animal vitality antithetical to the life of the spirit. But we cannot go much beyond this generalization, for Williams does little to define the nature and content of this view. He accepts it rather unselfconsciously with no clear sense of the assumptions it entails. He concentrates, instead, on making the individual's painful relationship to his family vivid and theatrically evocative.

Williams's concern with the interior psychological state repeatedly takes him past the boundaries of the realistic theater which O'Neill accepted in presenting the Tyrone family and which Miller tentatively exploited in the Loman family. His is a drama which, in its emphasis on inner reality, moves further and more consistently than Miller or O'Neill toward the subjective.[3] We have nearly left the domestic drama in talking about Tennessee Williams—nearly, but not quite. For if he moves from realism and from the family, he never quite abandons either. Indeed, part of the peculiarity of effect which Williams achieves depends on the maintenance of those connections. And in tracing their outlines, we are measuring the degree to which the realistic family situation continues to attract our playwrights, even those who are avowedly anti-realistic.

Williams's dramatic vision, as Esther Merle Jackson has usefully pointed out, can be seen to take its cue from the consciousness of one character in each play.[4] Looked at in this way, Williams is projecting a lyric moment of that character which is, for him, the play itself. The technical device Williams uses to justify such an effect—and it is significant here that Williams wants a realistic justification—would be the point of view of a character whose perceptions are not limited in, say, the Jamesian sense, but are distorted through memory, insanity, drugs, alcohol, or dreams. But even while we move into the bizarre or exaggerated situation emblematic of the gauzy mind of the protagonist, we are constantly aware that it approximates a realistic situation.

While Williams's family dramas are consistently more lyrical, looser, and more freewheeling than Miller's, they are not given over to the exploration of psychic irrationality. Nor do they exist primarily on the plan of symbolic abstraction or of idealization. Indeed, the whole matter of distortion—as important as it is to a precise understanding of Williams's tone—can be greatly overemphasized. Williams's plays, especially those dealing directly with the family, have a concreteness about them which suggests a calculated intensification of realistic conventions rather than a revolutionary break with these customs. Conversational prose speech, coherent and rationalized plot, everyday situations, and understandable motivation are not absent, but rather are slightly stylized to indicate the intense feelings they inadequately represent. Such exaggeration helps to emphasize the cruelty and destruction of family life. The reality of everyday family experience stands behind Williams's plays, and the effect of many of them depends on an audience saturated in realistic domestic drama.[5]

I think that the crux of the matter is that Williams wanted to break completely with the conventions of realism and that we tend to take his desire as the accomplished fact. In the remarks which preface *The Glass Menagerie* (1945), Williams speaks of the need to move beyond realism to a more "plastic theatre" and defends his flexible use of such devices as projections, music, and lighting in the name of revitalizing the drama:

> The straight realistic play with its genuine frigidaire and authentic ice-cubes, its characters that speak exactly as its audience speaks, corresponds to the academic land-scape and has the same virtue of a photographic like-ness. Everyone should know nowadays the unimportance of the photographic in art: that truth, life, or reality is an organic thing which the poetic imagination can represent or suggest, in essence, only through trans-formation, through changing into other forms than those which were merely present in appearance.
>
> These remarks are not meant as a preface only to this particular play. They have to do with a conception of a new, plastic theatre which must take the place of the exhausted theatre of realistic conventions if the theatre is to resume vitality as a part of our culture. [6]

That Williams is not an artist of the *trompe l'oeil* mode is certain. Perhaps the best example of the theatrical style Williams was reaching toward in his statement can be seen in *Camino Real,* produced eight years later. This play, as Jackson notes, marked a radical break with the realistic theater for Williams. [7] In its insistence on symbolic abstractions, in its episodic plot, and in its lyric intensity of language, *Camino Real* is *the* drama for Williams's plastic theater. Significantly, it does not deal with the family, and so it is also the most radical of his plays in its break with the traditions of American domestic drama.

Almost all of Williams's major plays have muted anti-realistic effects but they do not reproduce the style of *Camino Real.* And this seems to be a deliberate choice on Williams's part. It is not that he fails to write anti-realistic drama, but that he chooses to write something else, something in between "exhausted" realism and plastic theater. The result in his earlier work is a family play rendered plastically. Immediately after *Camino Real,* Williams wrote *Cat on a Hot Tin Roof* (1955), the closest thing to a standard domestic drama that he has done (only the 1960 comedy *Period of Adjustment* seems more orthodox.). This chronology suggests the reluctance of Williams to leave the principal subject and mode of American drama—family dilemmas and realistic domesticity.

Williams has an eclectic mind, and he draws his ideas from a wide variety of sources. [8] He does not pursue ideas for their own sake, but at his best uses them for whatever dramatic effect he needs at a particular moment. Still, the common subject in many— though not all—of his plays is that of family strife. This is particularly true of Williams's plays from 1945 to 1955. In other words, it is true of his best plays: *The Glass Menagerie, A Streetcar Named Desire* (1947), *Summer and Smoke* (1948), *The Rose Tattoo* (1951), and *Cat on a Hot Tin Roof.* [9] Clearly, in these works the struggle with and within the family has been a crucial topic.

After these plays, the question of an overall pattern in Williams's canon is a more difficult one. The chronology is not always clear. Williams has the habit of extensively rewriting his plays years after they have appeared in production and of making long plays out of earlier one-act plays and short stories. Furthermore, symbols and character types reappear constantly. Still, I think a general tendency can be seen in Williams's career to date: he began with plays about family breakdown and since 1955 has moved toward situations in which the characters, left without family but still longing for it, seek a version of domestic comfort. Although his later plays are not as often or as centrally about families, they are haunted by the ghost of the failed family. In other words, Williams found an artistic advantage in staying close enough to the principal tradition of American drama for his plays to have reference point. At the same time and with an original theatrical energy, he has given the effect of freeing his plays from this context. Reserving discussion of *The Glass Menagerie* for the moment, I would like to look briefly at Williams's other family plays to see how he echoes the domestic drama with a voice that is not so disembodied as it seems.

A Streetcar Named Desire is a good case in point. The main action is the fracturing of the old family and the failure to find a new one by Blanche Du Bois. Family failure is multiple in *Streetcar* and is in the background as well as the foreground of the play's action. Blanche, who remained at the family home, Belle Reve, lived through the loss of fortune, family members, and household. Her own marriage ended in her young husband's death, and she is guilt-ridden because of her own cruelty, which was in part responsible for his suicide. To escape from this and the slow, agonized dying of her relatives, Blanche became promiscuous. She arrives at her sister's apartment an example of the enervating decay of the Southern family of security, the last played-out and perverted representative of the beauty and idealism of its gentility.

The play's dramatic structure is, like that of many of Williams's plays, apparently episodic, but is actually closer to the three-act division which realistic drama inherited from the well-made play. The eleven scenes cluster around three units of action which show Blanche being defeated in her last attempts to find support and love through family. The first unit is Blanche's entrance into the world of the Kowalskis and her interference with her sister Stella's marriage in the name of spiritual progress. She is rejected by Stella, who embraces her husband Stanley in a clear choice of alternatives. The next unit is Blanche's attempt to seduce Stanley's friend, Mitch, into marriage, which fails when Stanley learns about her past. Now completely homeless, Blanche is finally destroyed in the last major movement of action and is taken to an asylum. But Blanche is not mad, exactly, only incapable of living within the crossfire of the forces at play in family life. At the end, at the most unexpected moment, she finds a gesture of the special feeling and support she needs and has always needed. The doctor's intuitive gentleness is there along with the terrifying prospect of the institutional "home": "Whoever you are—I have always depended on the kindness of strangers." [10] Those we know best are not nearly so kind.

As I have suggested, Williams opposes Blanche with the crude vitality of Stanley. He has none of Blanche's poetry and yearning for things as they should be ideally; he is full of animal energy, the life force of sex which underpins the family biologically. It is a force which is creative as well as destructive: Stella's labor pains are a counterpoint to her rejection of Blanche's interference in the marriage, and Stanley's rape of Blanche is an ugly contrast to her search for peace and security in marriage to gentle Mitch. Thus Blanche's fate is qualified in an interesting way. We are asked to sympathize with Blanche, even to see her destruction by family forces—with Stanley as the final agent—as tragic. Yet Stella, who rejects Blanche, is a healthy and positive character in many ways.

Early in the play, in rejecting Blanche's hysterical revulsion for her marriage, Stella seems to be opting for health and common sense: "I can't help your trembling if you insist on trembling!"[11] She shows no signs of Stanley's brutality or of Blanche's decadence. The price she pays for being caught between them is a willful self-deception at the end; but her cry for her child is poignant in its reaching for life. Stella is not, of course, the main dramatic interest even at the end; for Williams focuses the penultimate scenes on a lurid expressionistic evocation of Blanche's mind and dramatizes her anguished collapse even before she is raped. We are primarily involved in Blanche's fate as the victim, but the forces embodied in the family make positive as well as negative claims.

The fundamental point here, as in most of Williams's family plays, is that the family is hostile to the spiritual yearnings of his most sensitive characters. It twists the love-seeking of Blanche into nymphomania and finally destroys her. Bereft of family, she is a victim of the impossibility of expressing her need for its warmth and security except through the fleshly desires which create and destroy families. Williams treats the same oppositions in *Summer and Smoke* (1948). Alma Winemiller, like Blanche, yearns for a higher order of things. She does not disintegrate as Blanche does, but sets out on the road to promiscuity in her own belated attempt to find the love she has lost in John Buchanan. She is ultimately converted to a life of the flesh and rejects the deadening spirituality which she has championed and which her own family has represented. The childishness and kleptomania of her mother are a reaction to the suffocating pieties of the world of Reverend Winemiller; and they constitute a comic parody of the fate Alma rebels against. John revels in the flesh throughout the play but is saved at the end from the grossness of Stanley by his own (rather too neat) conversion to idealism. Williams marries him off to an innocent young thing (who develops normally, perhaps because she is sent away from her own corrupted mother at an early age). Williams reworked this play as *The Eccentricities of a Nightingale* (1967), and in the later version he increased his depiction of the suffocating ties of family life.

The dramatic struggle in *Summer and Smoke* between body and spirit is less dominated by the threat of explosive anger and is more schematic than in *Streetcar,* but it is equally painful. In both plays the characters who cannot live in families are more sensitive and finely tuned than those who can. But sensitive people need the family they are denied more desperately than do others. When Blanche thinks she will marry Mitch, she cries: "Sometimes— there's God—so quickly!" [12] Alma offers her sedative tablets to a young man she is picking up: "The prescription number is 96814. I think of it as the telephone number of God." [13] In the earlier play the embrace, the bit of tenderness and love which have replaced heaven, is absolutely the most to be hoped for. In Williams's later plays the more likely anodyne is chemical. These tiny hopes, by their very shrunken nature, measure the enormous difficulty of living with—and without—family.

Another Williams play that juxtaposes these same attitudes, though in a less successful way, is *Cat on a Hot Tin Roof.* Here the family of security is shown to be grasping, avaricious, full of "mendacity," to use the phrase of its leader, Big Daddy. The attractive characters—Big Daddy and his daughter-in-law, Maggie—hate their life in the plantation home and struggle to express the affection they genuinely feel. But in the family, affection is not enough. They are inundated by the other family members. Big Mama pokes and pries about (her husband has only pretended love for years); Gooper, the older son, and Mae, his wife, are caricatures with their horde of children and single-minded devotion to inheriting the family fortune.

Big Daddy struggles to keep order, but clearly he has contempt for his way of living. What he admires is the heritage of love which two homosexuals have left to the house by living there. His impending death gives him perspective on the importance of tenderness and affection in whatever form. Ochello and Straw, the bachelors, had the emotional harmony Big Daddy's family lacks.

The family of security is hateful, but Maggie's refusal to submit to the scheming of her brother-in-law wins the day. She will have the inheritance if she conceives a child. This she vows to do. In *Streetcar* the hatefulness of the family structure was in conflict with Stella's healthy perpetuation of it. The effect in *Cat* is less resonant, however. In this play rather than contrast two powerful claims, Williams is simply in favor of Maggie. She has "life," as Big Daddy says in one of the versions of the play, because Williams makes the other surviving characters two-dimensional (and for the most part unlikable). We are attracted to Maggie as the only fully drawn character left in the world of the play, and we are asked to see her possessiveness as a sign of humanity rather than another example of greed.

Only two of Williams's plays have affirmative images of family life. *Period of Adjustment* (1960), an undistinguished comedy, shows two couples surviving the fears and emptiness of their middle-class lives—the subtitle of the play is "High Point over a Cavern"—to come together at the end in reconciliation, ready and able to make love. *The Rose Tattoo* (1951) celebrates young Rosa finding love through independence from her mother in the subplot, while Serafina learns to give up the lonely ideal of her dead husband for the mutuality of her comic lover in the main action. The mother and daughter separate and are not reconciled at the end; but Serafina is pregnant, full of life again, and the two women are happy, each in her own love. It is apparently only in a Sicilian community in California that Williams can convincingly imagine something resembling a positive family life. As with Miller's *A View from the Bridge,* the special qualities of an alien family are advantageous to the American playwright.

In his next two full-length plays—*Orpheus Descending* (1957; a rewrite of *Battle of Angels* which was produced in 1940) and *Sweet Bird of Youth* (1959)—the families are sensationally destructive and perverse, but family relations are not the main subject so much as the violence of life itself, the conditions of biology and of time, apart from the family experience. The immolation of Val and the castration of Chance provide extreme and theatrically startling resolutions to the actions, but neither man is in conflict with his own family. (In the long one-act play, *Suddenly Last Summer*—1958—the revelation that son Sebastian has been cannibalized by the natives is the finale.) Williams is here beginning to shift away from the struggle within families as his primary dramatic material. When he returns to some semblance of domestic relations, as he does in *In the Bar of a Tokyo Hotel* (1969) and *Out Cry* (1973), the family struggle is no longer the primary dramatic action. In *Out Cry,* for example, its Pirandello-like compounds of role and personality will allow for all sorts of metaphysical interpretations. The brother-sister acting team, who are trapped in a theater, feel compelled to reenact a play which is probably a version of their earlier family life. At this level of reality their play is about life after the murder-suicide of their parents. The action moves into that situation intermittently as the characters enter a domestic world as isolated as their present one.

In such later works the family is gone but is not forgotten. There is now loneliness where there was family encounter, and Williams's characters are haunted by family loss. This is particularly true in *The Night of the Iguana* (1961), *The Milk Train Doesn't Stop Here Anymore* (1963), and *Small Craft Warnings* (1972). Perhaps the clearest statement of what these characters long for is made in the exchange in *The Night of the Iguana*. Shannon, a drunken, defrocked minister, has just proposed marriage to Hannah:

> HANNAH: We make a home for each other, my grandfather and I. Do you know what I mean by a home? I don't mean a regular home. I mean I don't mean what other people mean when they speak of a home, because I don't regard a home as a . . . well, as a place, a building . . . a house . . . of wood, bricks, stone. I think of a home as being a thing that two people have between them in which each can . . . well, nest—rest—live in, emotionally speaking. Does that make any sense to you, Mr Shannon?
>
> . . .
>
> SHANNON: When a bird builds a nest, it builds it with an eye for the . . . the relative permanence of the

> location, and also for the purpose of mating and
> propagating its species.
>
> HANNAH: I still say that I'm not a bird, Mr. Shannon,
> I'm a human being and when a member of that
> fantastic species builds a nest in the heart of anoth-
> er, the question of permanence isn't the first or
> even the last thing that's considered . . . necessarily?
> . . . always? [14]

Shannon's sexuality is a poor substitute for a home, that state of mind where mutuality is possible without pain. And home as an ideal has been reduced in Williams to the little byways, alleys, and odd moments in which some contact is made, where giving and taking are briefly possible. It is no longer the innocent family love or the search for social community. It is totally locked within the heart of his sufferers.

The major dilemmas of family life are imbedded in the dramatic action of Williams's plays, and the ideal that haunts his characters is family-related. Moreover, those plays which have been most successful artistically have been those mostly about the family—the plays up through *Cat on a Hot Tin Roof; Camino Real* is the only exception.

In the earlier plays Williams dramatized the family world in a state of collapse; in later ones family collapse is antecedent to the action. These two situations are combined in *The Glass Menagerie,* Williams's first successful play (and probably his most popular one [15]). The play is a perfect fusion of the two subjects and so is a figure for Williams's entire career. In it the family is long lost and, also, we witness its struggle before it is lost. Williams captures the poignancy of family memories in a way all his own, without sacrificing the core of dramatic conflict which makes such memories less static.

The play is a prime example of Williams's artistry in establishing the relation between his own dramatic world and the conventions of realistic domestic drama to which his audience owes great allegiance, as he well knew. The play occurs in the mind of Tom Wingfield, who drifts in and out of the action both as narrator and participant in a peculiarly appropriate way. From the moment at the beginning when the scrim of the tenement wall dissolves and we enter the Wingfield's apartment, we are reminded of the household of so many family plays. The realistic convention of the fourth wall is evoked as Tom remembers his family.

Tom's evocation is self-conscious, for as "stage manager" he has control over the setting. But Tom is also at the mercy of his memories and irresistibly must relive them. The play keeps us poised between these two styles, these two times, throughout. This is, in fact, its strongest and most subtle conflict. Like Tom, we are continually tempted into the world of a realistic family struggle, but never allowed to enter it completely. The projections and lighting keep the effect slightly stylized during the scenes, the fragmented structure blocks us from too long an absorption in the action, and the reappearance of Tom as narrator forces us back to the present. It is Tom's final reappearance in this role, when the action of the memory play is completed, which releases the tension created between the two styles and dramatizes, in a final rush of emotion, the irretrievable loss of the family which Tom can never escape.

Tom cannot shake the memory of his family from his mind; the dissolution of time and space in the play—that is, in his consciousness—heightens the importance of what he is remembering to make it the most significant thing about his existence. What he remembers—the bulk of the play—centers around two lines of action. The first is his desire to escape from his family just as his father had done before him: "He was a telephone man who fell in love with long distances." [16] Tom, a would-be writer, is caught between a domineering mother and a stultifying warehouse job. He escapes to the porch, to the movies, to the saloon. And finally, in the end, we learn that he has followed his father out into long distances. The second line of action, the principal one, concerns his mother, Amanda, and her attempts to establish some kind of life for Tom's crippled sister, Laura. Amanda pins her hopes on getting "sister" married, after Laura fails because of painful shyness to continue in business school. A "gentleman caller" is found, Jim O'Conner, "an emissary from the world of reality," but all of Amanda's hopes are crushed as he turns out to be already engaged.

The plot is slight stuff, as Williams himself knew. [17] The effect

of the play derives in part from the contrast between its two lines
of action. Amanda is given over to memories of her past life of
happiness as a young southern debutante in Blue Mountain, Mis-
sissippi, where on one incredible Sunday she had seventeen gentlemen callers. She imitates the manners and graciousness of those
days, a faintly ludicrous parody of southern gentility, the played-
out tradition of the antebellum South and its family of security.
But she has spirit, too, and responds to the problems of raising two
children in a St. Louis tenement during the Depression. Her practicality is what gives her dignity; as she cares for Laura we realize
how much Amanda herself needs to be cared for. Her refusal to
give in to her nostalgia, even while she indulges in it, enhances her
character and makes us susceptible to her longing.

Tom is smothered by such a woman. He fights with her, in
part, because she continually tells him what to do: how to eat; how
to sleep; how to get ahead. But he fights, also, because her standards represent the conventionality of family responsibility:

AMANDA: Where are you going?
TOM: I'm going to the *movies!*
AMANDA: I don't believe that lie!
*[Tom crouches toward her, overtowering her tiny figure.
   She backs away, gasping.]*
TOM: I'm going to opium dens! Yes, opium dens, dens
   of vice and criminals, hang-outs, Mother. I've
   joined the Hogan Gang, I'm a hired assassin, I
   carry a tommy-gun in a violin case! I run a string of
   cat-houses in the Valley! They call me Killer, Killer
   Wingfield, I'm leading a double-life, a simple,
   honest warehouse worker by day, by night a dynamic *czar* of the *underworld, Mother.* I go to
   gambling casinos, I spin away fortunes on the
   roulette table! I wear a patch over one eye and a
   false mustache, sometimes I put on green whiskers.
   On those occasions they call me—*El Diablo!* Oh, I
   could tell you things to make you sleepless! My
   enemies plan to dynamite this place. They're going

to blow us all sky-high some night! I'll be glad, very happy, and so will you! You'll go up, on a broomstick, over Blue Mountain with seventeen gentlemen callers! You ugly—babbling old—*witch* . . . .[18]

He can no more accept her memories of genteel home life in Blue Mountain than he can the spirit with which she has managed to carry on. Both suffocate him. The dead family world of the past is as stultifying as the present. Tom feels the need to escape both:

You know it don't take much intelligence to get yourself into a nailed-up coffin, Laura. But who in hell ever got himself out of one without removing one nail?
[As if in answer, the father's grinning photograph lights up. The scene dims out.][19]

The absent father, who still represents the memory of romantic family love to Amanda, is the possibility of romantic escape from family to Tom.[20] He loves his sister Laura, yet he will not accept the responsibility for her which Amanda demands of him. The Wingfields are only a ghost of the family of security, but even this demand to be close-knit repels the restless Tom.

Tom's love for Laura needs to emphasized, I think, not only because it is one part of the final image of the play—the moment of revelation toward which the action tends—but because it shows Williams's interest in the special qualities of those whom the world has hurt. They are the delicate and fragile people, too sensitive to be able to withstand the crude and harsh necessities by which life drives us along. They have an extraordinary awareness of hidden, almost mystical, qualities of spiritual beauty; and this openness dooms them to be crushed or perverted by the animal vigor of the world.

Laura's specialness is seen largely in contrast with Jim, her gentleman caller. He is, by all odds, the kindest of Williams's emissaries from reality, perhaps because his faith in the American

dream of self-improvement and success is so complete as to be itself
a touching illusion:

>JIM *[Going after him]:* You know, Shakespeare—I'm
>   going to sell you a bill of goods!
>TOM: What goods?
>JIM: A course I'm taking.
>TOM: Huh?
>JIM: In public speaking! You and me, we're not the
>   warehouse type.
>TOM: Thanks—that's good news. But what has public
>   speaking got to do with it?
>JIM: It fits you for—executive positions!
>TOM: Awww.
>JIM: I tell you it's done a helluva lot for me.
>*[Image on screen: Executive at his desk.]* [21]

Williams mocks Jim just enough in the use of the slide projection
so that we need not take him seriously, yet he makes Jim's naïveté
spring from high spirits and an openheartedness which is endearing.
He is healthy, happy, and full of hope, but set next to Laura and
her needs he is crude, clumsy, and shallow:

>You know what I judge to be the trouble with you?
>Inferiority complex! Know what that is? That's what
>they call it when someone low-rates himself! [22]

So much for the intricacies of the human personality. To Jim,
Laura's problems are easily solved and he sets about, in his well-
intentioned way, to cure her. First, he persuades her to dance; and
then, caught up himself in the romance of the moment, he kisses
her. But Laura needs more than a kiss, more in fact than Jim could
ever give her. She needs a tenderness and love that she will never
find. Her needs are so great that to satisfy them would mean alter-

ing the real world to fit her, changing it into a world like that inhabited by her glass animals, full of delicacy, beauty, and tender harmony.

When this incompatible couple waltzes into the glass menagerie, they begin to destroy it. At first, Laura does not mind. She is too thrilled with the prospect of being normal to care whether her glass unicorn has lost its distinctive horn. But the accident warns us of what Jim awkwardly confesses after the kiss—that he has made a mistake and will see her no more:

> I wish that you would—say something.
> *[She bites her lip which was trembling and then bravely*
> *smiles. She opens her hand again on the broken*
> *glass ornament. Then she gently takes his hand and*
> *raises it level with her own. She carefully places the*
> *unicorn in the palm of his hand, then pushes his*
> *fingers closed upon it.]*
> What are you—doing that for? You want me to have
> him?—Laura?
> *[She nods.]*
> What for?
> LAURA: A—souvenir. . . .[23]

Laura now knows that she belongs to a different world from Jim. He wandered into a zoo of exotic animals, but that was on his day off and he must return to the workaday world.

There will be no normal love of marriage and family for Laura nor for any of the Wingfields. Laura is too tender, too special, too fragile like her glass menagerie. It is Tom's painful sensitivity to Laura's predicament which makes him love her and which drives him from her. But he cannot escape Laura. The necessity of leaving her and the guilt over doing so, haunt him:

> Oh, Laura, Laura, I tried to leave you behind me, but I
> am more faithful than I intended to be! I reach for

a cigarette, I cross the street, I run into the movies
or a bar, I buy a drink, I speak to the nearest stranger—anything that can blow your candles out!
[Laura bends over the candles.]
For nowadays the world is lit by lightning! Blow out
your candles, Laura—and so good-bye. . . .
[She blows the candles out.][24]

Laura's painful encounter with the world's lightning represents all
of the Wingfields. Amanda's last glance at her husband's picture
reveals as much of her as does Tom's final speech of him. The
family is the supreme case of love trying to struggle against the
world, and the family fails. Fundamentally romantic, Williams
evokes the beauty of failure, the beauty which must fail.

While family life is impossibly difficult, Williams does not
actually reject it. Instead, he allows his characters—and his audience—the full "pleasures" of family nostalgia and suffering. It is
Williams's peculiar ability to do so without bathos. We can savor
the situation because, like Amanda, we are never lost in it uninter-
ruptedly. Williams insures his family memories against outright
sentimentality by a delightful (and convenient) comic touch. He
does not really create a comic perspective, which would change the
meaning of his vision and would suggest the sanity of compromise.
Rather, he edges the serious matter of his plays with humor. For
example, early in *Orpheus Descending* one of the minor characters
declares that most people find hate in marriage and an outlet in
money. Her laughter at this observation is a perfect Williams moment. It conveys his temporary emotional defense against the
painful truth. *Streetcar* is framed in the same way, with a dirty
joke at the beginning and an ironic double entendre at the end:
"This game is seven-card stud." Williams seldom maintains his
comic view, however, since it is for him, and for his strongest
characters, a temporary way of keeping the world at bay. When he
waxes "true," his characters speak directly, often lyrically, and the
ironic edge disappears. Maggie, in *Cat,* has this edge, this style as
part of her character. For her, it is a defense against the suffocating
world of her in-laws. At private moments she may drop this de-

fense; the curtain parts, and we see the loneliness, the isolation, and the gentleness within her. The painful inner lives of his characters remain as desperate as ever, only we are given alternate moments of rest from the hurt.

The distancing in *The Glass Menagerie* is fully and artfully done. In Tom's opening speech, for example, the touch of social comment which appears mocks the world of the middle class as well as itself:

> In Spain there was revolution. Here there was only shouting and confusion. . . . This is the social background of the play. [25]

Later, when this motif reappears, it is directly associated with the dilemmas of the Wingfield family. Their private world looks out on the social world in the same way that their windows look out on the alley. Tom says to the audience:

> Couples would come outside, to the relative privacy of the alley. You could see them kissing behind ash-pits and telephone poles. This was the compensation for lives that passed like mine, without any change or adventure....
> In Spain there was Guernica! [26]

And immediately Amanda unwittingly provides the mocking counterpoint:

> A fire-escape landing's a poor excuse for a porch. *[She spreads a newspaper on a step and sits down, gracefully and demurely as if she were settling into a swing on a Mississippi veranda.]* What are you looking at? [27]

A more often used technique in *The Glass Menagerie* to provide a comic edge is the projection of legends or images onto a wall
in the Wingfield apartment, an element which is frequently dropped
in production. [28] The published editions of the play continue to
retain them. Williams argues that their use is important to maintain
a sense of the play's structure beneath its episodic surface. [29] A
number of the projections do seem to have only this architectural
function: legends such as "After the Fiasco," "You Think I'm in
Love with Continental Shoemaker's?," "High School Hero;"
images such as typewriters or a wintry scene in the park. But many
are obviously funny, sardonic, or ironic as well. Amanda's memories of Blue Mountain are introduced with "Ou Sont Les Neiges
d'Antan?" Tom's desire for adventure brings forth the image of
a sailing vessel with a Jolly Roger. Music, too, is used to evoke
straightforward emotion. "Between each episode it [the theme
tune] returns as a reference to the emotion, nostalgia, which is the
first condition of the play." [30] But music also mocks the characters
as when Amanda's self-pitying reproach to Tom's rudeness is
introduced with "Ave Maria."

Perhaps the most complex use of these alternating effects is
near the end of the play. Laura and Jim waltz to "La Golondrina."
Their kiss is preceded by the symbol of Laura's freakish beauty—a
projected image of blue roses—and swelling music. Then, having
given us the emotional luxury of this melodrama, the legend becomes slightly ambiguous—"Souvenir" anticipates the broken
glass figure Laura will give to Jim, and it also comes directly after
the kiss and may refer to it as well. There is less doubt about the
next legend. Jim's cliché explanation of his feelings for another
girl brings forth the mock-enthusiastic "Love!" on the screen, and
Laura's tender gesture with the broken unicorn ends with a choice
of the legend "Things Have a Way of Turning Out so Badly" or
the harsh image "Gentleman Caller Waving Good-bye—Gaily."
Finally, when Jim tells Amanda he is engaged to another girl, we
read the sardonic "The Sky Falls."

Williams tries to have his sentiment and mock it, too, using
these devices both to intensify the family drama and to pull back
from it. These "plastic" elements, then, are Williams's way of
using the realistic situation while not being exclusively bound to

it. The core of the play is the attempt by Amanda to find a family and the desire by Tom to escape from family. This surface action is alternately heightened and diminished by these nonrealistic devices. We are asked to embrace the characters and to laugh at them, to empathize and then to sympathize. Much of the same strategy can be seen in the dialogue, once we are alerted to it. Amanda's telephone campaign to sell subscriptions to the magazine *Companion* is filled with this juxtaposition of tears and laughter. More poignantly, her memories of her home life in Blue Mountain are made up of a dramatic alternation between vivid nostalgia and shrewd practicality:

> Finally there were no more vases to hold them, every available space was filled with jonquils. No vases to hold them? All right, I'll hold them myself! And then I—*[She stops in front of the picture. Music plays.]* met your father! Malaria fever and jonquils and then— this—boy . . . . *[She switches on the rose-colored lamp.]* I hope they get here before it starts to rain. [31]

Nearly lost in the intensity of her memory, Amanda begins to speak as though the past were the present, only to be brought up short by the reality of her situation. The rose-colored lamp is both a reprise of her vulnerability to charm and an instance of her coping, in the only way she knows how, with the situation in which that vulnerability has placed her: she puts a good light on harsh truths, and she dresses up the faded room to catch the gentleman caller for sister. And one might even say that all the Wingfields get caught out in the rain, away from the warm safety of home. Thus, the drama is embodied in the rhetoric and through its sequential movement each emotionally resonant element is followed by a flat deflation.

Williams uses a similar technique to add a more complex texture to the raw emotions of the Wingfields' family battles. Tom's angry speech denouncing his mother as a witch is slightly muted by his satiric, fanciful tone. But if the direct emotion is reduced in volume, it can also be said that the sense of calculation which Tom's imagery implies makes the hurt Amanda receives all the keener for having been so carefully designed. And in the rare moments when mother and son can talk to, rather than at, each other, Williams manages this shift in tone with greatest delicacy:

> AMANDA: When I was a girl in Blue Mountain and it was suspected that a young man drank, the girl whose attentions he had been receiving, if any girl *was,* would sometimes speak to the minister of his church, or rather her father would if her father was living, and sort of feel him out on the young man's character. That is the way such things are discreetly handled to keep a young woman from making a tragic mistake!
>
> TOM: Then how did you happen to make a tragic mistake?
>
> AMANDA: That innocent look of your father's had everyone fooled! He *smiled*—the world was *enchanted!* No girl can do worse than put herself at the mercy of a handsome appearance! I hope that Mr. O'Connor is not too good-looking.
>
> TOM: No, he's not too good-looking. He's covered with freckles and hasn't too much of a nose.
>
> AMANDA: He's not right-down homely, though?
>
> TOM: Not right-down homely. Just medium homely, I'd say. [32]

The lines play first between Amanda's nostalgia and Tom's blunt irony, and then between her ecstatic memories (with the painful lesson they teach) and Tom's more gentle teasing. At moments such as these, the play's tone becomes a mode of encounter between characters, its surface ingenuity a way of revealing inner lives. The Wingfields exist most vividly when they appear to us caught between moments of direct revelation of their psyches and moments of indirect relief from that painful confrontation. In *The Glass Menagerie* the longing for the family of security is mocked but never abandoned, indulged even as it is shown up.

In *The Glass Menagerie* Williams consciously manipulated his subject matter and his tone, playing off the oppressiveness of the family of security against a teasing stylized realism. He did not grapple with the assumptions beneath the conflicting claims of personal freedom and security, nor did he construct a dramatic action which defined them. Rather, he relied on the evocative power of family strife, running the risk of being merely agitated and pathos-filled as in the soap opera. His family victims are at their most vivid at those points where they are both caught up in their lyrical self-indulgence and at the same time aware of the difficulty in communicating to those around them what they truly feel.

Williams does not test the family attitudes which are his subject. He has evoked family fears and frustrations without probing them. But it is important to recognize the genuine, if limited, appeal of Williams's strategy. He has asked us to see his plays as artifice and as reports on reality. And he has used the artificial, "plastic" elements both to intensify and to relieve the intensity of the family struggles. This paradox is a most intriguing one. He has counted on our familiarity with the family drama, reminded us of it, and then eluded its more rigid restrictions. He has been a realist, if only in part, to refresh our response to the dilemmas of family life. His best plays remind us of our quest for relatedness and independence and so depend on, and contribute to, the very tradition of American domestic drama which he proposed to escape.

NOTES

1. Talcott Parsons, "The Kinship System of the Contemporary United States," *American Anthropologist,* 45 (Jan.-March 1943), 32.

2. Born Thomas Lanier Williams in Columbus, Miss., he was dubbed "Tennessee" for his accent by his fraternity brothers at the University of Missouri. He seems to have adopted the name permanently about 1938 in his Bohemian years in

New Orleans: "I think it helped me. I think it caught people's eyes." Nancy Tischler, *Tennessee Williams: Rebellious Puritan* (New York, 1961), pp. 62-63. Quotation appears on p. 63.

3. For an extended analysis of American drama in terms of its expressionist elements, see Louis Broussard, *American Drama: Contemporary Allegory from Eugene O'Neill to Tennessee Williams* (Norman, Okla., 1962).

4. Esther Merle Jackson, *The Broken World of Tennessee Williams* (Madison, Wis., 1965), pp. 26-42.

5. Jackson's book, the most suggestive and insightful yet done on Williams, argues the opposite point: Williams is an anti-realist whose work embodies—at one point she says it inaugurates—a third phase in the development of modern, expressionist form. Ibid., pp. viii, 20-42.

6. Tennessee Williams, "Production Notes," *The Glass Menagerie* in *The Theatre of Tennessee Williams,* I (New York, 1971), 131—hereafter volumes in this edition cited as *Theatre.*

7. Jackson, *Broken World,* p. 110.

8. Jackson has tried to systematize Williams's thought by describing three rather vague "myths" around which Williams's plays are built: the myth of the theater, the myth of the American, and the myth of psychology. These "synthetic" myths, she feels, ally Williams with Kandinsky, Sartre, Nietzsche, Sophocles, Shakespeare, Strindberg, as well as Christian, Freudian, and Jungian systems. (Ibid., pp. 43-67.) On balance, it is more a tribute to her ingenuity than to Williams's profundity.

9. I do not mean to imply that because all his good plays are family plays, all the family plays are good. Some family plays are well below the mark set by his best works; e.g., *Kingdom of Earth (The Seven Descents of Myrtle)* (1968). I have excluded from consideration *You Touched Me!* (1945) which is a collaboration (with Donald Windham).

10. Tennessee Williams, *A Streetcar Named Desire* in *Theatre,* I, 418.

11. Ibid., p. 322.

12. Ibid., p. 356.

13. Tennessee Williams, *Summer and Smoke in Theatre,* II (1971), 254.

14. Tennessee Williams, *The Night of the Iguana* in *Theatre,* IV (1972), 356-357.

15. Jackson, *Broken World,* p. viii, note 1.

16. Williams, *Menagerie,* p. 145.

17. "A free, imaginative use of light can be of enormous value in giving a mobile, plastic quality to plays of a more or less static nature." Williams, "Production Notes," *Menagerie,* p. 134.

18. Ibid., pp. 163-164.

19. Ibid., pp. 167-168.

20. Tischler, *Williams,* p. 97.

21. Williams, *Menagerie,* p. 199.

22. Ibid., p. 220.

23. Ibid., pp. 230-231.

24. Ibid., p. 237.

25. Ibid., p. 145.

26. Ibid., p. 179.

27. Ibid., p. 180.

28. The original New York production and the recent revival both omitted the projections. Without them the play is moved even closer to the conventional realism of domestic drama, a tendency which can also be seen in the Broadway productions of *Streetcar,* which have deemphasized the expressionist elements in such scenes as those presenting symbolic images of Blanche's mental state.

29. Williams, "Production Notes," p. 132.

30. Ibid., p. 133.

31. Ibid., p. 194.

32. Ibid., p. 186.

6

THE FAMILY
WORLD OF
AMERICAN DRAMA

Authority is contrary to the whole value scheme of democratic freedom which we have chosen although not yet put fully into effect. It is our democratic faith that the smooth order, the good manners, and all the other advantages of authoritarian society are purchased at too high a price, and that the greatest happiness, despite difficulties and many individual breakdowns, lies in the long run in a freer social order in which family and primary group life are the most important segment.

Joseph Kirk Folsom [1]

Don't join too many gangs. Join few if any.
Join the United States and join the family—
But not much in between unless a college.

Robert Frost [2]

This is you. This is your life.

Announcer's logo for
the serial *Rosemary*

American drama replays its dilemmas again and again. The struggle to leave and the longing to stay are not only motives of individual plays. They inform the careers of playwrights and shape our drama as a whole. The history of American drama in the twentieth century, our drama of importance, is not simply one of progressive development or step-by-step change. It is a history caught in the logic of its own material; plays, playwrights, and generations alike circle back over old ground on their way to new.

Part of the difficulty of any history of American drama is that O'Neill burst on the scene after a century and a half of derivative and second-rate plays. He was our first important playwright and our most important playwright. Because he grasped the full significance of the materials of family life which make up our drama, our playwrights all stand in his shadow. This does not mean that they imitated him or that he created a "school" of followers. The case is more interesting than that. Among a diverse group of playwrights, with their various themes and innumerable character types, is a common tendency, a thread which ties them together: the source of dramatic energy is the action of family struggle and personal dilemma.

While changes from decade to decade are real, important patterns recur. The first achievements in realism in the twenties, the social comedy and drama in the thirties, the post-World War II emphasis on alienation and the individual, and the new voices and forms of the sixties—all show the marks of our allegiance to the drama of self and mutuality. Looked at in this way, continuities can be seen as well as discontinuities. The picture becomes interesting and confusing as patterns reappear, sometimes in unlikely places. It turns out there are many different families in American drama whose agitations and crises are variations of each other. O'Neill established our family drama, while Miller and Williams represent major attempts to extend the social and personal limits inherent in that material. Other important variations can be seen in the works of Lillian Hellman, Clifford Odets, Edward Albee, Lorraine Hansberry, and Thornton Wilder. I will look at their versions, at lines of similarity and difference, to suggest the compulsive, circular quality of our dramatic literature.

Lillian Hellman dramatized subjects other than the family but generally as an adapter. [3] As with Arthur Miller, her strength as a social writer seems directly related to the subject of the self against the family, although the Hubbard family, her most vivid creation, is otherwise nothing like the Lomans. The saga of the Hubbards begins in *Another Part of the Forest* (1942), although this play was written after *The Little Foxes* (1935). In it we see the beginnings of the family's internal struggle for power and domination, a struggle which is meant to particularize the ruthless economic power and domination which they wield over their community. The Hubbards are grasping, vicious predators feeding off the Reconstruction South as they claw their way upward. In *Another Part of the Forest* they are merchants in a broken agricultural economy; in *The Little Foxes* they help bring industrialism, which means more power and more profits for them.

The Hubbards are victimizers—in melodramatic terms, the villains. Their history begins with Marcus Hubbard, the father of the clan, ruling and exploiting his family just as the family does the community. *Another Part of the Forest* is a play in which the son triumphs over the father, but Ben's "liberation" is not an escape from family but an extension of it. He is the outcome of his father's ruthlessness, the fulfillment of his father's spirit. Ben becomes the dominant Hubbard. The wealth he has blackmailed from his father gives him power over others. His sister, Regina, who plays the role of ladylike subservience to gain some advantage for herself, longs fiercely for the same power. Her passion, which attracts men to her in both plays, is put under a terrible discipline. She becomes rock hard yet extraordinarily vital, a combination of cool villainy and hot desire that is developed in *The Little Foxes* into one of the most commanding and repellent female characters on the American stage.

In fact, *The Little Foxes* is a richer play on many counts. It is Hellman's most successful work, and the one where we see to full effect the viciousness of the Hubbard family. As agents of exploitation they are incomparable. Hellman, like Miller, writes in the tradition of the well-made play which Ibsen turned into a vehicle for serious drama. She carefully structures the action in a close-knit progression of events. Crescendos of violence are prepared for and built toward as the suspense rises within each act and in the play as a whole. The action is a series of power struggles from which Regina's daughter, Alexandra, will finally escape. She frees

herself from her mother's domination not to continue the family
exploitation but to end it:

> You couldn't [make me stay], Mama, because I want to
> leave here. As I've never wanted anything in my life
> before. Because now I understand what Papa was trying
> to tell me. All in one day: Addie said there were people
> who ate the earth and other people who stood around
> and watched them do it. And just now Uncle Ben said
> the same thing. Really, he said the same thing. *(Tensely)*
> Well, tell him for me, Mama, I'm not going to stand
> around and watch you do it. I'll be fighting as hard as
> he'll be fighting *(Rises)* someplace else. [4]

The social implications of this speech, intrinsically strong,
were even greater in 1939 with the Depression and the Spanish Civil
War on the minds of the audience. Dramatically, the cry for social
justice and the demand for action are expressed as the escape from
family. The oppressive family with its power struggles is the paradigm for a rapacious social order that needs to be changed. Alexandra is out to start a new life for herself and for the world. She
will not make the mistake of her father, whose fatal attraction to
Regina and a life of compromise with the Hubbards of the world
left him with no authority, physically and morally spent, without
the power to effectively oppose his wife. The best he can do is turn
things over to the younger generation. The counter to despair in the
face of Ben's cold confidence and Regina's hardness is the triumphant hope for freedom through the rejection of family.

The Little Foxes was Hellman's best, though not only, effort
at fusing family struggles with social forces. *Days to Come* (1936),
Watch on the Rhine (1941), and *The Searching Wind* (1944) all
made the attempt with varying success. In *Days to Come* and *The
Searching Wind* the public and private realms are meant to illustrate each other. The upper-middle-class characters mess up their
domestic lives with the same disregard for hard reality which they
have for social and political questions. These characters are dan-

gerous because they have power to affect others but lack judgment. In *Watch on the Rhine* Hellman does create something like a successful family with the Müllers when Sara Müller returns to her childhood home with her husband and children. This family does not last, however, for Müller must go off to his death as an underground agent in the fight against fascism. His son will follow when he comes of age. The heroism of Müller teaches Sara's mother and brother to bury the domestic hatchet.

In Hellman the healing of wounds is not as convincing as the opening of wounds. When she concentrates on that situation, it is, with or without social implications, much more vivid. *Toys in the Attic* (1960), for example, attempts no direct equation of the Berniers family with social forces. Its scope is narrow but within its limits there is an intensity of effect which is unmatched by any of her other plays, except for those dealing with the Hubbards. *Toys in the Attic* shows what happens if you do not leave home, even if the home contains "nice" people rather than Ben and Regina.

The family structure is maintained because of the continual failure of the brother, Julian, to make good in his business dealings. In fact, his sisters, who keep a home waiting for him, need his failure in order that he will need them. The Berniers's family life is based on the self-delusion of benign togetherness which hides the reality of power struggles, incestuous love, and warped personalities. It is a portrait of unrelieved unpleasantness. One of Julian's sisters does recognize the truth of their lives but, like the rest of her family (which comes to include Julian's vacuous, disturbed young wife), she finds nowhere to go at the end. As in the Tyrone family the Berniers have no one but each other, although Hellman does not explore the drama of their facing that fact as does O'Neill. The destructiveness of family is her subject. In most of her plays, even in *The Autumn Garden* (1951) where she attempts a looser, less concentrated structure of a larger household, the corrosive effect of enclosed family is the central situation of her dramatic world. She is at her best when presenting a well-made family war.

Clifford Odets also has family life at the center of his plays. Although he is a very different sort of social realist than is Hellman, he, too, uses the intolerable family situation as an indicator of the need for social change. The old family must be destroyed along with the failing social and economic system. The family battle is a paradigm for the political battle which needs to be waged. This can be seen most strikingly in *Awake and Sing!* (1935), Odets's first full-length play.

Originally, Odets titled his play *I Got the Blues*, and, taken together, the titles suggest the two dominant moods of the play (and of the Depression era)—frustration and faith. The first two acts of the play dramatize the frustration, while in the short third act decisive and positive choices are made. We see the members of the Berger family struggle to survive, to make something new of their lives, or to escape. All of them have dreams, and the play reveals these dreams and the frustration of their crowded, trapped lives. Until near the end of the play, the characters aimlessly acquiesce to the tyranny of the mother, Bessie, and allow her strength to hold their lives together.

It is the son, Ralphie, who learns to act, and he does so by facing down his mother. The suicide of the grandfather, Jacob, brings him to a realization of the shallowness and hypocrisy of his mother's values. He rejects her authority, claims Jacob's books and his room, and becomes the effective heir to his grandfather's ineffective preachments on making a better life. When he goes on to encourage his unhappily married sister, Hennie, to run off with the man she loves, it is the final breaking down of the old Berger family system and, dramatically, it is confirmation that the larger social system will change also. A new day has come to this family and Ralphie will carry his message down to the warehouse and eventually across America:

Sure, inventory tomorrow. Coletti to Driscoll to Berger—that's how we work. It's a team down the warehouse. Driscoll's a show-off, a wiseguy, and Joe talks pigeons day and night. But they're like me, looking for a chance to get to first base too. Joe razzed me about my girl. But he don't know why. I'll tell him. Hell, he might tell me something I don't know. Get teams together all over. Spit on your hands and get to work. And with enough teams together maybe we'll get steam in the warehouse so our fingers don't freeze off. Maybe we'll fix it so life won't be printed on dollar bills.[5]

Odets's subsequent plays are all, in one way or another, about domestic life even though the direct equation between family struggle and social struggle began to weaken in *Rocket to the Moon* (1938), *Clash by Night* (1941), and *The Big Knife* (1944) and disappeared in his last plays, *The Country Girl* (1951) and *The Flowering Peach* (1954). Michael J. Mendelsohn has suggested that Odets began his career in rebellion against the family and ended it in an affirmation.[6] According to Mendelsohn's argument, in the early short plays—*Waiting for Lefty* and *Till the Day I Die* (both 1935)—family loyalty must give way to working class solidarity as in each case a man abandons his brother in favor of the revolutionary good. In *Awake and Sing!* and *Paradise Lost* (1935) the family mirrors society's wrongs and must be abolished on that account. Starting with *Golden Boy* (1937) Mendelsohn sees a change in Odets from rebellion to "an essential groping for family by characters who are homeless."[7] *Night Music* (1940) shows this most strongly. By the time of *Country Girl* the family is reunited and no longer even dissolved. Finally, in *The Flowering Peach* the family is solidarity and love.

The outline of Mendelsohn's argument is instructive but one-sided. There is a mix of two contrary attitudes—yearning and rejection—in each of Odet's plays. The dominant attitude shifts in the direction Mendelsohn indicates—from rejection to yearning—but the opposite, alternate attitude is always present. For example, in *Awake and Sing!* the major dramatic fact is the breaking of Bessie's control over her family and so the breaking of the old system. But it is also important, though not as preeminent, that while Hennie leaves, Ralphie does not. He rejects his mother's values but chooses to stay in the household. Hennie must go to find her freedom but Ralphie can find his without making a similar break. We might say that Odets measures their capacities by their different fates. Ralphie learns to see beyond his immediate needs in a way Hennie does not. Both break out of the old system but Ralphie is more profoundly liberated since he can stay and work for the changes necessary.

This sort of ending is unusual in American drama, where staying within the family is most often a sign of defeat rather than of greater maturity. So it would be for Hennie. But Ralphie accommodates in a special way, which indicates Odets's reluctance to destroy the family totally, even in a play which uses the family struggle as a dramatic springboard to political struggle. The celebration of freedom from family tyranny has along with it a gesture of family maintenance.[8]

To argue that the plays from *Awake and Sing!* to *The Flowering Peach* have a shifting mixture of family rejection and family yearning is to say that Odets's plays embody elements of both the family of security and the family of freedom. He is attracted to the warmth and nurture of close family life yet distrusts it. In fact Odets tries to resolve his contradictory attitudes by dramatizing family destruction as leading to family affirmation. In this way he can have the energies of the struggle and the hope for harmony. In *Awake and Sing!* Jacob paraphrases Marx but with a change: "Marx said it—abolish such families."[9] Odets does not want to abolish *the* family, only *such* families. *Paradise Lost* finds a last-minute hope in the breakup of the old system. The rebellion in *Golden Boy* ends with an image of a family solidarity that might have been. *Night Music* looks ahead to the family that will fight for justice. The paradox seems to be that Odets has to destroy the family—dramatically—to save it—thematically.

Awake and Sing! and *The Little Foxes* appeared the same year and in some ways represent quite separate dramatic worlds. Hellman's realism has an historical setting in the rural South while Odets's is contemporary, urban, and Jewish; Hellman deals with—is fascinated by—the agents of social injustice as well as their victims while Odets is concerned only with the latter; Hellman's structure, derived from Ibsen, is one of tight, logical construction while Odets creates a surface of seemingly random, even haphazard, events and conversations, an ebb and flow of everyday life which, for two acts at least, is closer to Chekhov.[10] Yet these two plays share a dramatic pattern by which each puts family struggles at the service of an indictment of social and political conditions: in both plays the destructive family is dominated by a strong mother, who is in some sense villainous and against whom the father is ineffective; in both the death of a father-figure, who knows truer values but cannot act, educates and liberates the young person; and both have a triumphant resolution in which the young person declares opposition to the family's values. Liberation from the family stands for rebellion against an oppressive or rapacious system. The family is dramatized as a corrupting battleground which needs to be opposed and changed. The rebellion of the young person from parental ties is, then, an heroic act directly equated with social and political revolution. The final optimistic triumph is, in each play, an indication of the political sentiments of the times, but the core emotion which makes these sentiments ring out at the play's end is produced by the drama of self against family.

O'Neill finds the desire to escape from the family to be an act of self-destruction. In their early plays, Odets and Hellman equate the destructive family with the destructive society and see escape as heroic rebellion. Rather than the deadlocked families of O'Neill, they write of family change in relation to the social condition. Thus they seem to anticipate Miller's social concerns and so to "fit" between O'Neill and Miller. Their use of the family as social report is simpler than Miller's. It is the world writ small in which family relations equal politics. After their plays Miller begins to explore the complexity of family in relation to society. He uses the struggle to escape as one of several elements in his drama, and he searches out the responsibilities and costs involved.

Such a scheme has a rough development to it which is useful as long as we remember that it must be qualified by the overall careers of these playwrights. Odets's attitude toward the family is less consistent than Hellman's, less well thought through. He has a richer response to the possibilities of family life. From the beginning he is attracted to family mutuality as well. Hellman runs less risk of sentimentality, of simply wanting to have it both ways. She is more consistently repelled by family life. Yet in their later plays both begin to examine what life would be like if we did not escape from the family. There is a shift from the drama of rebellion to the drama of staying within the family. For Odets, this has positive aspects; for Hellman, it is negative. In both, family rebellion as social gesture gives way to family life which persists and is not broken.

This pattern repeats itself, but not in the next generation of Miller and Williams. Miller in a recent play and Williams from the outset emphasize the persistence of family memories and the sense of loss which haunts us. But they have not returned to the family as it is before rebellion, escape, and loss. Surprisingly, it is in the family plays of Edward Albee that elements of this pattern reassert themselves and we can see American drama beginning another recapitulation, using familiar materials in a new context.

Edward Albee seems to have little in common with either Odets or Hellman, to belong to a newer generation of American playwrights who have broken with the dilemma faced by O'Neill, Miller, and Williams. Albee is part of the avant-garde of the 1960s, a movement which defined itself in opposition to the Broadway status quo. Located Off-Broadway—later Off-Off-Broadway— these writers energetically thumbed their noses at the conventions of bourgeois realism. They sought to revitalize the theater by outraging the audience. To this end they embraced all manner of theatrical experimentation and political radicalism, were fond of the satiric put-on, and admired European writers, especially the existentialists and Brecht.

Albee's first plays—four one-acts—established him as the leading figure of this movement, and he was identified as the best American example of the Theater of the Absurd.[11] But if we look closely at his works, we can see early on a preoccupation with the bankruptcy of family life. This theme is in the background of *The Zoo Story* (1959), Albee's first play and the one which launched his career, and is touched on briefly in *The Death of Bessie Smith* (1960). In *The Sandbox* (1960) and *The American Dream* (1961)— which are expressionistic in style rather than realistic—he moved the family on stage to attack it directly. These plays are clever cartoons of family life. Using such characters as Mommy, Daddy, and Grandma, Albee satirizes the middle-class family as mindless, sterile, and cruel.

If life seems absurd in these plays, it is because something worthwhile has been destroyed by the family. Albee is disappointed by the outcome of the American dream, and his short plays edge toward a direct presentation of the family struggle. When Grandma stops the play at the end of *The American Dream,* it is for fear things will get out of hand; if the play continues it will have to show what really happens in family life. And that is no comedy for Albee. Some things are too important for laughter. There is a larger emotion to be conveyed, a more suffering fate to be presented. This is the subject of his first full-length play.

Who's Afraid of Virginia Woolf? (1962) picks up on the attitudes Albee sketched out in his one-acts. It is a full—perhaps fulsome—picture, and the play's size and energy suggest that this was what Albee had wanted to write about all along. Once more in American drama we are back on a realistic family battleground. In Albee's version George and Martha, a middle-aged couple, attack each other with great skill and cruelty because they fear the emptiness of their lives. In addition to the family strife in their backgrounds, the condition of their marriage is vicious disharmony, a fact which is compounded by their refusal to face it. Instead, they substitute and hide behind a private illusion of family. But this illusion, their "son," is self-defeating.

In their differing versions of the son's life, George and Martha present an especially bitter picture of the family. Each uses the son as a way to attack the other's inadequacies. As this particular battle rages, we have multiple images of family failure: Martha's claim that the son is ashamed of his father's weakness; George's disclosure that the son cannot stand Martha's sexual advances; and the spectacle of these stories being told, that is, the enactment of George and Martha's mutual need to invent the son and the purposes to which they put their fiction.

The subject is the American dream again, the dream of an ideal family life which Albee inverts in order to debunk. As a realist he wants to show us what domestic life is really like. But Albee also wants us to draw the widest possible lessons from what we see. The play strains to make these identifications. *Who's Afraid of Virginia Woolf?* is filled with touches which are meant to make it highly representative. The family equals fate, not only for the private person but for the nation and even western civilization. To begin with, the names George and Martha remind us of George and Martha Washington. Albee enjoys the irony in the historical fact that "the father of our country" had no children of his own. American life, then, is barren and we have had to create the fiction that it is otherwise. Whenever domestic metaphors appear, they indicate deception or fraud.

Then, too, Albee suggests all sorts of different tensions which are meant to symbolize cultural dislocation. For example, the rivalry between George and his guest, Nick, is identified with the tension between humanism and science, in turn a contest between unpredictable freedom and totalitarianism. He places George and Martha in a town named New Carthage, thus suggesting the Punic Wars and annihilation. The more contemporary enmity between America and China is also hinted at, along with nuclear warfare. What these clashes mean is summarized when George reads aloud from a history book. It amounts to a short soliloquy:

> 'And the west, encumbered by crippling alliances, and burdened with a morality too rigid to accommodate itself to the swing of events, must . . . eventually . . . fall.' *(He laughs, briefly, ruefully . . . rises, with the book in his hand. He stands still . . . then, quickly, he gathers all the fury he has been containing within himself . . . he shakes . . . he looks at the book in his hand and, with a cry that is part growl, part howl, he hurls it at the chimes. They crash against one another, ringing wildly. . . .)*[12]

We do not need to ask for whom these bells clang. Again in American drama we are shown that the prophecy of harmony has failed. "When you want to change something," says George, "you BANG! BANG! BANG! BANG!"[13] The pun links sex and violence. Private neurosis and domestic strife are meant to equal history. This bang may be the way the world ends.

The foreboding prophecy of our decline as exemplified in family failure is very pessimistic, but not hopelessly so. In the end illusions are faced and appearance gives way to reality in a final dramatic reversal. The most hidden truth is revealed when we in the audience learn (at the same time as do the guests, Nick and

Honey) that the son is a fiction. Such a pattern of action does not suggest meaninglessness or total despair. Moreover, after a long and carefully structured family war, George and Martha arrive at a changed relationship. Some significant difference is made in their lives. However harsh the words or emotions, the process of disillusionment brings them to a core of truth which is meant to be healthy.

In fact, what is beneath the surface of the vicious peekaboos played by George and Martha is sincere feeling; more particularly, love. For the greater part of the play, domestic warfare overwhelms any hints of genuine attachment. The marriage seems to be turning from hatred to final dissolution. The relationship has gone "snap." However, in the final act Albee reverses this movement. First he saves Martha from adultery (and hints that her reputation in this regard is exaggerated). Then, in a series of speeches we are shown that underneath Martha's brash exterior is a person of tenderness and vulnerability. She talks wistfully about her father and ends by revealing it is George whom she loves best and who best loves her. If this were an eighteenth-century play, we would note immediately that it is a drama of sentiment and say that Albee has redeemed Martha by showing she has a feeling heart. When Martha returns to her brawling ways, we are to see her in a new light for we are aware of the needs and weaknesses beneath that rough exterior. Martha can now be an object of pity as we see George close in on her with the news of their son's death.

George, too, is changed in the final act. He has been a weakling but turns out to be stronger than Martha. In announcing that he no longer cares for Martha (and pelting her with *snap*dragons), he may be only pretending in order to disarm her. More likely he thinks he means it. But in the process of destroying the illusion of the son, he apparently comes to realize he loves her still. A cruel game turns into therapy. At the point at which the son is revealed to have been imaginary, George and Martha find that they can share something, the confession of their sterility. What would have been ammunition for an attack becomes a touch of togetherness. The gentle tone of the final section which follows seems to confirm this mutuality of feeling. Having lasted through Saturday night, they are alone together at the beginning of Sunday to face each other in a tone not exactly hopeful but suggesting that hope might be possible. Now that false ideals and values are destroyed, something might come from facing each other truthfully.

After the outburst of his first long play, Albee is drawn back to the family subject in two of his subsequent works. He dramatizes other matters and experiments with more inaccessible forms but returns to the struggles of family life. Albee's career alternates between family plays, which express his anger and disappointment, and excursions into theatrical conundrums, which are meant to reassure his audience that he is not a traditional American playwright. The line of consistency in his career is his picture of the family at war: *A Delicate Balance* (1966) and *All Over* (1971) continue to present that image in between the metaphysical puzzle of *Tiny Alice* (1964), the experimental form of *Box and Quotations from Chairman Mao Tse-Tung* (1968), and the fantasy-allegory of *Seascape* (1975).[14]

It needs to be said, however, that while the family battleground is his recurring subject, Albee's presentation of it changes somewhat in the two later family plays. The possibility of escape from family confines seems much more remote as actual rather than symbolic families are presented. The tone of these plays is increasingly subdued, with periodic outbursts of emotion rather than the sustained energy of *Who's Afraid of Virigina Woolf?* Increasingly, Albee's characters give up the battle to escape from family. In Albee's earlier work there was less despair. Grandma jauntily opposed her family and George and Martha finally broke through its artifice, though their future was not guaranteed. But where George and Martha destroy their symbolic family to face one another truly, the characters in *A Delicate Balance* and *All Over* continue to use the family arrangement as a pretense behind which to hide. They are attracted to the family structure not because of the love or nurture it affords but because for Albee the family is the way we have devised to avoid facing the truth about our own selfish natures: we are alone, isolated, unable to give love but screaming to be loved. The family is an hypocrisy which we support by lying to ourselves. In *Who's Afraid of Virginia Woolf?* the characters just manage to break out of the lie. In *A Delicate Balance* and *All Over* the truth is so overwhelming that the characters refuse to accept it, though they cannot fully suppress it.

As with most American playwrights, Albee's motive is to show there is no family harmony. In reality (through realism) the family is a destructive battleground and the urge to dramatize the bloodshed is one of the main sources of energy. Family struggle is still *the* drama and the family world is claustrophobic. Clearly, Albee is reluctant to give up the subject, and he uses it to illustrate 1960s themes of conformity, alienation, and despair.

In Albee's most successful play, *Who's Afraid of Virginia Woolf?,* the dramatic pattern is a variation on a familiar design: a long wrangle after which the crucial action is to break out of the family. By echoing the escape motif, Albee is basing his play on a recurring pattern in American drama, one that we have seen in our major playwrights from O'Neill on. And, as with some of our playwrights, Albee moves from the subject of family breakdown to that of the family as a continuing situation. The alternative to showing escape is showing what happens if you stay; the complement to rebellion is oppression.

The family is a trap, as usual, in American drama. In Albee's version of an alienated family world, it is one we enter willingly. The image is not that of young people struggling to escape from their elders as in the early plays of Odets and Hellman. Nor are there the more complex family struggles of Miller and Williams. O'Neill's dilemma of counterclaims is too demanding. Albee's family is the villain because it is a projection of the spiritual defeat of its members. There is no freedom, only selfish ego; security is a deadly hypocrisy rather than an ambiguous support. The bourgeois family is beat. [15]

The avant-garde from which Albee came was not the only new movement in the theater of the 1960s. A generation of young black playwrights also began producing work. The realistic drama of family life seems to be an important staple for these writers, too, though its meaning differs. Any discussion of the trends and characteristics of recent black drama must be tentative, however dogmatic, for a great deal of experimentation (especially in one-act plays) has been going on in pursuit of a black aesthetic, a new tradition of style as well as of substance. Adrienne Kennedy and Leroi Jones have written especially powerful and original short pieces, but it is not at all clear that their radical experiments with form will have a lasting influence. Playwrights such as Ed Bullins and Charles Gordone may be more typical of this generation. Their style shows a basic allegiance to realism somewhat modified by expressionistic devices which allow them to range freely through a panorama of black life. Black drama, then, is still in the process of developing its mature traditions. Just how dominant a mode the realistic family play will be has yet to be decided, though it has certainly been important to date.

When speaking of plays of black family life, another factor should be kept in mind. The sociology which stands behind such plays is a complex and somewhat discrete variant within the general framework of the American family. Black family life has its own history and ideology, the formal debate on which began with E. Franklin Frazier's work and continues today. However, since the question here concerns the images produced by and for the dominant culture, it is useful to compare black family plays to the larger family world of American drama. When we do, we see an unusual picture; the black family is often a sustaining and nurturing force. This is true in such recent successes as *The River Niger* (1972) by Joseph A. Walker and *What the Wine-Sellers Buy* (1974) by Ron Milner. Not that there is any lack of family conflict in these works. And, as in many white family plays, this conflict is the vehicle for the themes of the plays. Protest against racism, pride in African heritage, and the question of achieving one's identity are the issues. In the dramatic action of these plays, the young protagonist associates his family with an evil—such as acquiescence to white domination—but learns to appreciate his family and its support in his fight against that evil, though he will fight it in a new way. Thus the family is neither rejected nor merely tolerated, but needed. This need can be shown through the failure of family life, too. In a play such as *Ceremonies in Dark Old Men* (1969) by Lonne Elder III, the decline of the family means the degeneration of the father and his sons, who refuse to accept responsibility for its maintenance. Here the destruction of the family is to be mourned as a loss, a casualty of social oppression and personal failing. Typically in plays of black family life, the struggle against the family ends neither in freedom nor in anguish, but in an affirmation, direct or implied, of the family as a life-giving resource. [16]

The best of these newer plays of black family life is still Lorraine Hansberry's *A Raisin in the Sun* (1959). Like Odets, Hansberry writes a realistic social drama of the struggle for life by little people, in this case the Youngers, a black family which is crowded into an apartment even smaller than that of the Bergers. They have, as one member of the family puts it, "acute ghetto-itus." Here, too, the family is held together by a strong mother, Lena, known as Mama; and the dead father-figure provides the possibility for change in their lives through the legacy of his insurance money. But escape from family is not the solution or even, really, the issue. Instead, the play celebrates the family as the anchor by which the individual maintains pride, sense of purpose, and resilience in the face of social injustice and personal despair.

For Mama, the four generations of Youngers and the example of her dead husband, Big Walter, have made her own struggles worthwhile; in fact, her family heritage has made survival possible by giving her an example of dignity and integrity. Her son, Walter, discovers the same resource. In the end he must decide if he will take money, which he desperately wants, from whites who wish to keep the Youngers out of the neighborhood. Mama forces him to make that decision in front of his own son:

> WALTER: What I am telling you is that we called you
> over here to tell you that we are very proud and that
> this is—this is my son, who makes the sixth genera-
> tion of our family in this country, and that we have
> all thought about your offer and we have decided
> to move into our house because my father—my
> father—he earned it. *(MAMA has her eyes closed
> and is rocking back and forth as though she were in
> church, with her head nodding the amen yes)*[17]

To Walter, the concrete fact of being together with his son has significance in itself and beyond itself. This double meaning gives him the strength to throw off his cynicism and to achieve his manhood. The moment is personal, familial, and timeful.

If Hansberry sees the family as a resource, her celebration

of it tries not to ignore or gloss over the real tensions among the Youngers. From Mama's first entrance on stage, we can see the potential for tyranny in her strong character. Mama's dominance is a balance of forces. Her severity with her daughter Beneatha's flippant remarks on religion is as much an indication of the daughter's immaturity as it is the mother's overbearing nature. Lena has earned the right to her beliefs by trying to live them; her daughter has no genuine reason to challenge them, only a sophomore's sophistication. Similarly, Walter's plan to make something of himself involves obtaining a liquor store license by graft and hustling, activities his mother distrusts. Not only are they morally suspect to her but they are outside the family experience and competence. The very extravagance of Walter's dreams and fantasies of business life shows how naive and innocent he is as a wheeler-dealer, a perfect mark. Walter and Beneatha talk about being grown-up, but if Mama dominates them it is in part because their actions do not bear out their words. They demand freedom, but Hansberry measures the legitimacy of that demand as well as Mama's too great strength.

A Raisin in the Sun has, then, a conflict between security and freedom. Hansberry is working toward a new formulation of this dilemma. She is beginning to explore its creative possibilities along with its destructive side. Dramatically, this potential is embodied in the rather simple ability of the characters to learn from each other, to change in reaction to claims made on them which they initially resist. When Mama and Walter are deadlocked—she with her need to keep the family secure and he with his need for personal achievement—we are faced with a situation of family counterclaims typical in American drama. At this point the tradition suggests several possible resolutions. Walter could break loose from Mama and emerge as the hero of the new black consciousness which frees itself from family ties and an older, debilitating habit of mind. If the emphasis was on Mama in this action, we would have the pattern of the Lomans; if it was on Walter, we would have something closer to the Bergers. If Walter broke free but wounded his psyche in the process, we would be reminded of the Wingfields. On the other hand, if no break occurs, several other patterns are available. Perhaps the family would be shown as an hypocrisy, as in later Hellman and Albee (in works which appeared about the same time); or we could be witnessing a replay of one of O'Neill's families—the heroic isolation of the Cabots, the mutual destruction of the Mannons, or the inescapable love and hate of the Tyrones.

The value of *A Raisin in the Sun* is in Hansberry's attempt to work out a somewhat different pattern, one which recognizes both claims but sees their interaction as a matter of continuing possibility rather than as a fixed dilemma. Mama's character is not rigid but capable of change. She can be more than one sort of person and can act in a different way. She learns and changes, and we see the effect of this first with Beneatha and then with Walter. Walter, too, has this capability, which depends on the family context. The family does not represent a fixed psychological set or a metaphysical certainty but a potential for turning agitation to interaction.

Hansberry effectively achieves this sense of possibility indirectly, through the rich vein of humor which runs through the play. Humor is a strategy of survival for the characters, a way by which they keep themselves in balance and restore their resilience in the face of difficult circumstances. Its effect on the play is to cut through the impossibility of a situation and to release forces in new ways. Hansberry seems to be saying that people do funny things (as well as admirable and stupid things) because of their needs. All these possibilities exist at a given moment.

The humor in *A Raisin in the Sun* is one of its strong elements and gives more credibility to a play which in other ways is not as rich and evocative as it needs to be to fulfill its own promise. The family drama here is worth our attention because of the new direction in which Hansberry tries to take it, not because she manages to travel a long ways in that direction. Her achievement is limited. The emphasis on the potential for change in her characters is handled too simply and so runs the risk of sentimentality. Hansberry senses that the tension between freedom and security in the family might be a humanizing one in that either impulse has the possibility of qualifying the worst effects of the other. But she does not dramatize this possibility so much as dramatize her faith in its existence. The question is how agitation becomes interaction. The answer, dramatically, comes in the imposition of the character of Mama. Her superiority is the mechanism by which Hansberry makes certain that the right change takes place. Because of Mama's relative strength, the actual risks to the family are reduced and what could be hard-won knowledge begins to look like a vindication of faith. At the end Walter and Beneatha leave the stage quarreling as they did at the beginning, *"and the anger is hard and real till their voices diminish,"*[18] says Hansberry in the stage directions. But Mama and Ruth, her daughter-in-law, are on stage chuckling and smiling at them, which serves to insulate us from their anger. Hansberry's insight that the conflicts and struggles will go on, that the issue could be not harmony but the capacity to make something of tension, comes perilously close to being turned into a theatrical joke—oops, here we go again.

A similar weakness exists in Mama's assertion of love for Walter when he is about to sell out the family heritage. This ought to be a difficult moment for Mama, too, since Walter is threatening to destroy the most cherished value in her world. But Hansberry does not show a struggle within Mama. Rather, the depth of Mama's love (in an earlier scene, the depth of her religious faith) is contrasted with the superficiality of Beneatha's reaction. Nothing can shake Mama's love. But what, then, of the possibility for change? Love becomes *the* solution rather than a resource, the danger that Walter will "dry up/Like a raisin in the sun" is reduced and we watch his final test comforted rather than fearful. In another context, there might be a vitalizing danger in the last sentences of Mama's speech on love: "When you starts measuring somebody, measure him right, child, measure him right. Make sure you done taken account what hills and valleys he come through before he got to wherever he is."[19]

Hansberry is edging toward an interesting paradox: if measurement of Walter by Mama is a real possibility, then measurement is also more powerful and believable as a source of strength for Walter. But unless Walter also can fail by the standard of Mama's family ethic, the drama soothes us instead of exploring the way in which two warring elements—in this case, judgment and love—can be sustaining and their tension turned to energy and strength. In American drama we are used to such a dilemma destroying either the individual or the family. When Biff Loman judges Willy, Biff then decides he must leave the family forever; in turn, Willy will not hear the judgment, only Biff's love, and kills himself for it. Hansberry is on the verge of denying that such family polarities are mutually exclusive and so of developing a new calculus for family drama. But while she hints at her insights, she never finds a fully satisfactory dramatic action to embody them. Instead, she falls back on the intervention of the Good Woman Leader to solve her dramatic problems. She sees a new content possible for the family drama but has not developed the form to reflect it.

Perhaps Hansberry's weaknesses show up more clearly than they would if her output had not been so limited. Unfortunately, her apprenticeship became her career; she died after completing one more play for production, *The Sign in Sidney Brustein's Window* (1964). [20] Still, in *A Raisin in the Sun* the image of black family life and the pattern of dramatic action on which it is based achieve a distinct variation of the main tradition of American family drama. The realistic presentation of family conflict begins in a familiar manner but the play goes on to show that the family can be supportive and capacitating. Although *The Sign in Sidney Brustein's Window* is not a family play, it does contain an exchange which sums up Hansberry's attitude. A nihilistic playwright (who resembles Edward Albee) says: "Trying to live with your father's values can kill you. Ask me, I know." "No, Sweetie," answers a prostitute who later commits suicide, "living *without* your father's values can kill you. Ask *me,* I know." [21]

In a new generation of playwrights we see old elements continuing. The reappearance of these images and patterns of action involves interesting complications. On the face of it, Albee is the writer in touch with new modes of perception and Hansberry is old-fashioned. Surely Albee's style is more avant-garde than Hansberry's. Even in his family plays he formalizes and ritualizes the action. Increasingly, the locale becomes vague; the action is reduced and nearly disappears into arias of talk; his plays move into a borderline area between realism and symbolism. But the core images of family life are familiar ones of family destruction and oppression. Hansberry sticks to the conventions of verisimilitude, to particulars and to a historically defined setting. The form of her play seems almost trite to us now. But in this old bottle, Hansberry tries to put some new wine. She begins with the same old struggles of family life but wants to recast the terms in which they are carried on.

Hansberry had few examples in American drama to draw on (she said Ireland's Sean O'Casey was her inspiration). In fact, we have had only one playwright who used family materials, celebrated this life, and produced major work. Thornton Wilder has written two plays which are clearly related to our drama in their family-centered images. In one in particular, the family struggle is at the heart of the work; there freedom and security conflict. Yet these plays are discrepancies in that family failure is not the inevitable result of exploring conflict and tension.

A novelist as well as a playwright, Wilder seems in the main to have reserved the family subject matter for his plays. This tendency helps underline the fact that American drama is domestic drama. But Wilder's contribution is singular, and where, exactly, he is to be located within our drama becomes a nice question. Simple chronology does not help. Wilder's important plays date from the late 1930s and early 1940s, but he is no more a part of that generation of playwrights than any other. In some ways he belongs to an earlier period in that his career as a writer began in the mid-1920s. His innovative theatrical style, worked out in the early 1930s, anticipated but did not directly influence the new forms of the 1960s. The combination of Wilder's break with realism, his hold on the family subject, his vision of it as a source of strength, and his artistic achievement puts him in a special category. Wilder's relationship to our generations of playwrights is best seen, perhaps, as the alternate response of American drama to the changing family system. His few, accomplished plays show other directions which our dramatists might take, but do not, even within the very terms of their obsession with family conflict. His example emphasizes our reiteration of the drama of family failure.

Wilder's reaction to the formal problems of American family drama in effect represents a critique of it. Most American playwrights have been realists and, in their restless explorations of family conflict, often have turned to expressionism not as an alternative to realism but as an extension of it, an attempt to make the family drama even more vivid. Wilder's experiments did not begin with realism and an attempt to modify and stretch it but stemmed from different premises about the nature of drama and its relation to life. The theater ought to be frankly theatrical, and to this end Wilder began removing the scenery and collapsing time. In such short plays as *Pullman Car Hiawatha, The Happy Journey to Camden and Trenton,* and *The Long Christmas Dinner* (all published in 1931)[22] a generalized reality is conveyed by the typical, average, and allegorical. The single event is itself and all such events, as Wilder imitates the typology of medieval drama. The action is one of theme and variation rather than of revelation, progress, or problem-solving. A perspective is created whereby the audience see these characters as functions of a larger pattern. A special sort of dramatic irony is achieved. The lives of the characters have a rhythm and shape of which they are not aware. There is an energy apart from their own more immediate desires.

Wilder's attacks on realism distort time and place but not in a harsh or grotesque manner. The events of daily life take on meaning because of the perspective he creates, and Wilder wishes to celebrate the most typical experiences of life. By stripping away the things of the stage, he forces us to pay attention to the few ordinary experiences which make up his action; and by repeating these events he suggests how valuable they are and how transitory our attention is to them. To the characters time may pass quickly or slowly but they continually miss that which is most rewarding about life.

For Wilder the family experience is at the center of what is both common and missed in life. In *Our Town* (1938), Wilder's first original long play,[23] it is the core of the everyday rhythms of life in Grover's Corners, New Hampshire. Wilder builds a picture of the town through a complex development and extension of the techniques he worked out in his experimental one-act plays. The result is a play which has become synonymous with the sweetness of everyday life but not, unfortunately, with Wilder's painful corollary, that we inevitably miss that sweetness. The fault is partly Wilder's and partly that of a public in search of a nostalgic escape from the "reality" (and associated realism) of our family drama.

In *Our Town* the events are unspectacular and low-keyed. We watch the daily habits and routines of two families, the Gibbses and the Webbs. It is a montage of small moments: church music and the smell of flowers, first love, family discipline, the town scandal, courtship, and marriage. The characters are allowed to show their desires, frustrations, and contentments just enough to establish the fact of their inner lives, at which point the Stage Manager moves us on to the next episode. The ordinary life of family, friends, and work is celebrated as part of a larger process that is fundamentally sound. The very mundane quality of this life is to provide us with a sense of snug containment by the overall life process.

It is at this point that *Our Town* might seem to deserve its fate of innumerable sentimental productions. Wilder runs such a risk, especially in the first two acts, and only barely saves himself through the hinting quips of the Stage Manager. The special perspective he wants us to experience as we view the play does have more to it than nostalgia for a cosmically secure routine, however. We see that time moves very quickly in the world of the play. It is much more fleeting than the characters realize. This fact is a bitter one as the Stage Manager well knows, and his awareness peeks out in laconic comments. The reality beneath appearance is indicated in a single word or phrase. Again and again he adds to his speeches on the nature of life a final remark which startles us with its dark quality. "All that education for nothing;" "It's what they call a vicious circle;" "Once in a thousand times it's interesting."[24] The Stage Manager does not sneer nor does he devalue ordinary domestic life. In such lines he gives us something stronger than cynicism, the blank truth; and invites us to accept it.

These hints suggest that the simplest matters of life have rich implications. In *The Happy Journey to Camden and Trenton* Wilder used one line of painful isolation to force us to reevaluate the pleasant family idyll which precedes it.[25] In *Our Town* he uses the entire third act. We see life from the point of view of the dead and watch Emily, who has just died in childbirth, relive one chosen day, her twelfth birthday. The wonder and beauty of its routines soon turn to pain, however, for the deeper meaning of Emily's experience is that she was not able to grasp her life at the time. She sees how isolated, lonely, and cut off she was from the family and from the very act of living. "Mama, just for a moment we're happy. *Let's look at one another.* "[26]

Knowing that we miss life's goodness—which is not the same as saying that life is good—is the point of the play's structure. We sentimentalize the past because we did not fully live it; and we never will. The play celebrates the common things of life not as occasions for nostalgia, which would be to claim easy knowledge of them, but because they are life, what our lives are made of, and they are the part we will never know in our lives. We see this only when, like Emily, we are graced with perspective. The Stage Manager and Emily give us a way to go beyond our initial sense of simple goodness.

> EMILY: Do any human beings ever realize life while
>   they live it?—Every, every minute?
> STAGE MANAGER: No. *(Pause)* The saints and poets,
>   maybe—they do. [27]

The Stage Manager gives us the blank truth again in his simple "no." Perhaps in art and religion some heightened awareness is possible. But then it is only temporary and, at least in the case of art, indirect. We are aware of Emily's loss while we are in the theater; we will forget our own when we leave.

The play ends with an affirmation of faith which is comforting but vague. Since the dead know the truth about life's inadequacy, their serenity must indicate other knowledge as well, truths which are also unknown to us. After Simon Stimson's outburst, a bitter denunciation of life which reminds us that the warm rhythms of Grover's Corners did not soothe him, Mrs. Webb turns our attention elsewhere, away from the human predicament and toward the stars. She does not deny the truth of what Simon has said, only that it is the whole truth. There is something in addition to the pain that drove him to suicide and that is represented by the star. It may be a figure for the life process itself, an essence separate from the accidents of particular lives. Earlier, the Stage Manager remarked: "There's something way down deep that's eternal in every human being."[28] In any case we are left with the predicament of our lives and the Stage Manager closes the play with a joke on that subject.

In *Our Town* the family represents the quintessence of our human difficulty. It is the center of the daily life in the play and each act is devoted more fully to it. It is to her family that Emily chooses to return in Act Three. Here, if anywhere, we should be able to see life and here, especially, we miss it. The pain of what is missed within *that* warm circle is especially shocking to Emily and so more vivid to us. Yet *Our Town* is about the family only in a certain way and up to a point. The Stage Manager always breaks in before any separate dramatic existence is established for the Gibbses and the Webbs. The montage of short episodes gives us a panorama in which we see the family imbedded in the community, its outlines clear but its inner workings only suggested.

Wilder's next play, *The Merchant of Yonkers* (1938)—later rewritten as *The Matchmaker* (1954)—also affirms the importance of domestic life. In it Wilder turns farce away from an instrument of attack to put it at the service of family values. The need to invent one's way out of situations, which is crucial to the action of farce, is a gesture of vitality in the face of rigid, life-denying roles. Instead of such roles being identified with the family as they often are in farce, Wilder suggests the opposite: domesticity means new life for the merchant. But the play is more interested in the fun of getting people married than in what happens when they are married. *The Skin of Our Teeth* (1942) is the Wilder play most fully about the family.[29]

The Skin of Our Teeth continues the non-realistic impulse of *Our Town* and the early one-act plays but in a different way. In this play the style bypasses the outline of likelihood in the daily events of *Our Town*. The allegorical tendency, which is always present in Wilder's emphasis on the typical, is given full rein. The Antrobus family is the family of Man, as the Greek root of their name indicates. George and Maggie Antrobus and their children Henry and Gladys are a suburban New Jersey family as well as the families of Adam and Eve, Noah, and other mythical models.

Wilder has a lot of fun with the resultant anachronisms. The family keeps pet dinosaurs; Mr. Antrobus invents the wheel and the alphabet; Homer, Moses, and other great figures take refuge in the Antrobus house; there are newsreels of the Ice Age; a 5,000th wedding anniversary is announced; the world's mammals gather at a Shriners' convention; and, in addition to a great deal more of this sort of thing, the actors, who have their own problems, regularly stop the play.

The joking quality of Wilder's allegory spills over into a lively emphasis on production. Where *Our Town* is spare and simple, almost stark visually, with set and props kept to an emphatic minimum, *The Skin of Our Teeth* is theatrical in an opposite way. Wilder draws on the resources of the theater to encourage a splashy, lively production. (No doubt this has cost the later play some popularity since it is difficult for amateurs to do.) The play is filled with color and sound and sight gags. Wilder uses slide projections, a voice from a loudspeaker, and dinosaurs that talk. The convention setting is meant to light up like a pinball machine, and on the other set the walls of the house tilt, right themselves, and disappear on their own or at the command of others. The spectacle of the theater is made to be the spectacle of humanity.

The Skin of Our Teeth is a play within a play. Miss Somerset, the "actress" who plays the character of Sabina, keeps interrupting with comments by which Wilder makes fun of himself as well as the genteel tastes and style of the conventional theater. This strategy is a useful one in getting his allegory accepted in good fun. Because Miss Somerset is something of a Philistine, he can insinuate the importance of his ideas while making light of them at the same time. Moreover, when Miss Somerset has to ad-lib because an actress has missed her cue, the two levels of the play begin to approach each other; in both you have to invent quickly to get along. But Miss Somerset is even more of a link because her own reaction to the play changes. At first she scorns the play and calls it nonsense. Then she begins to understand it but claims no comparison can be made to contemporary life: "Savages don't love their families—not like we do."[30] Later she contradicts herself when she refuses to play the divorce scene. Now the play is too painfully relevant. Finally, in the last act when an impromptu rehearsal is called, Miss Somerset stoutly defends the play. She has learned something from it.

The juggling of time in the play suggests one of its important themes: humanity's problems are unchanging. This idea is most obviously reflected in the structure of the play, which is circular overall. The action ends where it starts—with a mockery of the nineteenth-century well-made play—because history is unfinished. The play must go on and on as human beings repeat their sins and manage, barely, to save themselves from extinction through the strength of their virtues. Not only does the play begin again at its end but the first and third acts are started twice. And each act repeats the same patterns of a new crisis—the Ice Age, the Flood, World War—which is met with the Antrobuses fighting for survival after passing through the temptation of despair. The shape of history, like the art of the theater, involves fresh repetition, the illusion of the first time.

At the heart of this changeless pattern of history is the family and its dilemmas, which are shown in two ways: the contest between Sabina, the maid, and Mrs. Antrobus for the affection of Mr. Antrobus; and the acceptance/rejection by the Antrobuses of their son Henry, formerly known as Cain. We are told the love triangle is a rivalry which has been going on for some time. Each character is associated with a cluster of values which puts the rivalry immediately into a symbolic framework. Sabina is sex, but other things as well. Her sensuality is related to inspiration, freedom, and indulgence. For her, Mr. Antrobus invents the alphabet; for her, he is willing to leave his family under the watchword, "Enjoy Yourself." Sabina is selfish. She will keep two needles when she needs only one or steal bouillon cubes when the times call for sharing food. She is unprincipled ego and at her worst aims at misrule. And she lets the fire go out.

Mrs. Antrobus, on the other hand, is domesticity. Instead of "Enjoy Yourself," she proposes "Save the Family." She is practicality, order, and survival. She keeps the fire going and endures everything for her family, which is her glory and her limitation. She is sociable and generous but her family always comes first. She would, she freely admits, burn the last copy of Shakespeare's works to keep her children from catching a cold. As Sabina likes to point out, she is not pretty.

The case for Mrs. Antrobus is clear enough. Without her they would all perish. She is steadfast where Sabina is flightly and unreliable. In the time of ice she keeps the fire lit, and in the time of flood she has her sharp eye out for an ark. After the war she gets the household going again. When the walls need putting together, Sabina can be forced to help but Mrs. Antrobus is needed to finish the job. Yet Sabina, though she is always defeated by Mrs. Antrobus, will always be able to challenge her, too. It is not only that her sexuality cannot be denied—though given Mr. Antrobus's robust energies that is a strong lure—but also that she is linked to creative intellect. It is through Mr. Antrobus's inventions and achievements that the household finds a reason to go on after each disaster. This is true for Mrs. Antrobus, also. Her strength and constancy are based on more than an instinct for protecting her children. There is a value to life which makes such protection meaningful. If good cannot come out of evil, if Mr. Antrobus will no longer struggle to achieve, then she, too, is lost. Indirectly, Mrs. Antrobus needs Sabina. Or, rather, the world needs both of them to get on with its work.

The second family dilemma in *The Skin of Our Teeth* is what to do about Henry. With the mark of Cain on his forehead (which Mrs. Antrobus tries to rub out with the hem of her apron) and a murderous streak in his heart, Henry represents the evil in human nature. At first he does his killing as a young boy throwing rocks; later he advances to a slingshot; by the final act he has grown up to lead a world war. Mr. Antrobus can face the ice and the floods, even the war, better than he can deal with Henry in peace. After Henry murders the boy next door, Mr Antrobus momentarily gives up the survival struggle and begins to stamp out the fire which protects them from the approaching ice. When Henry murders the black man on the boardwalk, he runs off, but Mrs. Antrobus will not leave on the ark without him. He returns at the last minute when she calls him by his proper name, Cain. Her acceptance of him as part of the family at this point counterbalances her husband's despair over him earlier.

These two impulses come to a head in the last act after the war. Mr. Antrobus and Henry are now enemies. In fact, Henry is *the* enemy, the general of the army against whom Mr. Antrobus has fought. Each man swears to kill the other. A showdown is at hand. But it turns out not to be a simple dilemma. Neither man is as single-minded as he thinks he is. Henry claims to be self-sufficient, alone, and without connection, but for all his rebellion, he has returned home. Even his wartime killing was a gesture of relatedness since it was his father that he went after. Mr. Antrobus recognizes this in Henry and, throwing away his pistol, offers to try again to live together. His offer is not a promise of harmony but of struggle. Henry's rebellion has been fought in the name of freedom and Mr. Antrobus responds to this ideal. He admires the good aspect of his son's evil ways and wants to struggle for the one and against the other.

It is here that Wilder's drama takes an extraordinary turn. The two worlds of the play are fused when Henry and Mr. Antrobus face each other. Mr. Antrobus wants to accept the good in Henry and will tyrannize him to do so. Henry bristles and jumps for his father's throat. At this crucial point, Miss Somerset breaks in:

> Stop! Stop! Don't play this scene. You know what happened last night. Stop the play. *(The men fall back, panting. HENRY covers his face with his hands.)* Last night you almost strangled him. You became a regular savage. Stop it![31]

The meaning of the play has come home to the actors personally. The actor playing Henry relives the hatred he felt for his own father and the fiction of the play becomes a fact for him. The theater is like history in yet another way then, for the actors identify with their roles.

Wilder's touch is subtle here. He raises the question of whether the young actor was overtly tyrannized. Miss Somerset knew the family and thinks not. The question is not answered, however, to point us toward the more relevant issue. The responsibility for his attitude must be shared in the past and in the present:

> ANTROBUS *(in his own person, with self-condemnation, but cold and proud):* Wait a minute. I have something to say, too. It's not wholly his fault that he wants to strangle me in this scene. It's my fault, too. He wouldn't feel that way unless there were something in me that reminded him of all that. He talks about an emptiness. Well, there's an emptiness in me, too. Yes,—work, work, work,—that's all I do. I've ceased to live. No wonder he feels that anger coming over him.[32]

However it appeared to Miss Somerset, in reality blame turns out to be interconnected. Freedom and tyranny, love and hate, good and evil are dependent on each other. And we have mutual responsibility for them. Because it is an actor in the present moment of the play who senses this, the drama of its discovery is multiplied. Suddenly the theme of humanity's changeless patterns and the action of family dilemmas are brought together on a different level. The past of the play emerges in this present moment. The play jumps into new focus with an energy that forces us to reconsider the gaiety of the play as gaiety and something more. We have to confront the problem of mutual responsibility—in the Antrobus family, in the "actors" playing roles, and in ourselves in the audience. The allegorical remove from which we have been seeing the action is shifted and the play takes on a new density.

In a sense this is the moment toward which the play has been heading all along, and Wilder's effect, which forces us to change perspective, has parallels with the dramaturgy of *Our Town*. The Fortune Teller at the Sodom and Gomorrah revels has something of this function as well when she predicts the deaths of passing conventioneers (and members of the audience). We all have a common future, she says, but none of us can understand our past, where time went, and what happened to our good intentions. As in *Our Town* the irretrievable loss of the present moment is humanity's fate. But *The Skin of Our Teeth* is more interested in the family dilemma as the figure for our strengths and weaknesses, what keeps us going in spite of this fate. It is, in part, an elaboration of the star symbol at the end of the earlier play. In fact the star is mentioned in passing. Gladys tries to lift her father's spirits by showing what she has accomplished in school and offers to recite "The Star" by Longfellow.

An even more important symbol of the strength by which the family survives is the "promise." Mrs. Antrobus refers to it twice, both times at crucial moments. When Mr. Antrobus is threatening to break up the family, she claims the promise in a manner which might seem to equate it with wedding vows:

> MRS. ANTROBUS *(calmly, almost dreamily):* I didn't marry you because you were perfect. I didn't even marry you because I loved you. I married you because you gave me a promise. *(She takes off her ring and looks at it.)* That promise made up for your faults. And the promise I gave you made up for mine. Two imperfect people got married and it was the promise that made the marriage. [33]

But those vows are, in turn, a symbol for a deeper promise which is elaborated later. After the showdown with Henry, after Mr. Antrobus has recognized that not only is Henry related to him through his goodness but also through his evil, Mr. Antrobus is exhausted and unwilling to take up the task of rebuilding the world once again. Mrs. Antrobus answers that their survival depends on his bringing "something good out of this suffering." She continues:

> In the night, in the dark, we'd whisper about it, starving and sick.—Oh, George, you have to get it back again.

> Think! What else kept us alive all these years? Even
> now, it's not comfort we want. We can suffer what-
> ever's necessary; only give us back that promise. [34]

The promise, then, is not simply a legal or even moral obligation.
The deeper pledge being made is that something worthwhile can
come out of the contradictions of life. It is the assurance that the
oppositions in life, such as those between husband and wife, parents and children, can be accommodated.

For Wilder the family is the epitome of this humanizing
compromise. It is the arena wherein we necessarily face the most
basic contradictions. As he pictures it in *The Skin of Our Teeth,*
the family is subject to those same dualities which our realistic
family playwrights have also identified. In fact he doubles them in
that both Sabina/Mrs. Antrobus and Henry/Mr. Antrobus are
elaborations of the impulses toward freedom and security which
we have seen before. Neither opposition is resolved, and the allegory of the family is of life as survival and achievement through
this dialectic. If there is any progress, it is slow and hard won, as
when Mr. Antrobus comes to realize what he knew from the beginning, that he, too, was covered with the blood guilt. At the end the
masque of the Hours calms the play down after the emotional
turmoil between father and son (and between the actors playing
these roles). It suggests Wilder's philosophical idealism that our
achievements have been a few good ideas gradually accumulating
over the centuries. Wilder affirms the process—the struggle with
contradictions, particularly in the family—out of which these
ideas arise.

The Skin of Our Teeth is our most affirmative family play,
which makes it an anomaly. It is a part of our drama and a criticism
of it. It celebrates family life by drawing on the same dilemmas
which underpin most of our plays. It is non-realistic, in the style
of fantasy and myth rather than mundane probability, yet it works
to connect the struggles directly to the audience rather than to
provide them with an escape. Without evading issues—in fact, by
embracing them—Wilder asserts that our family dilemmas can be

creative as well as destructive, that an energizing synthesis can come from its oppositions.

Wilder claimed no greater originality for himself as playwright than one quality: "I give (don't I) the impression of having enormously enjoyed it."[35] Not a grand claim, but no mean one either in a national drama which seems to have been written under the pressure of severe disappointment. There is a burst of energy driving many of our plays which comes, I think, from a concomitant expectation of harmony. Anything less must result in destruction— for the family, for the individual, or for both. Perhaps this is why so often our best plays are first plays. At any rate, Wilder is remarkably free of that feeling.

American playwrights inherited their expectations from a changing family structure and a complex of ethical and emotional attitudes toward the family. From the outset the strains on the nuclear family system were felt in terms of intensity and isolation. But those very qualities also proved appealing in other ways because of their conjunction with deeply held attitudes. Our concern with the family was related to our expectations of what made up the good life, our desire to abandon social forms, and our assumptions about the democratic system. American ambivalence toward social structures came to be expressed in conflicting models of family life, Crèvecoeur's secure structure and Tocqueville's spontaneous (but worried) freedom. Even our popular images of the family have betrayed a deep uncertainty as to its place in a culture devoted to suspicion of institutions. Yet, in our drama we do not give up the realistic family war. This conservative reluctance wars with the radicalism implicit in our desire to break out of inherited forms.

Not only have our playwrights perpetuated American familialism, but they have refined and translated it into patterns of action which underpin our plays. The two family models of freedom and security are rendered as active and conflicting motives. The playwright arranges these forces into a pattern which provides the energy for his play. To escape from the confining structure of the family is the most common arrangement but not the only one. Defeat, longing, and loss are called into being by the initial gesture; and so we have the composite elements of American family tragedy, a dilemma of inescapable contradiction. The style and substance of our drama have been shaped by our attitudes toward family life; and the drama has made of these attitudes artistic constructs which, in turn, clarify them. Only a few American playwrights have ignored or avoided these conventions. There are no rival traditions.

If the discussion of the family as the key element in American drama suggests that our attitudes here are persistent and recurring, it allows us to juxtapose and relate dramatists who are in other ways quite dissimilar. The terms by which we see American drama can be recast. Our playwrights can be viewed as part of a larger, over-arching literary and cultural concern rather than as separate from each other and projecting only their private neuroses, anxieties, and psychic histories. It is hardly significant that Albee sneaks in quotations from Williams; it is amusing that Williams echoes a famous radio soap opera by using the portrait of the paterfamilias on stage; the connections become interesting as we note all the missing and dying fathers, the dominant mothers, and the insurance checks. [36] And when, beneath these items, we see that basic patterns of action in our plays are similar, then we have a common denominator which tells us about our playwrights and ourselves.

The American stage is typically one of family destruction where escape means freedom and failure tragic oppression. This battleground is entered again and again for we are uneasy in the face of what is lost when we escape. If we cannot live within the family, can we live without it? Our plays take us over the same questions in search of an answer. The separate tragedies of the Cabots and the self-destructiveness of the Mannons lead to the heroic love and hate of the Tyrones, who dominate this world. The Lomans and the Wingfields try to escape from such isolated deadlock. O'Neill, who revolutionized American drama, may in some respects be the last, great playwright of bourgeois family life. It is certain that he looked more deeply and fully into the relationship between the individual and the family than did those who followed him. Both Miller and Williams have sensed, as it were, the completeness of O'Neill's achievement and each has tried to move to new ground, Miller by emphasizing social context and Williams by exploiting theatrically the individual's inner life. But neither man has advanced the subject. The Hubbards, the Bergers, and George and Martha inhabit this world, too, epitomizing so much of our drama. In their various ways, Hellman, Odets, and Albee manage original variations on a common pattern in which the struggle against the family is equated with freedom or the absence of struggle with defeat. Much less common is the sort of family life which Hansberry suggests and Wilder allegorizes. What is finally true about this world, what all those who people it represent, is a preoccupation with the family which continues even in attempts to escape from it. We are never more committed to the family than when we reenact its destruction.

NOTES

1. Joseph Kirk Folsom, *The Family in Democratic Society* (New York, 1943), p. 350.

2. Robert Frost, "Build Soil" in *The Poetry of Robert Frost,* ed. Edward Connery Lathem (New York, 1969), p. 325.

3. *Montserrat* (1949) and *The Lark* (1955) are from European plays; *My Mother, My Father and Me* (1963) is an expressionist family play from a novel; and *Candide* (1956) is Hellman's adaptation for a musical. Only her first play, *The Children's Hour* (1934) is both original and, despite the title, not a family drama.

4. Lillian Hellman, *The Little Foxes* in *The Collected Plays* (Boston, 1972), p. 199.

5. Clifford Odets, *Awake and Sing!* in *Six Plays of Clifford Odets* (New York, 1939), p. 97.

6. Michael J. Mendelsohn, "Clifford Odets and the American Family," *Drama Survey,* 3 (Fall 1963), 238-243.

7. Ibid., p. 242.

8. Some might find irony implicit in the choices made by Ralphie and Hennie. As Gerald Weales notes, the daughter's escape to an island that sounds suspiciously like Cuba goes against Odets's public attitude toward the oppressed conditions of that island. See Weales, *Clifford Odets: Playwright* (New York, 1971), pp. 71-75. Similarly, Ralphie's reluctance to leave home might be argued a fatal mistake which, contrary to my point, will lead him into a life of failure like his grandfather's.

Weales rejects the possibility of irony with regard to Hennie and so do I for Ralphie. The triumph over Bessie and the satisfaction in uniting Hennie and Moe are so great that any such interpretation would be perverse.

9. Odets, *Awake and Sing!,* p. 55.

10. It may have been as much a matter of Odets writing for the ensemble style of the Group Theatre as it was any direct influence of the Russian: "I have often been

accused of aping Chekhov, which is in no sense a *mean* thing. But the real truth is that with the Group Theatre ensemble acting company, I wrote not one or two leading parts with a lot of supporting players, but the early plays were written with equal size parts for equal size actors. So that a play like *Awake and Sing[!]*, let us say, has seven leading parts in it. And that form was dictated by the composition of the Group Theatre acting company." Quotation from an interview in Michael John Mendelsohn, "Clifford Odets: A Critical Study," Diss. U. of Colorado 1972, p. 190.

11. Martin Esslin, *The Theatre of the Absurd* (Garden City, N.Y., 1969), pp. 266-270.

12. Edward Albee, *Who's Afraid of Virginia Woolf?* (New York, 1962), p. 174.

13. Ibid., p. 178.

14. Also, Albee has done three adaptations: *The Ballad of the Sad Cafe* (1963) and *Malcolm* (1966) are from novels; *Everything in the Garden* (1967) is from a play.

15. *Seascape* is not a family play but it does have domestic overtones. In it, Albee apparently is trying very hard to project a sense of hopeful beginnings. Perhaps it occupies a place in Albee's canon analogous to that of *The Flowering Peach* in Odets's—mutuality can be affirmed in fantasy. Miller's *The Creation of the World and Other Matters* (1972) might be relevant in this regard, also.

16. It would be interesting to determine the exact degree to which such plays reflect black attitudes toward the family as distinct from the images Broadway will select, accept, and allow. Are black families taken to be more "picturesque"? Or is there a conjunction between black defensive solidarity and white yearning for the more spontaneous emotions of black stereotype? In any case the primary fact for American drama is that in such plays the family is a positive force.

17. Lorraine Hansberry, *A Raisin in the Sun* (New York, 1959), p. 142.

For a slightly modified version of the play, see *Contemporary Black Drama: From "A Raisin in the Sun" to "No Place to Be Somebody,"* eds. Clinton F. Oliver and Stephanie Sills (New York, 1971), pp. 33-120. The editors do not comment on the source of their version.

18. Hansberry, *Raisin,* p. 145.

19. Ibid., p. 140.

20. A dramatic compilation of her writings has been done under the title, *To Be Young, Gifted and Black,* adapted by Robert Nemiroff (Englewood Cliffs, N.J., 1969). The collection, *Les Blancs,* ed. Robert Nemiroff (New York, 1972), has minor and late plays in draft at the time of her death.

21. Lorraine Hansberry, *The Sign in Sidney Brustein's Window* (New York, 1965), p. 132.

22. Prior to 1931, Wilder had written a number of what he called "three-minute plays," closet drama one-acts, generally on religious themes.

23. He had adapted André Obey's *Le Viol de Lucrece* in 1$932 under the title *Lucrece.*

24. Thornton Wilder, *Our Town* in *Three Plays by Thornton Wilder* (New York, 1957), pp. 10, 47, 78. Citations from Wilder refer to this edition unless otherwise noted.

25. Throughout the play the family travels gaily on a visit to the married daugh-

ter, Beulah. Only after they arrive, near the end of the play, do we learn what the family knows, that she has lost a baby in childbirth. "BEULAH *(whispering as her eyes fill with tears):* Are you glad I'm still alive, pa?"—*The Long Christmas Dinner and Other Plays in One Act* (New York, 1963), p. 108.

26. Wilder, *Our Town,* p. 99.

27. Ibid.

28. Ibid., p. 81.

29. Wilder's other full-length play, "A Life in the Sun; The Drunken Sisters" (1955), his version of Euripedes's *Alcestis* with a satyr play, is unpublished in English.

30. Thornton Wilder, *The Skin of Our Teeth,* p. 143.

31. Ibid., p. 238.

32. Ibid., p. 240.

33. Ibid., pp. 200-201.

34. Ibid., pp. 243-244.

35. Thornton Wilder, "Preface, ibid., p. xiv.

36. Albee borrows from *The Glass Menagerie* ("Up the spout") and *A Streetcar Named Desire* ("THE POKER NIGHT"; "Flores para los muertes"); see *Who's Afraid of Virginia Woolf?,* pp. 186, 195. The soap opera I have in mind is "Ma Perkins" where Pa's picture hangs over the mantelpiece and Ma, in times of stress, addresses the image of her dead husband.

BIBLIOGRAPHY

FAMILY LIFE (HISTORY, SOCIOLOGY, SOCIAL COMMENT)

Abbott, Lyman. *The Home Builder.* Boston: Houghton Mifflin, 1910.

Alcott, William A. *The Young Husband.* 1838; rpt. New York: Arno Press, 1972.

———. *The Young Wife.* 1837; rpt. New York: Arno Press, 1972.

Aldous, Joan, and Reuben Hill. *International Bibliography of Research in Marriage and the Family, 1900-1964.* Minneapolis: University of Minnesota Press, 1967.

"The American Family" Issue. *American Journal of Sociology,* 52 (May 1948).

Ariés, Philippe. *Centuries of Childhood: A Social History of Family Life.* Trans. Robert Baldick. New York: Knopf, 1962.

Bailyn, Bernard. *Education in the Forming of American Society: Needs and Opportunities for Study.* Chapel Hill: University of North Carolina Press, 1960.

Beasley, Christine. *Democracy in the Home.* New York: Association Press, 1954.

———. "How Can the Family Breed Democracy?" *Marriage and Family Living,* 15 (August 1953), 201-205.

Becker, Howard, and Reuben Hill, eds. *Family, Marriage and Parenthood.* Boston: D. C. Heath, 1955.

Bridges, William E. "Family Patterns and Social Values in America, 1825-1875." *American Quarterly,* 17 (Spring 1965), 3-11.

———. "Warm Hearth, Cold World: Social Perspectives on the Household Poets." *American Quarterly,* 21 (Winter 1969), 764-779.

Burgess, Ernest W., Harvey J. Locke, Mary Margaret Thomas. *The Family: From Institution to Companionship.* 3rd ed. New York: American Book Co., 1963.

Calhoun, Arthur W. "The American Family." *Annals of the American Academy,* 160 (March 1932), 7-12.

———. *A Social History of the American Family From Colonial Times to the Present.* 3 vols. Cleveland, Ohio: Arthur H. Clark Co., 1917-1919.

Cavan, Ruth Shonle. *The American Family.* New York: Crowell, 1953.

———. *American Marriage: A Way of Life.* New York: Crowell, 1959.

Chapman, Dennis. *The Home and Social Status.* New York: Grove Press, 1955.

Connor, Paul. "Patriarchy: Old World and New." *American Quarterly,* 17 (Spring 1965), 48-62.

Cuyler, Reverend Theodore L. "Introduction" to *Mother, Home, and Heaven.* New York: E. B. Treat, 1878.

Demos, John. *A Little Commonwealth: Family Life in Plymouth Colony.* New York: Oxford Press, 1970.

Farber, Bernard. *Family: Organization and Interaction.* San Francisco: Chandler Publishing Co., 1964.

———. *Guardians of Virtue: Salem Families in 1800.* New York: Basic Books, 1972.

Folsom, Joseph Kirk. *The Family and Democratic Society.* New York: J. Wiley & Sons, 1943.

Fowler, C[harles] H[enry], and W. H. DePuy. *Home and Health and Home Economics: A Cyclopedia of Facts ....* New York: Phillips & Hunt, 1880.

Gilman, Charlotte Perkins. *The Home: Its Work and Influence.* New York: McClure, Phillips & Co., 1903.

Goode, William J. *The Family.* Englewood Cliffs, N.J.: Prentice-Hall, 1964.

———. "Social Engineering and the Divorce Problem." *Annals of the American Academy,* 272 (November 1950), 86-94.

———. *World Revolution and Family Patterns.* New York: Free Press, 1963.

Goodsell, Willystine. *A History of Marriage and the Family.* Rev. ed. New York: Macmillan, 1934.

Green, Arnold W. "The Middle Class Male Child and Neurosis." *American Sociological Review,* 11 (February 1946), 31-41.

Groves, Ernest R., and Lee M. Brooks. *Readings in the Family.* New York: J. B. Lippincott, 1934.

Gruenberg, Sidonie Matsner. "Changing Conceptions of the Family." *Annals of the American Academy,* 251 (May 1947), 128-136.

Hague, William. *Home Life: Twelve Lectures.* Philadelphia: American Baptist Publication Society, 1855.

Handlin, Oscar and Mary. *Facing Life: Youth and the Family in American History.* Boston: Atlantic-Little, Brown & Co., 1971.

Higginson, Thomas Wentworth. *Common Sense About Women.* Boston: Lee & Shepard, 1882.

Howard, George Elliott. *The Family and Marriage: An Analytical Reference Syllabus.* Lincoln: University of Nebraska, 1914.

Kolb, William L. "Book Review of Three Guides to Marriage." *American Sociological Review,* 15 (February 1950), 153-154.

———. "Family Sociology, Marriage Education and *The Romantic Complex:* A Critique." *Social Forces,* 29 (October 1950), 65-72.

———. "Sociologically Established Family Norms and Democratic Values." *Social Forces,* 26 (May 1948), 451-456.

Koos, Earl L[omon]. "Class Differences in Family Reactions to Crisis." *Marriage and Family Living,* 12 (Summer 1950), 77-78, 99.

―――. "Middle-Class Family Crises." *Marriage and Family Living,* 10 (Spring 1948), 25, 40.

Laslett, Peter. *The World We Have Lost.* Rev. ed. London: Methuen, 1971.

Lynes, Russell. *The Domesticated Americans.* New York: Harper & Row, 1963.

Mace, David R. "Personality Expression and Subordination in Marriage." *Marriage and Family Living,* 15 (August 1953), 205-207.

Martinson, Floyd M. *Marriage and the American Ideal.* New York: Dodd, Mead, 1960.

Miller, Nathan. "The European Heritage of the American Family." *Annals of the American Academy,* 160 (March 1932), 1-6.

Mogen, J. M. "A Century of Declining Paternal Authority." *Marriage and Family Living,* 19 (May 1957), 234-239.

Morgan, Edmund S. *The Puritan Family: Religion and Domestic Relations in Seventeenth-Century New England.* New York: Harper & Row, 1966.

―――. *Virginians at Home: Family Life in the Eighteenth Century.* Williamsburg, Va.: Colonial Williamsburg, 1952.

Mowrer, Ernest R. "Recent Trends in Family Research." *American Sociological Review,* 6 (1941), 499-511.

Nimkoff, M[eyer] F[rancis], ed. *Comparative Family Systems.* Boston: Houghton Mifflin, 1965.

―――. *Marriage and The Family.* Ed. William F. Ogburn. Boston: Houghton Mifflin, 1947.

Nye, F[rancis] Ivan, and Felix M. Berardo. *Emerging Conceptual Frameworks in Family Analysis.* New York: Macmillan, 1966.

Parsons, Talcott. "The Kinship System of the Contemporary United States." *American Anthropologist,* 45 (January-March 1943), 22-38.

Parsons, Talcott, Robert F. Bales, et. al. *Family, Socialization and Interaction Process.* Glencoe, Ill.: Free Press, 1955.

Parsons, Talcott, and Winston White. "The Link Between Character and Society." In *Culture and Social Character: The Work of David Riesman Reviewed,* pp. 89-135. Ed. Seymour Martin Lipset and Leo Lowenthal. Glencoe, Ill.: Free Press, 1961.

Parsons, Talcott, and Winston White. "The Mass Media and the Structure of Society." *Journal of Social Issues,* 16, no. 3 (1960), 67-77.

Rabb, Theodore K., and Robert I. Rotberg, eds. *The Family in History, Interdisciplinary Essays.* New York: Harper & Row, 1973.

Randolph, Sarah Nicholas. *The Domestic Life of Thomas Jefferson.* New York: Harper & Brothers, 1871.

Redfield, Margaret Park. "The American Family: Consensus and Freedom." *American Journal of Sociology,* 52 (November 1946), 175-183.

Riesman, David, Reuel Denney, and Nathan Glazer. *The Lonely Crowd: A Study of the Changing American Character.* New Haven: Yale University Press, 1950.

Rodman, Hyman, ed. *Marriage, Family and Society: A Reader.* New York: Random House, 1965.

Russo, David J. *Families and Communities: A New View of American History.* Nashville, Tenn.: American Association for State and Local History, 1974.

Scanlan, Thomas Michael. "The American Family and Family Dilemmas in American Drama." Diss. University of Minnesota, 1970.

Schücking, Leven Ludwig. *The Puritan Family: A Social Study from the Literary Sources.* Trans. Brian Battershaw. New York: Schocken Books, 1970.

Sennett, Richard. *Families Against the City: Middle Class Homes of Industrial Chicago, 1872-1890.* Cambridge: Harvard University Press, 1970.

Shorter, Edward. *The Making of the Modern Family.* New York: Basic Books, 1975.

Sirjamaki, John. *The American Family in the Twentieth Century.* Cambridge: Harvard University Press, 1959.

Smelser, Neil J. *Social Change in the Industrial Revolution: An Application of Theory to the British Cotton Industry.* Chicago: University of Chicago Press, 1959.

Smith, Page. *Daughters of the Promised Land: Women in American History.* Boston: Little, Brown & Co., 1970.

Sorokin, Pitrim A. *The Crisis of Our Age: The Social and Cultural Outlook.* New York: E. P. Dutton, 1941.

Starrett, Helen Ekin. *Letters to Elder Daughters: Married and Unmarried.* Chicago: A. C. McClurg, 1888.

Stott, Leland A. "The Problem of Evaluating Family Success." *Marriage and Family Living,* 13 (Summer 1951), 149-153.

Taves, Marvin J. "A Direct vs. an Indirect Approach in Measuring Marital Adjustment." *American Sociological Review,* 13 (October 1948), 538-541.

Taylor, William R. *Cavalier and Yankee: The Old South and American National Character.* New York: G. Brazillier, 1961.

Tocqueville, Alexis de. *Democracy in America.* Ed. Phillips Bradley. 2 vols. New York: Knopf Borzoi, 1945.

Truxal, Andrew G., and Francis E. Merrill. *Marriage and the Family in American Culture.* Englewood Cliffs, N.J.: Prentice-Hall, 1953.

Waller, Willard. *The Family: A Dynamic Interpretation.* Rev. Reuben Hill. New York: Dryden Press, 1951.

Winch, Robert F. *The Modern Family.* Rev. ed. New York: Holt, Rinehart & Winston, 1963.

Woods, Frances Jerome. *The American Family System.* New York: Harper & Brothers, 1959.

Zimmerman, Carl C[lark]. *Family and Civilization.* New York: Harper & Brothers, 1947.

PLAYS

Albee, Edward. *All Over.* New York: Atheneum, 1971.

———. *The American Dream.* New York: Coward-McCann, 1961.

———. *Box; Quotations from Chairman Mao Tse-Tung: Two Inter-Related Plays.* New York: Atheneum, 1969.

———. *A Delicate Balance.* New York: Atheneum, 1966.

———. *Seascape.* New York: Atheneum, 1975.

———. *Tiny Alice.* New York: Atheneum, 1965.

———. *Who's Afraid of Virginia Woolf?.* New York: Atheneum, 1962.

———. *The Zoo Story; The Death of Bessie Smith; The Sandbox.* Intro. by author. New York: Coward-McCann, 1960.

Anderson, Maxwell. *Eleven Verse Plays, 1929-1939.* New York: Harcourt, Brace & Co., 1940.

———. *Saturday's Children.* New York: Longmans, Green & Co., 1927.

Barry, Philip. *States of Grace: Eight Plays.* Ed. Brendan Gill. New York: Harcourt Brace Janovitch, 1975.

Behrman, S[amuel] N[athaniel]. *4 Plays: The Second Man; Biography; Rain from Heaven; End of Summer.* New York: Random House, 1955.

Eliot, T[homas] S[tearns]. *The Complete Poems and Plays of T. S. Eliot.* London: Faber, 1969.

Famous American Plays of the 1920s. New York: Dell Laurel, 1959.

Famous American Plays of the 1930s. New York: Dell Laurel, 1959.

Famous American Plays of the 1940s. New York: Dell Laurel, 1960.

Famous American Plays of the 1950s. New York: Dell Laurel, 1962.

Famous American Plays of the 1960s. New York: Dell Laurel, 1972.

Hansberry, Lorraine. *A Raisin in the Sun.* New York: Random House, 1959.

———. *The Sign in Sidney Brustein's Window.* New York: Random House, 1965.

Hellman, Lillian. *The Collected Plays.* Boston: Little, Brown, 1972.

Inge, William. *4 Plays: Come Back, Little Sheba; Picnic; Bus Stop; The Dark at the Top of the Stairs.* New York: Random House, 1958.

Jefferson, Joseph. *Rip Van Winkle.* In *Representative American Plays: From 1767 to the Present Day,* pp. 399-431. Ed. Arthur Hobson Quinn. 7th ed. New York: Appleton-Century-Croft, 1957.

Mersand, Joseph, ed. *Three Comedies of American Family Life.* New York: Washington Square Press, 1960.

Miller, Arthur. *After the Fall.* New York: Viking Press, 1964.

———. *Arthur Miller's Collected Plays.* Intro. by author. New York: Viking Press, 1957.

———. *The Creation of the World and Other Business.* New York: Viking Press, 1973.

———. *The Price.* New York: Viking Press, 1968.

Moses, Montrose J., ed. *Representative Plays by American Dramatists: From 1765 to the Present Day.* 3 vols. New York: E. P. Dutton, 1918-1925.

Odets, Clifford. *The Big Knife.* New York: Random House, 1949.

———. *Clash by Night.* New York: Random House, 1942.

———. *The Country Girl.* New York: Viking Press, 1951.

———. "The Flowering Peach." New York Public Library Theatre Collection.

———. *Night Music.* New York: Random House, 1940.

————. *Rocket to the Moon.* New York: Random House, 1939.

————. *Six Plays of Clifford Odets.* New York: Modern Library, 1939.

O'Neill, Eugene. *The Later Plays of ....* Ed. Travis Bogard. New York: Modern Library, 1967.

————. *Long Day's Journey into Night.* New Haven: Yale University Press, 1956.

————. *More Stately Mansions.* Shortened by Karl Ragner Gierow and ed. Donald Gallup. New Haven: Yale University Press, 1965.

————. *Nine Plays.* Intro. Joseph Wood Krutch. New York: Modern Library, 1943.

————. *The Plays of ....* 3 vols. New York: Random House, 1951.

————. *Ten "Lost" Plays.* New York: Random House, 1964.

Rice, Elmer. *Seven Plays.* New York: Viking, 1950.

Shaw, [George] Bernard. *Complete Plays with Prefaces.* 6 vols. New York: Dodd Mead, 1962.

Strindberg, August. *Plays.* Trans. Elizabeth Sprigge. Chicago: Aldine Publishing Co., 1962.

Wilder, Thornton. *The Angel That Troubled the Water and Other Plays.* New York: Harper & Row, 1963.

————. *Childhood.* New York: S. French, 1960.

————. *Infancy.* New York: S. French, 1961.

————. *Three Plays by Thornton Wilder.* New York: Harper & Row, 1957.

Williams, Tennessee. *American Blues: Five Short Plays.* New York: Dramatists Play Service, 1948.

————. *Dragon Country: A Book of Plays.* New York: New Directions, 1970.

————. *Kingdom of Earth; The Seven Descents of Myrtle.* New York: New Directions, 1968.

————. *The Milk Train Doesn't Stop Here Anymore.* Norfolk, Conn.: New Directions, 1964.

————. *Out Cry.* New York: New Directions, 1973.

————. *Small Craft Warnings.* London: Secker & Warburg, 1973.

————. *The Theatre of Tennessee Williams.* 4 vols. New York: New Directions, 1971-1972.

————. *27 Wagons Full of Cotton and Other One-Act Plays.* Norfolk, Conn.: New Directions, 1953.

LITERARY CRITICISM AND HISTORY

Alexander, Doris. "Eugene O'Neill as Social Critic." *American Quarterly,* 6 (Winter 1954), 349-363.

Armens, Sven. *Archetypes of the Family in Literature.* Seattle: University of Washton Press, 1966.

Bedard, Margaret Mary. *Marriage and Family Relations in Current Fiction: A Content Analysis of Forty "Best Sellers."* Washington, D.C.: Catholic University of America Press, 1950.

Bentley, Eric. *The Life of the Drama.* New York: Atheneum, 1964.

Bernbaum, Ernest. *The Drama of Sensibility: A Sketch of the History of English Sentimental Comedy and Domestic Tragedy, 1696-1780.* Boston: Ginn & Co., 1915.

Broussard, Louis. *American Drama: Contemporary Allegory from Eugene O'Neill to Tennessee Williams.* Norman: University of Oklahoma Press, 1962.

Cargill, Oscar, N. Bryllion Fagin, and William J. Fisher, eds. *O'Neill and His Plays: Four Decades of Criticism.* New York: New York University Press, 1961.

Clark, Barrett H. *Eugene O'Neill: The Man and His Plays.* New York: Dover Publications, 1947.

Coveney, Peter. *The Image of Childhood: The Individual and Society: A Study of the Theme in English Literature.* Baltimore: Penguin, 1967.

Earnest, Ernest. *The American Eve in Fact and Fiction, 1775-1914.* Urbana: University of Illinois Press, 1974.

E[aton], W[alter] P[ritchard]. "Jefferson, Joseph." *Dictionary of American Biography.* Ed. Dumas Malone. New York: Scribner's, 1933.

Ellis, Ann W. *The Family Story in the 1960s.* London: Bingley, 1970.

Esslin, Martin. *The Theatre of the Absurd.* Garden City, N.Y.: Doubleday Anchor, 1969.

Falk, Signi Lenea. *Tennessee Williams.* New York: Twayne, 1961.

Fergusson, Francis. *The Idea of a Theatre.* Garden City, N.Y.: Doubleday Anchor, 1949.

Fiedler, Leslie. *The Return of the Vanishing American.* New York: Stein & Day, 1968.

Gassner, John. *Form and Idea in Modern Theatre.* New York: Dryden Press, 1956.

Gassner, John, ed. *O'Neill: A Collection of Critical Essays.* Twentieth Century Views. Englewood Cliffs, N.J.: Prentice-Hall, 1964.

Gelb, Arthur and Barbara. *O'Neill.* New York: Harper & Row, 1974.

Groff, Edward. "Point of View in Modern Drama." *Modern Drama,* 2 (1959), 268-282.

Hawkins, Chauncey J. *Will the Home Survive.* New York: Thomas Whittaker, 1907.

Hogan, Robert Goode. *Arthur Miller.* Minneapolis: University of Minnesota Press, 1964.

Hynes, Joseph A. "Arthur Miller and the Impasse of Naturalism." *South Atlantic Quarterly,* 62 (1963), 327-334.

Jackson, Esther Merle. *The Broken World of Tennessee Williams.* Madison: University of Wisconsin Press, 1965.

Jefferson, Joseph. *"Rip Van Winkle"; The Autobiography of Joseph Jefferson.* New York: Appleton-Century-Croft, 1950.

Lawrence, D[avid] H[erbert]. *Studies in Classic American Literature.* Garden City, N.Y.: Doubleday Anchor, 1953.

Levin, Harry. "Literature as an Institution." In *Criticism: The Foundations of Modern Literary Judgment,* pp. 546-553. Ed. Mark Schorer, Josephine Miles, and Gordon McKenzie. Rev. ed. New York: Harcourt, Brace, 1958.

Marx, Leo. *The Machine in the Garden: Technology and the Pastoral Ideal in America.* New York: Oxford University Press, 1964.

Maxwell, Gilbert. *Tennessee Williams and Friends.* Cleveland, Ohio: World Publishing Co., 1965.

Meyer, Kenneth John. "Social Class and Family Structure: Attitudes Revealed by the Earliest American Novels, 1789-1815." Diss. University of Minnesota, 1965.

Miller, Arthur. "The Family in Modern Drama." *Atlantic Monthly,* 197 (April 1956), 35-41.

———. "Tragedy and the Common Man." *Theatre Arts,* 35 (March 1951), 48-50.

Moss, Leonard. *Arthur Miller.* New York: Twayne, 1967.

Nelson, Benjamin. *Tennessee Williams: The Man and His Work.* New York: I. Obolensky, 1961.

Newman, William J. "Review of *Arthur Miller's Collected Plays.*" *Twentieth Century,* 164 (1958), 491-496.

Raleigh, John Henry. *The Plays of Eugene O'Neill.* Carbondale: Southern Illinois University Press, 1965.

Shaeffer, Louis. *O'Neill: Son and Artist.* Boston: Little, Brown, 1973.

———. *O'Neill: Son and Playwright.* Boston: Little, Brown, 1968.

Strang, Lewis. *Famous Actors of the Day.* Boston: L. S. Page & Co., 1900.

Tischler, Nancy Marie. *Tennessee Williams: Rebellious Puritan.* New York: Citadel Press, 1961.

Valency, Maurice. *The Flower and the Castle: An Introduction to Modern Drama.* New York: Macmillan, 1963.

Waterman, Arthur E. "Joe Jefferson as Rip Van Winkle." *Journal of Popular Culture,* 1 (1968), 371-378.

Weales, Gerald. *American Drama Since World War II.* New York: Harcourt, Brace & World, 1962.

———. *Clifford Odets: Playwright.* New York: Pegasus, 1971.

Welland, Dennis. *Arthur Miller.* New York: Grove Press, 1961.

Williams, Edwina Dakin (as told to Lucy Freeman). *Remember Me to Tom.* New York: Putnam, 1963.

Williams, Raymond. *Modern Tragedy.* Stanford: Stanford University Press, 1966.

Wilson, Garff B. *A History of American Acting.* Bloomington: University of Indiana Press, 1966.

Wingate, Charles E. L., and Frederic E. McKay, eds. *Famous American Actors Today.* New York: T. Y. Crowell, 1896.

Winter, William. *Other Days: Being Chronicles and Memories of the Stage.* New York: Moffat, Yard & Co., 1908.

SOAP OPERA

Edmondson, Madeleine, and David Rounds. *The Soaps: Daytime Serials of Radio and TV.* New York: Stein & Day, 1973.

Harmon, Jim. *The Great Radio Heroes.* New York: Ace Books, 1967.

Herzog, Herta. "On Borrowed Experience: An Analysis of Listening to Daytime Sketches." *Studies in Philosophy and Social Science,* 9 (1941), 65-95.

Lazarsfield, Paul F., and Frank K. Stanton, eds. *Radio Research, 1942-43.* New York: Essential Books, 1943.

Rhymer, Paul. *The Small House Halfway Up in the Next Block: Paul Rhymer's "Vic and Sade."* Ed. Mary Frances Rhymer. New York: McGraw-Hill, 1972.

"Soap Opera." *Fortune,* 33 (March 1946), 119-123, 146, 148, 151.

Stedman, Ray. *The Serials: Suspense and Drama by Installment.* Norman: University of Oklahoma Press, 1971.

Thurber, James. *The Beast in Me and Other Animals.* New York: Harcourt, Brace, 1948.

Tilley, Winthrop. "Fleda Vetch and Ellen Brown, or, Henry James and the Soap Opera." *Western Humanities Review,* 10 (1956), 175-180.

Wakefield, Dan. *All Her Children.* Garden City, N.Y.: Doubleday, 1976.

Warner, W. Lloyd, and William E. Henry. "The Radio Day-Time Serial: A Symbolic Analysis." *Genetic Psychology Monographs,* 37 (1948), 7-64.

OTHER LITERATURE

Bradstreet, Anne. "To My Dear and Loving Husband." In *The American Tradition in Literature,* I, 38-39. Ed. Sculley Bradley et al. 2nd ed. 2 vols. New York: Norton, 1962.

Crèvecoeur, J. Hector St. John. *Letters from an American Farmer.* Garden City, N.Y.: Doubleday Dolphin, 1961.

Irving, Washington. *Selected Writings of ....* Ed. Saxe Commins. New York: Modern Library, 1945.

Johnston, Johanna, and Murry Karmiller, eds. *Family Tree: An Anthology ....* Cleveland, Ohio: World Publishing Co., 1967.

Somerville, Rose M., ed. *Intimate Relationships: Marriage, Family, and Lifestyles through Literature.* Englewood Cliffs, N.J.: Prentice-Hall, 1975.

Tavuchis, Nicholas, and William J. Goode, eds. *The Family through Literature.* New York: McGraw-Hill, 1975.

GENERAL

Boorstin, Daniel J. *The Lost World of Thomas Jefferson.* New York: H. Holt, 1948.

Griswold, A[lfred] Whitney. *Farming and Democracy.* New Haven, Conn.: Harcourt, Brace, 1952.

Hofstader, Richard. *The Age of Reform: From Byron to F.D.R.* New York: Knopf, 1955.

Jefferson, Thomas. *The Jefferson Cyclopedia.* Ed. John P. Foley. New York: Funk & Wagnalls Co., 1900.

———. *Notes on the State of Virginia.* New York: Harper & Row Torchbook, 1964.

———. *The Writings of ....* Ed. Paul Leicester Ford. 10 vols. New York: G. P. Putnam's Sons, 1892-1896.

———. *The Writings of ....* Ed. H. A. Washington. 9 vols. Washington, D.C.: Taylor & Maury, 1853-1854.

Marx, Karl. *Essential Works of Marxism.* Ed. Arthur P. Mendel. New York: Bantam Books, 1961.

Miller, Perry. *Errand Into the Wilderness.* Cambridge: Harvard University Press, Belknap Press, 1956.

Polanyi, Karl. *The Great Transformation.* Boston: Beacon Press, 1957.

Smith, Henry Nash. *Virgin Land: The American West as Symbol and Myth.* New York: Random House Vintage, 1957.

INDEX

Titles of soap operas and other serials appear in quotation marks with no parenthetical identification following.

ABOUT THE AUTHOR

Tom Scanlan, a specialist in American and modern drama, has taught at Lincoln University and George Washington University. He has published in *The Virginia Quarterly Review.*

P2